Barnes & Noble Guide to Children's Books

BARNES
&NOBLE
BOOKS
NEW YORK

Annotations by Holly Rivlin
Additional annotations by Michael Cavanaugh and Brenn Jones
Editors: Michael Cavanaugh and Brenn Jones
Art Director: Lynn Binder
Senior Production Editor: Lynne Arany
Book design: Ellen Marin
Copy Editor: Helen Chumbley
Proofreader: Hilary Dyson

Special thanks to Marcella Fernandez and the staffs of our
Manhattan Barnes & Noble Children's Departments.

Please note: Title availability and price subject to change
at the discretion of the individual publishers. Books not currently
in stock at your local bookstore may be special ordered,
or you may order online at barnesandnoble.com.

1999 Barnes & Noble Books

ISBN 0-7607-0811-8

Printed and bound in China

99 00 01 02 03 M 9 8 7 6 5 4 3 2 1

LFA

Table of Contents

Welcome to the Barnes & Noble Guide to Children's Books

CHILDREN TODAY LIVE IN AN EXCITING MEDIA-DRIVEN ERA of television, video games, and computers. Yet no medium is able to stir a child's imagination like the pages of a book. Reading with a child is still one of the warmest and most magical experiences we can share. This time together helps children to develop reading skills, and gives them the key to the rich and enchanting world of children's literature.

In these pages we will try to explain the basic differences between the various categories of children's books. The books we have chosen to present are some our favorites. We have started with books for babies, and continue through to young fiction, the springboard into adult reading. Some of these titles you will recognize, while others will be a surprise. This list of books is truly the tip of the iceberg. Think of a subject—any subject—and there is likely a children's book that covers it.

Enter any children's bookstore, and you will see the enormous selection of children's books available. We have focused our guide within the boundaries of fiction. This does not in any way detract from the importance or quality in the tremendous selection of nonfiction books available to today's young readers.

To a little baby, a book is a bright object to chew, throw, and play with. But in time the pictures take on meaning, and the words become more than symbols. Word association begins.

It's a wonderful moment for parents when they see their child sitting alone with a book, trying to make out the words and grasp the story. Favorite characters become friends. Madeline, Curious George, Winnie-the-Pooh, and Ferdinand the Bull are only a few of the characters your children will never forget. Someday your children will introduce these immortal characters to their own children.

We hope you come away from this guide with a new enthusiasm for children's books. Remember that the titles we include here are really just a few of the many great books published each year. Don't just take our word for it, or the word of award committees—find your own classics, give your own awards! And, above all, enjoy!

Michael Cavanaugh

Michael Cavanaugh

Editor, Barnes & Noble Books

A Special Hello!

THE WORLD OF CHILDREN'S BOOKS IS BROUGHT TO YOU BY countless individuals. Authors, illustrators, and editors are among those working behind the scenes to provide the treasure trove of material. We have asked three incredibly talented creators of children's books to give us a little insight into their world.

Representing the colorful world of preschool books is the author and illustrator David Carter. From the genre of picture books is the illustrator Hilary Knight. And finally, out of the diverse and splendid realm of fiction, we have the award-winning author E. L. Konigsburg. We are pleased to present their thoughts.

v

Words from the Author

I am often asked by children where I get my ideas for books. I have spent many hours contemplating this question, and I still do not have the answer.

In the beginning of my career as an author, illustrator, and paper engineer, I honestly did not give much thought to why I created my books. They just happened; they were a compilation of many influences. I have always been an artist. I have always been very stimulated by visual images. To this day the first thing I do when I pick up any book, including a novel, is look for pictures.

A few years ago I received an e-mail from a student of children's literature. She asked a couple of questions about my work and one in particular got me to thinking. She asked me to describe an average day in the life of eight-year-old David Carter. My answer was simple. I would play outside all day, spending hours on end in the fields around my home, lifting up rocks and boards in search of bugs. It was always very exciting to lift up the rocks because I never knew what I would find. I actually started to chuckle at this answer. Lifting something to find a bug was one of my greatest thrills as a child, and that is exactly what I had created, unconsciously, in *How Many Bugs in a Box?* I still cannot explain the creative process that goes on in my mind, but discovering that link between my childhood curiosities and thrills, and my books, has something to do with where my ideas come from.

My goal in creating a book is to engage this natural curiosity, to entertain with surprise and silliness, and whenever possible, to educate—because for me, the end result of curiosity is learning.

In recent years the term *interactive* has become popular in reference to computer software. Pop-up books are also interactive; of course, to a big kid like myself, the term *interactive* is nothing more than a big word for play. I believe children learn by playing. One of the things that I like most about pop-up books is that a child who may not be reading yet can interact, or play, with the book. My hope is that this will draw the young reader into the book and hopefully into reading in general.

If my books can entertain and excite a child who is not a reader, and draw him or her into books and reading, then I have accomplished my goal.

Have fun,

David A. Carter

David Carter

Check pages 18–19 of the Preschool section for even more books by David Carter!

GLITTER BUGS
0-689-81857-2
Little Simon
$7.99

NUMBERS
0-689-81041-5
Little Simon
$6.99

BED BUGS
0-689-81863-7
Little Simon
$14.95

JINGLE BUGS
0-671-72924-1
Little Simon
$16.00

GIGGLE BUGS
0-689-81859-9
Little Simon
$12.95

A Lift-and-Laugh Book by David A. Carter

A Pop-up Bedtime Book by David A. Carter

A Merry Pop-up Book with Lights and Music!

Words from the Artist

In a career as an illustrator of over sixty books, my first book was *Eloise*, which—by luck or perfect circumstance—was a *total* collaboration with the late, great Kay Thompson.

For reasons known only to publishers, artists and authors rarely mix. (There are those who say that's fortunate.) The year I was born (1926) prevented me from working with several authors whose books I illustrated. Charles Dickens's *Captain Boldheart and the Magic Fishbone*, for one. Edward Lear would have insisted on drawing *The Owl and the Pussycat* himself, I suppose, had he been around. Ogden Nash didn't depart until after I had done his *Animal Garden*, but we never did meet. What a missed opportunity for me. On Judith Viorst's first children's book, *Sunday Morning*, for which I drew the pictures, I heard from that delightful writer—after publication—that I had drawn a duplicate of her bedroom comforter. Mental telepathy, but not much fun as a working relationship. And when you author your own books—there are no laughs at all.

Kay Thompson was different.

It was nonstop cyclone talk about music, painting, food, and Hollywood in the 1940s, her rapier wit decapitating luminaries along the way. It was also complete dedication to the book at hand . . . until you dropped from sheer exhilarated exhaustion.

Since she has "joined the choir" (a Kay-ism borrowed from her pal Noel Coward), all Eloise books will be coming back, and a flood of memories for me of an extraordinary collaboration.

Hilary Knight

Hilary Knight

Hilary Knight

ELOISE IN PARIS
0-689-82704-0 Simon & Schuster $17.00

Check page 76 of the Picture Books section for more Eloise!

Words from the Author

I have been pondering the meaning of *award* and trying to differentiate it from *reward*.

Fact: A paycheck is a reward.
Fact: A medal is an award.
   Conclusion: Reward means profit. Award means merit.

Fact: Sometimes grown-ups (example: teachers) give kids rewards (example: extra credit) for reading 2,000 pages.
Fact: Grown-ups don't give kids awards for reading 2,000 pages unless they are counselors in summer camp where everyone gets an award for something.
   Conclusion: Rewards are quantitative; awards are qualitative.

Fact: Sinclair Lewis, Eugene O'Neill, Pearl S. Buck, William Faulkner, Ernest Hemingway, John Steinbeck, Saul Bellow, Isaac Bashevis Singer, and Toni Morrison altogether did not get as much money for their novels as Tom Clancy got for *Rainbow Six*.
Fact: Clancy bought a football team. The others won the Nobel Prize.
   Conclusion: Rewards, measurable in dollars, can outweigh the awards, which are singular and incalculable.

Creating children's books that have been loved by three generations has been a reward. You can give yourself a reward, but your books have to win the awards. *From the Mixed-up Files of Mrs. Basil E. Frankweiler* won a Newbery Medal. *The View from Saturday* won one, too. Winning two Newbery Medals is sugar and spice and everything nice. Also non-fattening.

And that's a fact.

E.L. Konigsburg

E. L. Konigsburg

E. L. Konigsburg

THE DRAGON IN THE GHETTO CAPER
0-689-82120-4 Aladdin $4.50

UP FROM JERICHO
0-689-82120-4 Aladdin $4.50

*Check pages 153-154 of the Fiction section
for more books by E. L. Konigsburg!*

THROWING SHADOWS
0-689-82120-4 Aladdin $4.50

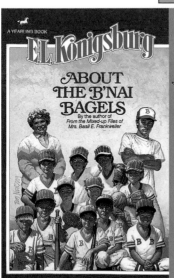

ABOUT THE B'NAI BAGELS
0-440-40034-1 Yearling $3.99

THE VIEW FROM SATURDAY
0-689-80993-X Atheneum $16.00

**JENNIFER, HECATE, MACBETH, WILLIAM
MCKINLEY, AND ME, ELIZABETH**
0-440-44162-5 Yearling $4.50

How to Use the Internet to Look for Children's Books

In this guide, we have tried to give the reader an overview of some books we find especially appealing. But there are so many great children's books, it is impossible to take them all in . . . or is it?

On the World Wide Web, anything is possible. Online shopping is becoming more and more popular. Customers can now browse the Web for the thousands of children's books available. We asked our friends at *barnesandnoble.com* to talk about how easy and fun it is to look for children's books on the Internet.

In Madeleine L'Engle's Newbery Medal–winning book, *A Wrinkle in Time*, Meg and Charles Wallace rely on the help of Mrs. Whatsit to rescue their father. The children have to do the rescuing themselves, but Mrs. Whatsit and her friends, Mrs. Who and Mrs. Which, give the children some guidance along the way. However, the advice of these ladies can be almost as obscure as it is helpful—leaving Meg and Charles Wallace to scratch their heads in confusion at times.

Turning to the Internet for advice on developing a healthy love of reading in your child can be a little like asking Mrs. Whatsit for book recommendations. You might eventually get some help, but at first every answer you find will raise several more questions. That's why an online bookseller like **barnesandnoble.com** can be not only a convenience for busy parents, but also a help in discerning which are the right books to give young readers.

The online division of Barnes & Noble, the world's largest bookseller, **barnesandnoble.com** has created a special area just for parents who want to read reviews and learn what the authors have to say about children's literature. Using any available Web browser, you can type in **http://www.barnesandnoble.com** to go to the site. From there, if you click on the choice that allows you to browse our subject areas, you'll find the "Kids" subject area. In addition to finding reviews of new releases and classics, you'll also be able to see lists of recommended books in a variety of categories: books for bedtime, books about bugs, picture books adults will love, and even "rollicking read-alouds." You can purchase any of the books that you find there and think will appeal to your youngster, usually at a substantial discount, and have the order delivered to your home or office, generally within just a few days or less.

Another popular area at the **barnesandnoble.com** site is "The Reader's Catalog," which provides recommendations for both adult and children's books. This amazing catalog of more than 40,000 books has been compiled by the editors and friends of the *New York Review of Books.* It

allows you to browse in a number of categories, or search for specific titles. There's also a feature that lists four excellent children's books chosen at random—which can be particularly helpful for a parent who's at a loss for the next reading material to give a son or daughter.

The Internet is a pretty big place, however, and you'll want to venture out to get a few other ideas for your child's reading. To help you, here are some other suggestions:

The Children's Literature Web Guide is an excellent place to begin exploration. It has links to other sites specifically devoted to children's literature, as well as discussion boards and quick reference lists of award-winning and best-selling books for kids. You'll also find links to other resources for parents, teachers, and even writers and illustrators. **http://www.acs.ucalgary.ca/~dkbrown/**

The New York Public Library has put together **"On-Lion" for Kids**—its name inspired by the two great stone lions that guard the library system's flagship building. It offers a whole range of choices, including recommended reading lists built around different celebrations of the year (such as Hispanic Heritage Month, Thanksgiving, and Kwanzaa); information on authors, titles, and favorite characters; and links to science and technology Web sites that young nonfiction lovers will enjoy. **http://www.nypl.org/branch/kids/**

The children's literature "gopher" site from the **New Mexico State University Library** isn't much to look at—a gopher site can be accessed by most Web browsers, but unlike a Web site, it doesn't usually contain pictures or images—but the information is invaluable for anyone interested in children's literature. You can access back issues of book reviews from selected children's literature journals and find digitized versions of some of the classic texts in children's fiction. You wouldn't want to sit at the computer to read to your child, of course, but these full-length versions of texts can be printed out and savored, chapter by chapter. **gopher://lib.nmsu.edu:70/11/.subjects/Education/.childlit**

The **Youth Division of the Internet Public Library** is organized by the Dewey decimal system—so kids start to learn how to find other books even as they explore the different resources and links on this simple but excellent site. At its heart, it's a directory of links to other Web sites, many of them book-related, but the descriptions are so kid-friendly, you'll wish you could just hang out in the library a little bit longer before moving on! **http://www.ipl.org/youth/**

If the preceding sites whet your appetite for the world of children's literature and education, then by all means check out the **Fairrosa Cyber Library** and its online collection of articles, book reviews, archives of discussion group posts, information about authors, and electronic texts of classic children's books. The site is definitely oriented toward parents and teachers, not children themselves, but for what it is, it's very comprehensive. **http://www.users.interport.net/~fairrosa/**

One of the greatest honors a parent can receive is when someone younger—someone still impressionable, and still unsure of his or her place in the world—asks: "Will you read to me?" In *A Wrinkle in Time,* young Charles Wallace asks Meg's new friend Calvin to read to him before bed . . . and the two of them become fast friends themselves. We wish the same for you and your young book lover.

How to Use This Book

- Each section is easily recognizable by the color banner at the top:

  Baby Books—Pink
  Preschool—Yellow
  Picture Books—Blue
  Poetry & Anthology—Purple
  Early Readers—Green
  Fiction—Orange
  Special Needs—Sage
  Barnes & Noble Books—Gray

- At the beginning of each section is an introduction containing helpful hints for choosing books.

- The sections are alphabetized by author, or, in some cases, such as in the Baby Books and Early Readers sections, by series.

- We have annotated some titles, while line-listing others by the same author or in the same series.

- When available we have listed the author and illustrator. To wet your beak, we have incorporated our favorite illustrations in the guide.

- Each listing will have the price at the time of this guide's publication, the ISBN (a book code that distinguishes each edition), page count, and the publisher.

- In our book we use the following symbols to highlight selected titles:

  A = Award Winners
  T = Appropriate for Toddler Age

- In addition to an author, title, and illustrator index, we have provided an index by subject.

Baby Books

CERTAINLY ONE OF THE BEST WAYS TO DEVELOP a future reader is to introduce a baby to a book. In a baby's world, a book is a plaything, a thing of joy . . . it is FUN.

In baby books, little ones get plenty of visual stimulation—they recognize other babies and the simple objects that make up their daily life. At first, the printed word or words mean nothing . . . but just wait. When babies have enough time with a book, the words become more that just squiggles on a page. The toddler begins to associate the word with the picture.

In this section we present four kinds of baby books:

BOARD BOOKS: These are made with sturdy cardboard pages that can be wiped clean.

TOUCH & FEEL: Attached to these sturdy books are cloth, feathers, fur, and familiar "feely" things for little ones to discover.

CLOTH BOOKS: Made of safe washable material, these are perfect for baby's bedtime.

BATH BOOKS: Bath books, constructed of soft, durable plastic, can take a lot of abuse.

Quiet is
the kitten
washing herself.

Quiet is
the toy
upon the shelf.

What to look for . . .

- Simple text and art

- Repetition and bouncy rhymes

- Bright and familiar photos. There should be a connection between the baby's surroundings and the book's photos.

- A sturdy book that can handle many spills

- Rounded corners for safety's sake

- A book of the right size and shape for little hands. Part of the baby's learning experience is recognizing that pages are for turning.

- A book you will enjoy as well. The baby will recognize your own enjoyment of the shared experience.

BOARD BOOKS

These popular first books for babies are printed on sturdy cardboard, so they can take the wear and tear that babies can give!

BUNNYKINS™ BOARD BOOKS

The beautiful artwork from the Royal Doulton™ collection forms the basis for these delightful board books.

BUNNYKINS FAMILY FUN DAY
In this family outing we all visit the park and take a train trip to the beach.

12pp Board Book $4.95
0-9645524-0-X Ziccardi

In the same series:
All 12pp Board Book
$4.95 Ziccardi

BUNNYKINS TOGETHER FOREVER
0-9645524-3-4

GOODNIGHT BUNNYKINS
0-9645524-1-8

A SURPRISE FOR DADDY BUNNYKINS
0-9645524-2-6

CHUNKY BOARD BOOKS

With a variety of stories and illustrations, **Chunky Board Books** gently teach basic concepts. The small books' baby-friendly format (safe rounded corners and "wipe clean" pages) puts parents at ease.

lamb

FARM ANIMALS
Cute and cuddly barnyard animals populate this charming book. The photos are clear and bright for little eyes.

28pp Board Book $3.99
0-394-86254-6 Random House

In the same series:
All 28pp Board Book
$3.99 Random House

BABY'S ABC
0-394-87870-1

BABY'S ANIMAL FRIENDS
0-394-89583-5

BABY'S FIRST WORDS
0-394-86945-1

IN & OUT UP & DOWN
0-394-85151-X

LITTLE CRITTER® ABC'S
0-679-87356-2

THE LITTLE QUIET BOOK
0-394-82899-2

RICHARD SCARRY'S LOWLY WORM WORD BOOK
0-394-84728-8

CHUNKY SHAPE BOOKS

THE VELVETEEN RABBIT
This sweet little book tells how toys become real. The story has been simplified and illustrated with pictures soft and warm.

22pp Board Book $3.99
0-679-83617-9 Random House

In the same series:
All 22pp Board Book
$3.99 Random House

GOOD NIGHT, SLEEP TIGHT! SHHH . . .
0-679-80845-0

NOAH'S ARK
0-679-83600-4

RICHARD SCARRY'S CARS AND TRUCKS FROM A TO Z
0-679-80663-6

THOMAS AND THE FREIGHT TRAIN
0-679-81599-6

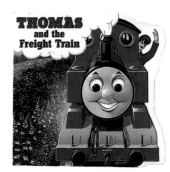

Baby Books

DK BOARD BOOKS

DK Board Books use the brightest, most colorful images around to hold the interest of the youngest of readers.

MY FIRST WORD BOARD BOOK
32pp   Board Book $7.95
0-7894-1514-3   DK

MY LITTLE ABC BOARD BOOK
32pp   Board Book $6.95
0-7894-2781-8   DK

MY LITTLE ANIMALS BOARD BOOK
32pp   Board Book $6.95
0-7894-2783-4   DK

LITTLE SPOT BOARD BOOKS

Eric Hill's creation of the little dog Spot was a preschooler's dream come true. These easy-to-follow books have simple stories and concepts the entire family will find charming.

Eric Hill
SPOT'S FIRST WORDS
Everybody's favorite dog helps toddlers associate words and pictures in this delightful book.
14pp   Board Book $3.95
0-399-21348-1   Putnam

By the same author in this series:
All 14pp   Board Book
$3.95   Putnam

SPOT AT HOME
0-399-21774-6

SPOT IN THE GARDEN
0-399-21772-X

SPOT'S TOY BOX
0-399-21773-8

PUDGY BOARD BOOKS™

For years the **Pudgy Book** line has provided families with books on almost every toddler subject. The **Pudgy Books'** unique shape make them easier for babies to hold.

A dog doesn't quack.

A dog woof-woofs.

WHO SAYS QUACK?
"A dog doesn't quack. A dog woof-woofs." In this book parents and babies attempt to identify the animal who quacks. The sounds of several barnyard animals are introduced with adorable photographs, and at the end of the book we finally meet a family of ducks. *Quack!*
18pp   Board Book $3.95
0-448-40123-1   Grosset

In the same series:
All 18pp   Board Book
$3.95   Grosset

THE PUDGY BOOK OF BABIES
0-448-10207-2

THE PUDGY BOOK OF FARM ANIMALS
0-448-10211-0

THE PUDGY BOOK OF MOTHER GOOSE
0-448-10212-9

THE PUDGY BUNNY BOOK
0-448-10210-2

THE PUDGY PEEK-A-BOO BOOK
0-448-10205-6

PUDGY PAL BOARD BOOKS™

This part of the **Pudgy Book** line introduces nursery rhymes and fairy tales to the little ones. Each book is die-cut into an appealing shape with rounded corners.

THE UGLY DUCKLING
This classic tale reinforces that it's okay to be different. Simplified words and pictures show how the little duck becomes a swan.
18pp   Board Book $3.95
0-448-40184-3   Grosset

In the same series:
All 18pp   Board Book
$3.95   Grosset

CHICKEN LITTLE
0-448-10223-4

THE CITY MOUSE AND THE COUNTRY MOUSE
0-448-10226-9

JACK AND THE BEANSTALK
0-448-40857-0

THE LITTLE RED HEN
0-448-10218-8

NOAH'S ARK
0-448-40185-1

THE NUTCRACKER
0-448-40546-6

Baby Books

SESAME STREET ® BOARD BOOKS

In a world full of TV and movie tie-ins, there is one place we all feel safe—on *Sesame Street!* Each of these colorful books inspired by the popular PBS program is produced with the same quality and sensibility we have come to trust from Big Bird and friends.

ELMO'S GUESSING GAME

Elmo will be proud of you when you choose the correct item for him in various situations. This Sesame Street book teaches useful concepts in a fun and friendly way.

12pp   Board Book $4.95
0-307-12398-7   Golden

In the same series:
ERNIE & BERT CAN . . . CAN YOU?
26pp   Board Book $3.99
0-394-85150-1   Random House

ERNIE FOLLOWS HIS NOSE
12pp   Board Book $4.95
0-307-12321-9   Golden

HIDE AND SEEK WITH BIG BIRD
12pp   Board Book $4.99
0-679-80785-3   Random House

SO TALL BOARD BOOKS™

This series boasts some of the most popular board books of all time. The tall 5" x 9" format gives a baby lots to see and do on each page. Simple rhymes, stories, and easy concepts are the hallmarks of the **So Tall**'s.

Gyo Fujikawa
BABIES

Gyo Fujikawa is one of the truly great preschool book artists. Her soft style of painting is pleasing and always interesting—you can visit the illustrations again and again without getting bored. In *Babies* she has given us a bundle of babies busy doing what babies do. As in all her books, Fujikawa's baby landscapes portray many different ethnic groups.

18pp   Board Book $4.95
0-448-03084-5   Grosset

In the same series:
All 18pp   Board Book
$4.95   Grosset

BABY ANIMALS
0-448-03083-7

BABY'S 123
0-448-40265-3

BABY'S ABC
0-448-40130-4

BABY'S MOTHER GOOSE
0-448-03077-2

BABY'S WORDS
0-448-40926-7

PEEK-A-BOO! I SEE YOU!
0-448-03092-6

RUB-A-DUB-DUB
0-448-40521-0

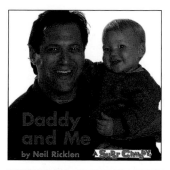

SUPER CHUBBY ® BABY PHOTO BOARD BOOKS

Babies *love* to look at other babies. Each book in this series has delightful photos of babies acting and reacting within their world. One simple word per page helps develop a baby's growing vocabulary.

Neil Ricklen
DADDY AND ME

This super board book beautifully portrays things Daddy does with baby. As always, Ricklen's photography is attention grabbing for both children and adults.

24pp   Board Book $4.99
0-689-81266-3   Little Simon

By the same author in this series:
All 24pp   Board Book
$4.99   Little Simon

BABY'S CLOTHES
0-689-81264-7

BABY'S COLORS
0-689-81239-6

BABY'S HOME
0-689-81269-8

NON-SERIES TITLES

Byron Barton
THE THREE BEARS

Byron Barton's lovely simple artwork is a perfect fit for the famous tale of Goldilocks and the three bears.

32pp   Board Book $7.95
0-694-00998-9   HarperFestival

Hippos wear pajamas just a little tight.

Sandra Boynton
SNOOZERS

These seven short-short stories bring chuckles before bedtime. The clever table of contents with finger tabs allows the child to flip immediately to his or her favorite story.

18pp   Board Book $7.99
0-689-81774-6   Little Simon

By the same author:
All 14pp   Board Book
$4.99   Little Simon

A TO Z
0-671-49317-5

BLUE HAT, GREEN HAT
0-671-49320-5

BUT NOT THE HIPPOPOTAMUS
0-671-44904-4

DOGGIES
0-671-49318-3

THE GOING TO BED BOOK
0-671-44902-8

HORNS TO TOES AND IN BETWEEN
0-671-49319-1

MOO, BAA, LA LA LA!
0-671-44901-X

OPPOSITES
0-671-44903-6

Lucy Cousins
MAISY'S COLORS

It won't take long for any adult to see why Maisy has become a favorite of children everywhere. The mouse with the cute, pink nose and whiskers is very charming as she conducts a green train, rides a blue boat on a blue sea, and stands in a yellow sandbox. Lucy Cousins's clean, artistic designs make this venture into the world of colors highly pleasing.

24pp   Board Book $9.99
0-7636-0159-4   Candlewick

By the same author:
MAISY GOES TO SCHOOL
16pp   Board Book $12.99
1-5640-2085-1   Candlewick

MAISY GOES TO THE PLAYGROUND
16pp   Board Book $12.95
1-5640-2084-3   Candlewick

Pat Cummings
MY AUNT CAME BACK

This clever rhyme tells the story of a little girl and her aunt who travels the world. The aunt returns from each destination bearing marvelous gifts. In the end, the little girl gets to go along—and bids us farewell in several languages!

12pp   Board Book $5.95
0-694-01059-6   HarperFestival

Lois Ehlert
COLOR ZOO

What do a tiger, a mouse, and a fox have in common? They are all formed from shapes. Using die-cut pages, Lois Ehlert introduces animals, shapes, and color in this brilliantly designed board book.

24pp   Board Book $6.95
0-694-01067-7   HarperFestival

By the same author:
COLOR FARM
24pp Board Book $6.95
0-694-01066-9 HarperFestival

Mushrooms

Anne Geddes
GARDEN FRIENDS
Baby birds . . . baby hedgehogs . . . baby mushrooms! These real babies, dressed in ornate costumes, create a fantasy world beautifully captured by photographer Anne Geddes.

14pp Board Book $5.95
1-55912-342-7 Cedco

By the same author:
All 14pp Board Book
$5.95 Cedco

COLORS
1-55912-013-4

DRESS-UPS
1-55912-014-2

FACES
1-55912-015-0

Tana Hoban
BLACK ON WHITE
Many child-care experts believe babies are better able to see and recognize shapes when they are presented in black and white. A butterfly, a leaf, an elephant, and a small child are among the solid black images presented against a white background.

10pp Board Book $4.95
0-688-11918-2 Greenwillow

By the same author:
WHITE ON BLACK
10pp Board Book $4.95
0-688-11919-0 Greenwillow

Peter Linenthal
LOOK LOOK!
Stunning high contrast, black-and-white spreads are an eyeful for baby. The objects are all familiar and very, very happy.

16pp Board Book $6.99
0-525-42028-2 Dutton

A. A. Milne
Illustrated by Ernest H. Shepard
POOH SOLVES A MYSTERY
Where is Eeyore's tail? Pooh himself sets out to find it. You can help Pooh search by opening the sliding panels to reveal where the missing tail is . . . and isn't!

12pp Board Book $5.99
0-525-45987-1 Dutton

By the same author:
All 12pp Board Book
$5.99 Dutton

EEYORE HAS A BIRTHDAY
0-525-46118-3

POOH AND PIGLET GO HUNTING
0-525-46117-5

TIGGER HAS BREAKFAST
0-525-45989-8

Helen Oxenbury
WORKING
How does a baby work? By eating, washing, drinking, and sleeping! This classic board book features simple drawings of a round-faced baby's nine-to-five, from high chair and carriage to bathtub and crib. Each of the seven two-page spreads is accompanied by one easy word.

14pp Board Book $3.95
0-671-42112-3 Little Simon

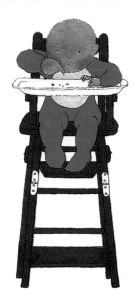

By the same author:

DRESSING
14pp   Board Book $4.95
0-671-42113-1   Little Simon

FRIENDS
14pp   Board Book $4.95
0-671-42111-5   Little Simon

Jan Pieńkowski
ZOO

Lions and camels and bears—oh my! This delightful board book helps little folks learn the names of animals in the zoo.

14pp   Board Book $4.99
0-689-82098-4   Little Simon

By the same author:

All 14pp   Board Book
$4.99   Little Simon

123
0-689-82096-8

ABC
0-689-82095-X

SHAPES
0-689-82097-6

John Prater
OH WHERE, OH WHERE?

A dear little bear is playing hide-and-seek with his daddy. The action is shown in adorable pictures accompanied by a rhyme that is reminiscent of the song "Where Oh Where Has My Little Dog Gone?"

24pp   Board Book $6.95
0-7641-5109-6   Barron's

By the same author:
WALKING AROUND THE GARDEN

"One step, two steps . . ." is the way the little bear gets around. With his dad watching closely, the little tyke makes his way from the garden up to the bedroom where a story and a goodnight kiss are the perfect way to end the day.

24pp   Board Book $6.95
0-7641-5111-8   Barron's

Karen Gray Ruelle
Illustrated by Lizi Boyd
THE BOOK OF BREAKFASTS

When a dog crunches and a pig munches, it must be time for breakfast! The morning meal is a delight when you and your toddler see how animal friends eat.

10pp   Board Book $4.95
0-15-201064-5   Red Wagon

By the same author:
THE BOOK OF BATHS
10pp   Board Book $4.95
0-15-201003-3   Red Wagon

THE BOOK OF BEDTIMES
10pp   Board Book $4.95
0-15-201001-7   Red Wagon

Charles G. Shaw
IT LOOKED LIKE SPILT MILK

"Sometimes it looked like a Sheep. But it wasn't a Sheep." So what was it? In this imaginative book, a cloud appears to be a bird, a tree, an ice-cream cone, and other objects familiar to children. The white images set against a deep blue background are striking. This wonderful book can be used as a guessing game or gentle read-aloud.

24pp   Board Book $4.95
0-694-00491-X   HarperFestival

Sian Tucker
MY TOYS

Using both pastels and primary colors, Sian Tucker beautifully presents familiar objects of play. One simple word per page is perfect for language development.

16pp   Board Book $4.99
0-689-81983-8   Little Simon

By the same author:

All 16pp   Board Book
$4.99   Little Simon

COLORS
0-689-81980-3

GOING OUT
0-689-81981-1

MY CLOTHES
0-689-81982-X

Lee Wade
THE CHEERIOS® PLAY BOOK

It's finally okay to play with your food! Each of the interactive pages has embossed holes in which to place Cheerios. The Cheerios help finish the picture by becoming wheels or bubbles and so on. NO milk, please!

12pp   Board Book $4.99
0-689-82280-4   Little Simon

Jane Wattenberg
MRS. MUSTARD'S BABY FACES

Beaming babies, jolly babies, happy babies—crying babies, cranky babies, crabby babies! Each page in this charming gatefold board book has a big baby face on it. One side is the happy side and the other is the not-so-happy side.

14pp   Board Book $5.95
0-87701-659-3   Chronicle

By the same author:
MRS. MUSTARD'S BEASTLY BABIES
14pp   Board Book $5.95
0-87701-683-6   Chronicle

William Wegman
123

How do weimaraners count to ten? William Wegman's famous dogs show you how. Count seven paws, then see Fay and friends lying side by side to form the number 7!

14pp   Board Book $6.95
0-7868-0103-4   Hyperion

By the same author:
TRIANGLE SQUARE CIRCLE
14pp   Board Book $6.95
0-7868-0104-2   Hyperion

FROM *Max's Birthday*

Monica Wellington
BABY IN A BUGGY

This oversized book with board pages is bright enough to catch the attention of the most fidgety baby. Wellington begins her book with the question, "What does baby see?" Then each spread shows us such simple objects as a hat, a swing, and roller skates. What makes this book special is the wonderful contrasting colors for these simple and pleasing pictures. The flower page is so bright Mom might wish it were a wall hanging!

14pp   Board Book $4.99
0-525-45295-8   Dutton

Rosemary Wells
MAX'S BIRTHDAY

Max the rabbit loves presents, but he finds the gift his sister gives him—a toy lobster—to be a little scary! When the lobster runs around and around, Max yells, "NO!" But when the lobster finally stops, Max shouts, "AGAIN!" Rosemary Wells's books about Max provide little lessons for preschoolers.

10pp   Board Book $5.99
0-8037-2268-0   Dial

By the same author:
All 10pp   Board Book
$5.99   Dial

MAX'S BATH
0-8037-2266-4

MAX'S BEDTIME
0-8037-2267-2

MAX'S FIRST WORD
0-8037-2269-9

MAX'S RIDE
0-8037-2272-9

MAX'S TOYS
0-8037-2271-0

Norman Bridwell
CLIFFORD'S FURRY FRIENDS

Norman Bridwell's big red dog has been a favorite among babies and preschoolers for years. Here babies are introduced to Clifford—and then to his animal friends, each of whom children can pet and describe.

16pp   Touch & Feel $8.95
0-590-86402-5   *Scholastic*

Jack Hanna
LET'S GO TO THE PETTING ZOO WITH JUNGLE JACK

At Jungle Jack's petting zoo, babies can feel a llama's woolly fur, a flamingo's feathery tale, and a chick's fuzzy down. Along the way Jack poses questions to stimulate the imagination.

16pp   Touch & Feel $10.95
0-385-41694-6   *Doubleday*

Dorothy Kunhardt
PAT THE BUNNY

"Judy can pat the bunny. Now YOU pat the bunny." Those words have been read countless times since the publication of this classic in 1940. With textures, peekaboo, mirrors, and more, this timeless book and its two sequels make babies gurgle with glee.

18pp   Touch & Feel $8.95
0-3071-2000-7   *Golden*

In the same series:

Edith Kunhardt
PAT THE CAT
18pp   Touch & Feel $7.95
0-3071-2001-5   *Golden*

PAT THE PUPPY
18pp   Touch & Feel $7.95
0-3071-2004-X   *Golden*

Dorothy & Edith Kunhardt
PAT THE BUNNY AND FRIENDS (3 BOOK GIFT SET)
Each 18pp   Touch & Feel $17.95
0-3071-6209-5   *Golden*

Matthew Van Fleet
FUZZY YELLOW DUCKLINGS

With textures to feel, and colors, shapes, and funny animals to view and name, this terrific book keeps toddlers busy and content. The last page folds out into a naming game. "Can you guess the reason for this animal parade? Turn the page over and see what they've made!"

16pp   Touch & Feel $10.95
0-8037-1759-8   *Dial*

Pat & Eve Witte
Illustrated by Harlow Rockwell
THE TOUCH ME BOOK

"What feels ticklish? Feathers are ticklish. Feel it with your nose—All sneezy, giggly ticklish!" Each spread offers babies a chance to feel a new material, whether smooth like glass or scratchy like sand.

16pp   Touch & Feel $7.99
0-3071-2146-1   *Golden*

CLOTH BOOKS

Made of safe, soft materials, cloth books can go in the wash after unfortunate spills! The books have simple verse and pictures, and are perfect for a bedtime cuddle.

Lucy Cousins
FLOWER IN THE GARDEN
8pp   Cloth Book $6.99
1-56402-029-0   Candlewick

By the same author:
All 8pp   Cloth Book
$6.99   Candlewick

HEN ON THE FARM
1-56402-032-0

KITE IN THE PARK
1-56402-031-2

TEDDY IN THE HOUSE
1-56402-030-4

Eric Hill
ANIMALS
10pp   Cloth Book $4.95
0-399-22524-2   Putnam

By the same author:
CLOTHES
10pp   Cloth Book $4.95
0-399-22521-8   Putnam

HOME
10pp   Cloth Book $4.95
0-399-22522-6   Putnam

Jan Pieńkowski
ANIMALS
8pp   Cloth Book $4.50
0-689-80433-4   Little Simon

By the same author:
All 8pp   Cloth Book
$4.50   Little Simon

FRIENDS
0-689-80433-4

FUN
0-689-80432-6

PLAY
0-689-80431-8

Sian Tucker
TOOT TOOT
8pp   Cloth Book $5.50
0-671-89117-0   Little Simon

fire truck

By the same author:
All 8pp   Cloth Book
$5.50   Little Simon

QUACK QUACK
0-671-89116-2

RAT-A-TAT-TAT
0-671-89115-4

YUM YUM
0-671-89114-6

Other Cloth Books:
BABY BOO!
8pp   Cloth Book $6.99
0-679-81544-9   Random House

BABY'S FIRST BOOK
10pp   Cloth Book $4.99
0-394-87470-6   Random House

BABY'S LITTLE ENGINE THAT COULD™
10pp   Cloth Book $4.95
0-448-02785-2   Platt & Munk

BABY'S MOTHER GOOSE
10pp   Cloth Book $4.95
0-448-02790-9   Putnam

BUNNY RATTLE
10pp   Cloth Book $5.99
0-394-89956-3   Random House

NIGHTY-NIGHT TEDDY BEDDY BEAR
12pp   Cloth Book $4.99
0-394-88244-X   Random House

THOMAS THE TANK ENGINE SAYS GOOD NIGHT
12pp   Cloth Book $4.99
0-679-80791-8   Random House

Boxed Gift Cloth Books
Jan Pieńkowski
BRONTO'S BRUNCH
8pp   Cloth Book $19.99
0-525-45354-7   Dutton

Other Boxed Gift Cloth Books:
FARM FACES
8pp   Cloth Book $14.95
0-8362-1491-9   Piggy Toes

ZOO FACES
8pp   Cloth Book $14.95
0-8362-1492-7   Piggy Toes

BATH BOOKS

Another type of book for babies is the bath book. Made of durable plastic, bath books can be taken into the tub or outside and can endure the worst baby spills! All bath books by major publishers have been safety tested and are completely nontoxic. In these bath books, toddlers will find familiar characters and new friends to make. There are some helpful lessons too— for example, in Potty Time. There are a wide variety of bath books to choose from. Here are a few of our favorites . . .

Eric Hill
SPOT GOES SPLASH
10pp   Bath Book $4.95
0-399-21068-7   Putnam

By the same author:
All 10pp   Bath Book
$4.95   Putnam

SPOT'S FRIENDS
0-399-21066-0

SPOT'S TOYS
0-399-21067-9

SWEET DREAMS, SPOT!
0-399-21069-5

Beatrix Potter
BENJAMIN BUNNY: A BEATRIX POTTER BATH BOOK
10pp   Bath Book $3.99
0-7232-0018-1   Frederick Warne

By the same author:
All 10pp   Bath Book
$3.99   Frederick Warne

JEMIMA PUDDLE-DUCK: A BEATRIX POTTER BATH BOOK
0-7232-3512-0

MR. JEREMY FISHER: A BEATRIX POTTER BATH BOOK
0-7232-3513-9

MRS. TIGGY-WINKLE: A BEATRIX POTTER BATH BOOK
0-7232-0019-X

PETER RABBIT: A BEATRIX POTTER BATH BOOK
0-7232-3584-8

Other Bath Books:
BABAR'S BATH BOOK
8pp   Bath Book $4.99
0-679-83434-6   Random House

BABY'S FIRST RATTLE
8pp   Bath Book $4.95
0-671-47668-8   Little Simon

ELMO WANTS A BATH
6pp   Bath Book $4.99
0-679-83066-9   Random House

ERNIE'S BATH BOOK
6pp   Bath Book $4.99
0-394-85402-0   Random House

I'M A LITTLE FISH
8pp   Bath Book $4.99
0-671-44435-2   Little Simon

LITTLE DINOSAUR SPLASH
8pp   Bath Book $4.99
0-679-86563-2   Random House

POTTY TIME!
8pp   Bath Book $8.00
0-394-89403-0   Random House

SPLISH! SPLASH!
8pp   Bath Book $4.99
0-679-89022-X   Random House

WALLY WHALE AND HIS FRIENDS
8pp   Bath Book $7.99
0-85953268-2   Child's Play

Preschool

PRESCHOOLERS ARE FULL OF CURIOSITY AND WONDER. Their minds are ready to grasp full concepts, words, and stories. This is the perfect time to get children involved with books. They will quickly begin to pick favorites and associate learning with fun.

Preschool books are on a higher level than baby books, but on a slightly lower level than picture books. These are books for the formative years.

In addition to hardcover and paperback, preschool books come in a variety of novelty formats. Among them are:

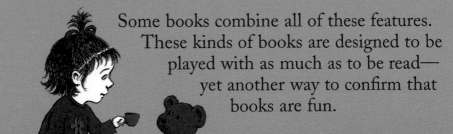

POP-UP: Paper-engineered pages make pictures three dimensional.

LIFT-THE-FLAP: Sturdy pages, and flaps to lift that reveal hidden words or pictures.

PULL TAB: Pulling the tabs changes the pictures.

Some books combine all of these features. These kinds of books are designed to be played with as much as to be read— yet another way to confirm that books are fun.

What to look for . . .

- A book that clearly covers the concept you are trying to teach

- A book that helps develop your preschooler's sense of humor

- An easy and fun story line

- Clear and easy-to-read words

- Colorful illustrations that intrigue the child

Jane Aaron
WHEN I'M ANGRY

Anger is an emotion that we all must deal with. For children it can be frustrating and sometimes frightening. This helpful storybook includes a parent's guide by Dr. Barbara Gardiner.

34pp   Hardcover $15.00
0-307-44019-2   Golden

Pam Adams, illustrator
OLD MACDONALD HAD A FARM

In this barnyard classic, die-cut pages reveal pigs, sheep, dogs, and the like. The die-cuts are cleverly formatted to reveal the *baa baa*'s and *bow wow*'s the animals make.

16pp   Paperback $6.99
0-8595-3053-1   Child's Play

Aliki
MANNERS

Leave it to the multitalented Aliki to create a fun and friendly book on a subject that makes most kids go ugh! Cheerful panel illustrations on subjects like "Too Loud is Too Loud," "Nobody's Perfect," and "Gossip and Whispers" provide gentle lessons on manners and tact. "A lack of manners in certain places can bother others and cause red faces." This book is appropriate for preschoolers and for children slightly older.

32pp   Hardcover $16.00
0-688-09198-9   Greenwillow

By the same author:
FEELINGS

36pp   Hardcover $16.00
0-688-03831-X   Greenwillow

Jonathan Allen
WAKE UP, SLEEPING BEAUTY! AN INTERACTIVE BOOK WITH SOUNDS

What a riot this book is! How can Prince Eggbert wake up Sleeping Beauty? By pulling the tabs, you can hear him try—with cymbals, a guitar, a gong, and jackhammer. When Prince Eggbert gives up, along comes Prince Kelvin. And wait 'till you hear him give her that famous kiss! Sound chips, placed in the thick back board of the book, make the clear and strong noises. Have fun!

16pp   Hardcover $16.99
0-8037-2212-5   Dial

Dina Anastasio
Illustrated by Mavis Smith
IT'S ABOUT TIME

The centerpiece of this book is a large watch face, whose movable hands are used to follow the story of Tim and his dog Ticker. There is a fair amount of text, so an adult should be available to help the preschooler along. By leading Tim and Ticker through their day, little ones will be telling time . . . well, in no time at all.

22pp   Hardcover $9.95
0-448-40551-2   Grosset

Mike Artell
LEGS

Legs, legs, everywhere. A mystery animal, revealing only legs, is hidden in each picture. Aided by a rhyming text, children are challenged to guess the animal each set of legs belongs to.

22pp   Lift-the-Flap $10.95
0-689-80621-3   Little Simon

Alan Baker
GRAY RABBIT'S ODD ONE OUT

Gray Rabbit is missing his favorite book. As he groups the various belongings in his room, he finds there is one item in each pile that does not belong with the rest. The preschooler will have great fun helping Rabbit find the incorrect item. As in each of the Rabbit books, this one is full of gorgeous illustrations and easy-to-read text.

24pp   Hardcover $7.95
1-85697-585-1   Kingfisher

By the same author:
All 24pp   Hardcover
$7.95   Kingfisher

BLACK AND WHITE RABBIT'S ABC
1-85697-951-2

BROWN RABBIT'S DAY
1-85697-584-3

BROWN RABBIT'S SHAPE BOOK
1-85697-950-4

GRAY RABBIT'S 1, 2, 3
1-85697-952-0

WHITE RABBIT'S COLOR BOOK
1-85697-953-9

Angela Banner
ANT AND BEE BOOKS

Angela Banner's pint-sized Ant and Bee books encourage older children to read to younger children. Certain words in the text are highlighted for the younger child to read, and colorful pictures help tell the stories of the two adventuresome British pals.

All 94pp   Hardcover
$7.95   Heineman

ANT AND BEE: AN ALPHABETICAL STORY
0-434-92966-2

ANT AND BEE AND THE ABC
0-434-92967-0

ANT AND BEE AND THE RAINBOW
0-434-92972-7

ANT AND BEE AND THE SECRET
0-434-92959-X

ANT AND BEE TIME
0-434-92961-1

AROUND THE WORLD WITH ANT AND BEE
0-434-92958-1

HAPPY BIRTHDAY WITH ANT AND BEE
0-434-92963-8

MORE ANT AND BEE
0-434-92965-4

ONE, TWO, THREE WITH ANT AND BEE
0-434-92964-6

Maggie Bateson and Herman Lelie
A VICTORIAN DOLL HOUSE

This wordless wonder of paper engineering is a world unto itself. Unfold the book fully so the front and back covers meet, and you have a two-story dollhouse set in the Victorian era. It is complete with working doors, stairs, tables, cabinets, and even a chandelier. Not only is this book hours of fun, but it also serves as a child's room decoration.

8pp   Hardcover $19.95
0-312-06228-1   St. Martins Press

Stella Blackstone
Illustrated by Debbie Harter
BEAR IN A SQUARE

Find the bear in the square . . . then find the hearts in the queen's hair. Each bright, fun spread has shapes to find, and each shape reappears in a sidebar and in an index at the back of the book.

28pp   Hardcover $13.95
1-901223-58-2   Barefoot

Lindley Boegehold
Illustrations by Pam Wall
THE GUMMI BEAR COUNTING BOOK

"One lonely Gummi Bear, what's he going to do? Along comes a friend and then there are . . ." Colorful Gummi Bears decorate this cute rhyming counting book. Go Gummies!

22pp Hardcover $4.95
1-85967-601-4 Lorenz

Paulette Bourgeois
Illustrations by Brenda Clark
THE FRANKLIN BOOKS

Paulette Bourgeois brings a wonderful, inviting, family-friendly tone to all her Franklin books. Preschoolers can relate to Franklin, a young turtle who does all the things little kids do. Mom and Dad help Franklin face his challenges in an upbeat way.

FRANKLIN IS MESSY

Franklin wants to play "Knights" with his friends, but he can't find the cardboard sword he made. Why? Because his room is a *mess.* And Franklin's father is not pleased about it—he finds an apple core in Franklin's drawer. Together Franklin and his father get boxes from the basement, and paint and label them so that Franklin will have a place for everything.

32pp Paperback $4.50
0-590-48686-1 Scholastic

FRANKLIN AND THE THUNDERSTORM

32pp Paperback $3.99
0-590-02635-6 Scholastic

From *Clifford the Big Red Dog*

FRANKLIN AND THE TOOTH FAIRY
32pp Paperback $4.50
0-590-25469-3 Scholastic

FRANKLIN FIBS
32pp Paperback $3.95
0-590-47757-9 Scholastic

FRANKLIN GOES TO SCHOOL
32pp Paperback $4.50
0-590-25467-7 Scholastic

FRANKLIN HAS A SLEEPOVER
32pp Paperback $4.50
0-590-61759-1 Scholastic

FRANKLIN IS BOSSY
32pp Paperback $3.95
0-59047757-9 Scholastic

FRANKLIN IS LOST
32pp Paperback $4.50
0-590-46255-5 Scholastic

FRANKLIN PLAYS THE GAME
32pp Paperback $4.50
0-590-22631-2 Scholastic

FRANKLIN'S BAD DAY
32pp Paperback $3.99
0-590-69332-8 Scholastic

FRANKLIN'S BLANKET
32pp Paperback $3.95
0-590-25468-5 Scholastic

Norman Bridwell
CLIFFORD THE BIG RED DOG

Emily Elizabeth has a dog. A big red dog. His name is Clifford and he is the biggest, reddest dog on her street. First published in 1963 as a small black-and-red paperback, Clifford has emerged as one of the most popular children's characters ever. In Clifford's first and most famous adventure, we get to know his doggy habits.

32pp Hardcover $12.95
0-590-40743-0 Scholastic

By the same author:
CLIFFORD AND THE BIG STORM
32pp Paperback $3.25
0-590-25755-2 Scholastic

CLIFFORD AND THE GROUCHY NEIGHBORS
32pp Paperback $2.99
0-590-44261-9 Scholastic

CLIFFORD GOES TO HOLLYWOOD
32pp Paperback $2.99
0-590-44289-9 Scholastic

FROM Arthur's Really Helpful Word Book

CLIFFORD THE SMALL RED PUPPY
32pp   Hardcover $10.95
0-590-43496-9   Scholastic

CLIFFORD'S BIG BOOK OF STORIES
62pp   Hardcover $9.95
0-590-47925-3   Scholastic

CLIFFORD'S THANKSGIVING VISIT
32pp   Paperback $3.25
0-590-46987-8   Scholastic

Marc Brown
ARTHUR'S REALLY HELPFUL WORD BOOK

This book could not be more aptly named. Marc Brown's Arthur has long been one of children's favorite characters, and here he teaches them tons of words. Big colorful spreads are crammed with items—each item with its name written beside it. Extra pictures and words associated with the activity in the picture run along the border of the page. In addition, a few sentences summarize each spread.

This is a great book for teaching word association.

36pp   Hardcover $12.99
0-679-88735-0   Random House

By the same author:
ARTHUR GOES TO SCHOOL
12pp   Lift-the-Flap $11.99
0-679-86734-1   Random House

ARTHUR'S NEIGHBORHOOD
12pp   Lift-the-Flap $11.99
0-679-86737-6   Random House

Rod Campbell
DEAR ZOO

When the narrator writes the zoo to request a pet, the zoo obliges with pets through the mail. Each page shows the animal behind a flap (a crate, basket, or box). But the animals are too big, grumpy, tall, or jumpy. In the end, a small case reveals a puppy, the perfect pet.

20pp   Lift-the-Flap $10.95
0-02-716440-3   Little Simon

David A. Carter
ALPHA BUGS

These bugs will dazzle your children into learning the alphabet. Each page has a letter and a bug (or bugs) that pop-up, twirl, and dance. Full of pull-tabs and flaps, this is a great candidate for a rainy day or quiet time.

24pp   Pop-up $16.95
0-671-86631-1   Little Simon

By the same author:
LOVE BUGS

Each spread of this heart-shaped valentine features an elaborate, beautifully engineered pop-up of bugs who love love. A bouquet of rose bugs helps say, in a cute and creepy-crawly way, "I love you!"

10pp   Pop-up $12.95
0-671-86629-X   Little Simon

BUGS IN SPACE
14pp   Pop-up $14.95
0-689-81430-5   Little Simon

BUGS THAT GO BUMP IN THE NIGHT
14pp   Pop-up $14.95
0-689-80120-3   Little Simon

FEELY BUGS
12pp   Touch & Feel $13.95
0-689-80119-X   Little Simon

HOW MANY BUGS IN A BOX?
20pp   Hardcover $13.95
0-671-64965-5   Little Simon

MORE BUGS IN BOXES
20pp   Hardcover $13.95
0-671-69577-0   Little Simon

CURIOUS CRITTERS: A POP-UP MENAGERIE

Ever wonder what a Sopranosaurus looks like? Mixed-up animals pop right out of the pages of this extravagant and fantastical book.

10pp Pop-up $16.95
0-689-81586-7 Little Simon

SAYS WHO?

"I swim in the ocean and rest on the warm rocks. ARK! ARK! Says who?" Children guess what animal is behind the rock, lift the flap, and are greeted by a friendly seal waving his flipper. So it goes in this delightful guessing game.

10pp Lift-the-Flap $13.95
0-671-72923-3 Little Simon

HOOT!
I'm an
OWL.

Mike Casey
Illustrated by Jenny Stanley

RED LACE, YELLOW LACE

This book aids with one of the first challenges children face—tying a shoe. Real shoe laces are tied to a large cardboard shoe. One lace is red, while the other is yellow. In a bouncy rhyme, the book takes the child through each step.

20pp Board Book $10.95
0-8120-6553-0 Barron's

Anne Civardi
Illustrated by Stephen Cartwright

GOING TO THE DENTIST

Going to the dentist can be a scary event for little ones. Color pictures and factual, friendly explanations help ease concerns they may have. The following books in the series deal with other potentially intimidating situations.

16pp Paperback $4.50
0-7460-1515-1 Usborne

By the same author:

GOING ON A PLANE
16pp Paperback $4.50
0-7460-1507-0 Usborne

GOING TO SCHOOL
16pp Paperback $4.50
0-7460-1269-1 Usborne

GOING TO THE DOCTOR
16pp Paperback $4.50
0-7460-1505-4 Usborne

THE NEW BABY
16pp Paperback $4.50
0-7460-1271-3 Usborne

Joanna Cole
Illustrated by Maxie Chambliss

I'M A BIG BROTHER

New babies are special—but so is being a big brother. This reassuring book is a tremendous boost to any older brother dealing with a new baby. A helpful note to parents is included.

28pp Hardcover $5.95
0-688-14507-8 Morrow

Lucy Cousins

MAISY GOES TO BED

The grooving mouse is back again. With pull-tabs and lift-the-flaps, preschoolers see Maisy get a glass of milk, brush her teeth, get into her pajamas, and get into bed. Maisy lends a special touch to any bedtime.

16pp Lift-the-Flap $13.95
0-316-15832-1 Little, Brown

By the same author:

MAISY GOES SWIMMING
16pp Lift-the-Flap $13.95
0-316-15834-8 Little, Brown

Nick Denchfield
Illustrated by Ant Parker

CHARLIE THE CHICKEN

Charlie the Chicken eats lots of barley. That's why he has such a big fat . . . tummy! Charlie goes on to eat lots of wheat, corn, and other barnyard goodies, which make him big and strong. But in the end, we see Charlie is not nearly as big and strong as his mother!

12pp Pop-up $12.95
0-15-201451-9 Little Simon

Carla Dijs

MOMMY, WOULD YOU LOVE ME IF . . . ?

In this sweet, simple pop-up book, a little pig wonders if mommy would love him if he were a lion, an elephant, a giraffe, etc. Each pop-up page shows what the little piglet would look like as another animal. Of course, mommy loves him just the way he is!

12pp Pop-up $8.99
0-689-80813-5 Little Simon

By the same author:

DADDY, WOULD YOU LOVE ME IF . . . ?

12pp Pop-up $8.99
0-689-80812-7 Little Simon

Blaise Douglas
Illustrated by Tania Hurt-Newton

WHEN I GROW UP I WANT TO BE . . .

Children can dream of being anything. Here they visualize themselves as firefighters, astronauts, deep-sea divers, and in many other thrilling grown-up professions. A photo of the child, when placed in the back

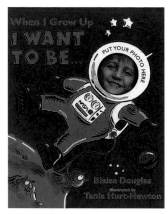

page of the book, can be viewed through a cutout hole on all the exciting pages. A funny rhyme accompanies each illustration.

28pp Hardcover $9.99
1-56402-866-6 Candlewick

Kin Eagle
Illustrated by Rob Gilbert

HEY, DIDDLE DIDDLE

You may think you know this popular old rhyme, but the talented team of Eagle and Gilbert will make you think differently! The cow in this version doesn't stop at the moon—he makes it all the way to Mars! Meanwhile, the dish and the spoon go to a wild party with

a baboon and a very funny cast of characters. Music is provided in the back of the book for a family sing-a-long.

32pp Hardcover $15.95
1-879085-97-6 Whispering Coyote

By the same author:

IT'S RAINING, IT'S POURING

32pp Hardcover $14.95
1-879085-88-7 Whispering Coyote

Ed Emberley

GO AWAY, BIG GREEN MONSTER!

This ingenious book puts a child in charge of his or her fears. Through a series of cutouts the monster reveals itself. First with two yellow eyes, then with a bluish-greenish nose . . . and he grows and grows as you turn the pages. But keep turning . . . and the monster slowly disappears. "And DON'T COME BACK! Until I say so."

32pp Hardcover $14.95
0-316-23653-5 Little, Brown

GO AWAY,
two little squiggly
ears!

Eric Hill
WHERE'S SPOT?

Spot has not eaten his dinner so his mother, Sally, sets out to find him. She looks in the clock, in the piano, in the closet, and under the bed. The preschooler gets to open each door to look for Spot, but behind each one hides a different animal! Finally the little pup is found in a basket, and his mom approvingly looks on as he finally sups. Eric Hill's Spot books are terrific lift-the-flap adventures, and are a must for every preschooler!

FROM *Where's Spot?*

20pp Lift-the-Flap $12.95
0-399-20758-9 Putnam

By the same author:
SPOT GOES TO A PARTY
20pp Lift-the-Flap $12.95
0-399-22409-2 Putnam

SPOT GOES TO SCHOOL
20pp Lift-the-Flap $12.95
0-399-21073-3 Putnam

SPOT GOES TO THE BEACH
20pp Lift-the-Flap $12.95
0-399-21247-7 Putnam

SPOT GOES TO THE FARM
20pp Lift-the-Flap $12.99
0-399-21434-8 Putnam

SPOT SLEEPS OVER
20pp Lift-the-Flap $12.99
0-399-21815-7 Putnam

SPOT'S BIRTHDAY PARTY
20pp Lift-the-Flap $12.99
0-399-20903-4 Putnam

SPOT'S FIRST CHRISTMAS
20pp Lift-the-Flap $12.95
0-399-20963-8 Putnam

SPOT'S FIRST WALK
20pp Lift-the-Flap $12.99
0-399-20838-0 Putnam

Tana Hoban
I READ SIGNS
Tana Hoban's crisp photographs show children the shapes, colors, and words of everyday signs.

32pp Paperback $4.95
0-688-07331-X Mulberry

By the same author:
26 LETTERS AND 99 CENTS
32pp Paperback $4.95
0-688-14389-X Mulberry

CONSTRUCTION ZONE
32pp Hardcover $15.00
0-688-12284-1 Greenwillow

EXACTLY THE OPPOSITE
32pp Hardcover $16.00
0-688-08861-9 Greenwillow
Paperback $4.95
0-688-15473-5 Morrow

JUST LOOK
44pp Hardcover $16.00
0-688-14040-8 Greenwillow

SO MANY CIRCLES, SO MANY SQUARES
32pp Hardcover $15.00
0-688-15165-5 Greenwillow

Janie Louise Hunt
ROUND AND SQUARE: A THROUGH THE WINDOW BOOK OF SHAPES

Cutout windows of different shapes are featured in this pastel-colored book. There is a glossary for the shapes presented, and a few questions to stimulate thinking.

24pp Hardcover $9.95
0-7613-0281-6 Millbrook

By the same author:
BIG AND SMALL: A THROUGH THE WINDOW BOOK OF OPPOSITES
24pp Hardcover $9.95
0-7613-0280-8 Millbrook

ONE, TWO, THREE: A THROUGH THE WINDOW BOOK OF COUNTING
24pp Hardcover $9.95
0-7613-0282-4 Millbrook

RED AND YELLOW: A THROUGH THE WINDOW BOOK OF COLORS
24pp Hardcover $9.95
0-7613-0279-4 Millbrook

Debra Leventhal
Illustrated by Monica Wellington
WHAT IS YOUR LANGUAGE?

It's never too early to learn about the rest of the world and the words we speak. This book teaches kids words in such languages as Swahili, Chinese, Inuktitut, and Arabic. A pronunciation guide helps parents and children. In addition, sheet music is provided, so the book can be sung as a song.

32pp   Paperback $5.99
0-14-056315-6   Puffin

Claire Llewellyn
MY FIRST BOOK OF TIME

The hours of the day, seasons of the year, and the time it takes for all of us to grow are some of the concepts covered in this comprehensive book of time. Included is a glossary of words and a fold-out clock with movable hands.

32pp   Hardcover $14.95
1-879431-78-5   Dorling Kindersley

Alice Low
Illustrated by Aliki
MOMMY'S BRIEFCASE

Reading glasses, a newspaper, and lunch are among the items children will find in this part storybook, part briefcase. Children love going through the items Mommy brings to work. Finally, Mommy comes home for a family dinner and quiet time—"the best part of the day."

32pp   Hardcover $14.95
0-590-47282-8   Scholastic

Mercer Mayer
LITTLE CRITTER®'S READ-IT-YOURSELF STORYBOOK

Little Critter has become a favorite of children everywhere, and these six stories get children excited about reading. With carefully chosen vocabulary, this book is both challenging and entertaining.

192pp   Hardcover $15.99
0-307-16840-9   Golden

No, Froo-Froo!
Come back!

Barbara Barbieri McGrath
THE M&M'S® COUNTING BOOK

Learning to count is great fun when using M&M's® as counters. The reward for learning is getting to eat those chocolate treats.

32pp   Paperback $6.95
0-88106-853-5   Charlesbridge

By the same author:
Illustrated by Roger Glass
MORE M&M'S® MATH
32pp   Paperback $6.95
0-88106-994-9   Charlesbridge

Illustrated by Brian Shaw
THE BASEBALL COUNTING BOOK
32pp   Paperback $6.95
0-88106-333-9   Charlesbridge

Corinne Mellor
Illustrated by Jonathan Allen
CLARK THE TOOTHLESS SHARK: A POP-UP, PULL-TAB BOOK

Mrs. Shark names her new baby Clark, a good strong name for a future ferocious shark. But Clark is toothless! This isn't all bad—being toothless enables Clark to help Sid the Squid escape from a stingray. Sid hides in Clark's mouth! Sid then introduces Clark to mermaids, who fashion out of a sunken treasure the teeth Clark so dearly covets. Pull-tabs and flaps make this silly outing great fun. The final flap reveals Clark's new gold teeth.

20pp   Pop-up $16.95
0-307-17606-1   Golden

Margaret Miller
BIG AND LITTLE

Big sisters and little sisters, big blocks and little blocks, big trucks and little trucks, and other size-related things fill the pages of this vibrant book of photos.

24pp Hardcover $15.00
0-688-14748-8 Greenwillow

By the same author:
GUESS WHO?
24pp Hardcover $15.00
0-688-12783-5 Greenwillow

NOW I'M BIG
24pp Hardcover $15.00
0-688-14077-7 Greenwillow

A. A. Milne
Illustrated by Ernest H. Shepard
POOH'S FIRST CLOCK

How to better learn to tell time than with Pooh? Original illustrations from the Pooh series highlight special times of the day. Gears click away as little ones turn the hands of the built-in clock.

12pp Board Book $12.99
0-525-45983-9 Dutton

By the same author:
WINNIE-THE-POOH'S GIANT LIFT-THE-FLAP BOOK

Pooh and friends teach us the alphabet, colors and shapes, numbers, and more. Included in this oversized book are large colorful spreads of *The Hundred Acre Woods* and Milne's famous characters. Each spread is filled with flaps and many hidden things to learn.

10pp Lift-the-Flap $9.99
0-525-45841-7 Dutton

FROM *My Very First Mother Goose*

WINNIE-THE-POOH'S LIFT-THE-FLAP REBUS BOOK

In this rebus version of "A House Is Built at Pooh Corner for Eeyore," flaps reveal the words that are depicted by pictures. Several pop-ups add to the fun.

14pp Lift-the-Flap $13.99
0-525-44987-6 Dutton

WINNIE-THE-POOH'S POP-UP THEATER BOOK

A three-dimensional theater scene pops up from every other page of this beautiful book. Pull-tabs on the theaters allow the child to move the characters as the story is read. The theater plays out stories taken from actual Pooh books.

10pp Pop-up $15.99
0-525-44990-6 Dutton

Bernard Most
COCK-A-DOODLE-MOO

Sounds abound in this wacky storybook. The rooster has lost his voice, and as a result all of the farm animals keep sleeping. The rooster enlists the cow's help, and eventually the whole farm wakes in laughter to "Cock-a-Doodle-Moo."

32pp Paperback $12.00
0-15-201252-4 Red Wagon

Iona Opie
Illustrated by Rosemary Wells
MY VERY FIRST MOTHER GOOSE

Mother Goose books come in many formats and have been illustrated by various artists. None have captured the action of the rhymes as splendidly as Rosemary Wells. In the introduction, Iona Opie calls Rosemary Wells "Mother Goose's second cousin." One glance though these beautiful pages will convince you that this is true.

108pp Hardcover $21.99
1-56402-620-5 Candlewick

David Pelham
A IS FOR ANIMALS

Learning the alphabet is animalicious in this pretty pop-up. Preschoolers may recognize the vulture, wallaby, and flamingo, and will learn what narwhals, quetzals, and xenopses look like.

12pp   Pop-up $16.95
0-671-72495-9   Little Simon

By the same author:
ABC FUN: APPLEBEE CAT'S ACTIVITY ADVENTURE

Pull-tabs bring several concepts together in this clever alphabet book. Each spread presents two letters of the alphabet and a question that is answered by pulling the tab. For example, one spread reads "Kk is for key / Ll is for . . ." When the tab is pulled, the word "lock" appears, while the key in the picture secures the lock. The last spread—featuring a pop-up zoo—provides a terrific ending.

26pp   Hardcover $10.99
0-525-45827-1   Dutton

SAM'S SNACK

You've never seen a packed lunch like this before! In this lunch-box book, Sis vents her jealousy of Sam by planting all kinds of creepy crawlies in among his food. This ingenious pop-up is spiced with playful verse that helps the reader guess each gross surprise. *Yuck!* Kids love it!

10pp   Pop-up (Boxed) $11.99
0-525-45266-4   Dutton

SAM'S SANDWICH
18pp   Pop-up $9.95
0-525-44751-2   Dutton

SAM'S SURPRISE
20pp   Pop-up (Boxed) $11.99
0-525-44947-7   Dutton

THE SENSATIONAL SAMBURGER
20pp   Pop-up $12.99
0-525-45426-8   Dutton

Ib Penick, paper engineer
Illustrated by Loretta Lustig
THE POP-UP BOOK OF TRUCKS

Vroom! If you are a kid who wants to learn what trucks do, this is the book for you.

12pp   Pop-up $10.00
0-394-82826-7   Random House

Kate Petty and
Charlotte Firman
BEING BULLIED

Most kids are bullied at one time or another. Feeling left out, making friends, and how to deal with bullies are some of the issues addressed here. Always talking honestly to Mom, Dad, or an adult supervisor is encouraged.

24pp   Paperback $5.95
0-8120-4661-7   Barron's

Jan Pieńkowski
DINNER TIME

"I'm going to eat you for my dinner" is the catch phrase in this wacky pop-up book by one of the masters of preschool humor. Each beastie eats the previous beastie with a "pop-up" mouth that opens wide. A silent shark brings this popular romp to a close.

10pp   Mini-Pop-up $6.99
0-8431-2963-8   PSS

By the same author:
LITTLE MONSTERS
10pp   Mini-Pop-up $4.95
0-8431-2964-6   PSS

OH MY, A FLY
10pp Mini-Pop-up $4.95
0-8431-2965-4 PSS

SMALL TALK
10pp Mini-Pop-up $4.95
0-8431-2966-2 PSS

PLANES AND OTHER THINGS THAT FLY

The preschooler can make helicopters, space shuttles, and other flying machines take off by pulling the tabs in this exciting pop-up. Pieńkowski's hot-air balloon literally floats off the page.

12pp Pop-up $7.99
0-525-45852-2 Dutton

BIG MACHINES
12pp Pop-up $7.99
0-525-45854-9 Dutton

BOATS
12pp Pop-up $7.99
0-525-45851-4 Dutton

TRUCKS AND OTHER WORKING WHEELS
12pp Pop-up $7.99
0-525-45853-0 Dutton

Watty Piper
Illustrated by George & Doris Hauman

THE LITTLE ENGINE THAT COULD™ THE COMPLETE ORIGINAL EDITION

A staple of American childhood, Watty Piper's classic continues to inspire nearly seventy years after its first printing. None of the train engines will take the dolls, food, or toys over the mountain. But then along comes the Little Blue Engine. "I'm not very big," she says. But with the famous phrase "I think I can—I think I can," the Little Blue Engine

FROM *The Little Engine That Could*™

makes it over the mountain and into children's book history.

40pp Hardcover $6.99
0-448-40520-2 Platt & Munk
Mini-hardcover $4.99
0-448-40071-5 Platt & Munk

By the same author:
Illustrated by Richard Walz

THE LITTLE ENGINE THAT COULD™
10pp Pop-up $10.99
0-448-18963-1 Platt & Munk

PLAYSCHOOL
MY FIRST ACTIVITY BOOK

A child's concentration, recognition, and motor skills are all developed by this multifaceted playing field of a book. The first spread is a touch-and-feel section, and is followed by a matching game, a counting game, and finally a challenge to fit the given plastic pieces in the appropriate holes.

8pp Hardcover $14.99
0-525-45471-3 Dutton

Henry Pluckrose
MATH COUNTS SERIES

Basic math concepts that every preschooler is confronted with are approached in this series. Bright, clear photographs are accompanied by gently guiding questions.

All 32pp Paperback
$4.95 Children's Press

CAPACITY
0-516-45451-X

COUNTING
0-516-45452-8

NUMBERS
0-516-45454-4

SIZE
0-516-45457-9

SORTING
0-516-45458-7

WEIGHT
0-516-45460-9

Beatrix Potter

PETER RABBIT AND FRIENDS: A STAND-UP STORY BOOK

The world of Peter Rabbit beautifully comes to life in this part book, part three-dimensional play. Peter, Mr. McGregor, and the Puddle-Ducks frolic in four pastoral country scenes.

8pp Pop-up $14.99
0-7232-4343-3 Warne

By the same author:

PETER RABBIT: A LIFT-THE-FLAP REBUS BOOK

16pp Lift-the-Flap $12.99
0-7232-3798-0 Warne

PETER RABBIT'S ABC 123

40pp Hardcover $10.99
0-7232-4188-0 Warne

You can drink from your cup
And feed yourself.

Fiona Pragoff

IT'S FUN TO BE ONE

Fiona Pragoff's books of photography show how things change as a child reaches age one and age two. Sturdy wipe-clean pages combat baby goo.

20pp Hardcover $6.95
0-689-71813-6 Aladdin

By the same author:

IT'S GREAT TO BE TWO

20pp Hardcover $6.95
0-689-71814-4 Aladdin

David Prebenna

LIFT-AND-PEEK INTO NOAH'S ARK

The folks that brought us *The Beginner's Bible* here present Noah and crew in this busy lift-the-flap book. Preschoolers can become acquainted with the story of Noah's Ark, and can help Mrs. Noah find the eight matching pairs of small creatures.

10pp Lift-the-Flap $10.99
0-679-87530-1 Random House

Raffi
Illustrated by Ashley Wolff

BABY BELUGA

Preschool singing sensation Raffi has been keeping young ears and minds busy for well over ten years now. Here, Baby Beluga, one of Raffi's most charming songs, is brought to life in a picture story form. The sheet music is presented on the last page of all the Raffi books.

32pp Paperback $5.99
0-517-58362-3 Crown

By the same author:
Illustrated by Jose Aruego and Ariane Dewey

FIVE LITTLE DUCKS

32pp Paperback $5.99
0-517-58360-7 Crown

Illustrated by Eugenie Fernandes

ONE LIGHT, ONE SUN

32pp Paperback $6.50
0-517-57644-9 Crown

Illustrated by Sylvie Kantorovitz Wickstrom

WHEELS ON THE BUS

32pp Paperback $5.99
0-517-57645-7 Crown

Edwina Riddell

MY FIRST DAY AT PRESCHOOL

Daily life at preschool is depicted by thirteen children (who are each given a name). Snack time, story time, and playtime are among the scenes that should put anxious preschoolers at ease.

24pp Paperback $5.95
0-8120-1878-8 Barron's

Anne Rockwell

PLANES

Children are usually fascinated with flying machines. Anne Rockwell brings big planes to little kids in a very simple and effective format. Seaplanes, model airplanes, hang gliders, and helicopters zoom in the sky.

24pp Paperback $4.99
0-14-054782-7 Puffin

By the same author:

BOATS

24pp Paperback $4.99
0-14-054988-9 Puffin

FIRE ENGINES

24pp Paperback $4.99
0-14-055250-2 Puffin

TRAINS

24pp Paperback $4.99
0-14-054979-X Puffin

This old man, he played one,
He played knick-knack on my drum.

1

With a knick-knack, paddy-whack,
give a dog a bone,
This old man came rolling home.

FROM *This Old Man*

Tony Ross, illustrator
THIS OLD MAN

"This old man, he played one, /
He played knick-knack on my
drum . . ." Pull the tab and sing
along to the popular song! Tony
Ross's comical drawings illustrate
the old man in all of his
exuberance.

12pp   Hardcover $10.95
0-689-71386-X   Aladdin

Shelley Rotner and Anne Woodhull
Illustrated by Shelley Rotner
COLORS AROUND US

This is one of the most
beautifully designed preschool
books on the market. Each two-
page spread uses superb
photographs to illustrate a color.
A few simple words per page prod
the senses and the imagination.

14pp   Hardcover $12.95
0-689-80980-8   Little Simon

Robert Sabuda
COOKIE COUNT

This fantasy land of candy glistens
with elaborate pop-ups and
découpage illustrations. On the
way to 10, we get "7 Linzer hearts
divine, 8 sugar cookies that shine."
The last spread pops-up to form
an awesome gingerbread house.

20pp   Pop-up $19.95
0-689-81191-8   Little Simon

Barney Saltzberg
WHERE, OH, WHERE'S MY UNDERWEAR?

"Where, oh, where's my
underwear? Where, oh, where
can they be?" A young elephant
searches about the house for his
missing undies. Of course, little
does the elephant know, his
underwear is having a good time
at the playground without him!

10pp   Pop-up $9.95
1-56282-694-8   Hyperion

Richard Scarry

Richard Scarry (1919-1994) was
born in Boston and received early
art training at the Boston
Museum of Fine Arts School.
During WWII, he served as an
art director in the Mediterranean
and North Africa. After the war
he moved to New York City
where, in 1946, he started
illustrating children's books. His
first big success, *Best Word Book
Ever*, is still tremendously
popular. Scarry's zany, detailed
illustrations provide children with
endless entertainment.

BUSIEST BUSYTOWN EVER!

When you open this most
unusual book, the pages keep
folding out until you get a seven-
foot town! Die-cut in the shape
of Busytown, Scarry's jam-packed
pages keep kids busy for hours.

24pp   Hardcover $12.95
0-689-80905-0   Little Simon

By the same author:
CARS AND TRUCKS AND THINGS THAT GO

Every car your child can think of
and more, from a "Bigshot car" to
a "Cheese car," can be found in

this imaginative compendium. A classic for many years, this book entertains even the most demanding preschooler.

70pp Hardcover $13.95
0-307-15785-7 Golden

PIG WILL AND PIG WON'T: A BOOK OF MANNERS

Pig Will has a smile on his little face while Pig Won't has a most displeasing frown. Pig Will is helpful and shares . . . but Pig Won't isn't very helpful and is in fact rather selfish. At the end of the book, Pig Won't comes to his senses and becomes a kinder, gentler pig.

20pp Hardcover $4.99
0-679-86653-1 Random House

BEST WORD BOOK EVER

70pp Hardcover $13.95
0-307-15510-2 Golden

BUSY, BUSY TOWN

48pp Hardcover $13.99
0-307-16803-4 Golden

FUNNIEST STORYBOOK EVER

44pp Hardcover $14.00
0-394-82432-6 Random House

WHAT DO PEOPLE DO ALL DAY?

62pp Hardcover $14.00
0-394-81823-7 Random House

The best street in any neighborhood!
SESAME STREET PRESCHOOL BOOKS

Tom Leigh
THE SESAME STREET WORD BOOK

Big Bird, Ernie and Bert, Cookie Monster, and all the other friends from Sesame Street teach little folks all sorts of words. Big colorful spreads clearly label items we find in the doctor's office, at school, at the farm, at the airport, and in other places around town.

48pp Hardcover $10.99
0-307-10374-9 Golden

Anna Ross
Illustrated by Joe Mathieu
ELMO'S LIFT-AND-PEEK AROUND THE CORNER BOOK

No one can resist the little red guy with the personality of total cuteness! This book with over sixty flaps gives Sesame Street fans hours of entertainment. Explore the famous street with Elmo as your guide, play

matching games, and look for storybook treasures. This lift-and-peek is more fun than a barrel of . . . Elmos!

10pp Lift-the-Flap (with board pages) $11.99
0-679-87188-8 Random House

By the same author:
ELMO'S BIG LIFT-AND-LOOK BOOK

10pp Lift-the-Flap (with board pages) $11.99
0-679-84468-6 Random House

Constance Allen
Illustrated by Maggie Swanson
TICKLE ME MY NAME IS ELMO

24pp Hardcover $3.99
0-307-16164-1 Golden

Joe Mathieu
SESAME STREET LIFT-AND-PEEK PARTY!

10pp Lift-the-Flap $12.99
0-679-88979-5 Random House

R. U. Scary
Illustrated by Tom Brannon
LIFT AND EEEEK! MONSTER TALES™: THERE'S A MONSTER IN THE CLOSET

16pp Lift-the-Flap $8.99
0-679-87415-1 Random House

Jon Stone
Illustrated by Mike Smollin
THE MONSTER AT THE END OF THIS BOOK

24pp Hardcover $3.99
0-307-16025-4 Golden

Nick Sharratt
A CHEESE AND TOMATO SPIDER

"Yummy! A strawberry flavored volcano." *Eh?* In this amusing mix and match book, almost anything is possible. Flipping the split pages gives the reader countless goofy images.

24pp Hardcover $12.95
0-7641-5112-6 Barron's

Norma Simon
Illustrated by Pam Paparone
FIRE FIGHTERS

Of all sorts of trucks, fire engines are the most fascinating to little folks. In this simple story, Dalmatians assume the brave role of fire fighters. Pam Paparone's illustrations are bright and to-the-point.

24pp Hardcover $13.00
0-689-80280-3 Simon & Schuster

Art Spiegelman
OPEN ME . . . I'M A DOG!

This book on a leash isn't a book at all. It's a dog, of course! At least, according to the dog in the book, it is. A wizard has cast a spell on our dog and turned him into a book. Before that, our poor narrator was a giant bullfrog, and a German shepherd (a real shepherd, and in Germany!). Readers will laugh aloud. Please handle the dog (book?) with love and care.

32pp Hardcover $14.95
0-06-027320-8 HarperCollins

Anastasia Suen
Illustrated by Chih-Wei Chang
BABY BORN

"Baby born in winter's sleep snowflakes fall snuggle deep." This charming, lulling rhyme soothes babies and preschoolers alike. Detailed watercolors give the book a true feeling for the seasons of the year.

16pp Lift-the-Flap $6.95
1-880000-68-7 Lee & Low

Iza Trapani
THE ITSY BITSY SPIDER

Trapani takes us beyond the water spout incident and follows the itsy bitsy spider's adventure through the day. Trapani's spider is very peaceful. In the end, she builds a beautiful web and rests happily in the sun.

32pp Hardcover $15.95
1-879085-77-1 Whispering Coyote

Sian Tucker
1 2 3 COUNT WITH ME

Children love Sian Tucker's simple images and wonderful, vibrant colors. While many counting books end at 10, Tucker takes us all the way to 20. Each number has a caption, which is embellished by lifting the flap.

24pp Lift-the-Flap $12.95
0-689-80828-3 Little Simon

Ellen Stoll Walsh
MOUSE PAINT

The cat is asleep, so it's time for the mice to paint! Each of three mice jumps into a jar of paint—one red, one yellow, and one blue. The red mouse then jumps in a yellow puddle, the yellow mouse in a blue puddle, and the blue mouse in a red puddle. The mice learn to make new colors, and so do we, the readers!

32pp Hardcover $13.00
0-15-256025-4 Harcourt Brace

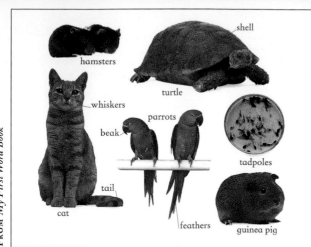

FROM *My First Word Book*

shell
hamsters
turtle
whiskers
parrots
beak
cat
tail
feathers
tadpoles
guinea pig

Tim Warnes
WE LOVE PRESCHOOL

Preschoolers can learn how to say hello, play, learn, and say good-bye in this fun romp based on the tune of "Here We Go Round the Mulberry Bush."

10pp   Lift-the-Flap $9.95
0-76130430-4   Millbrook

Angela Wilkes
MY FIRST WORD BOOK

This complete book of objects and words is great for a preschooler's vocabulary. "Things to eat and drink," "In the toolshed," "At the supermarket," "Pets," "At the seaside," and "Sports" are among the various subjects. A helpful index is included.

64pp   Hardcover $14.95
1-879431-21-1   Dorling Kindersley

Ken Wilson-Max
LITTLE RED PLANE

"Up, up, up, and away!" By lifting the flaps, children take charge of the distinctive red plane. Preschoolers are thrown into the cockpit, where they can command the control panels, fly through the clouds, and ease down for a safe landing.

12pp   Lift-the-Flap $14.95
0-590-43008-4   Scholastic

By the same author:
BIG YELLOW TAXI

10pp   Lift-the-Flap $14.95
0-590-42884-5   Scholastic

Paul O. Zelinsky
THE WHEELS ON THE BUS

You set the wheels in motion, and pull-tabs keep the action moving in this glorious little book. Clever paper-engineering and Zelinsky's gorgeous art lend a stylized and imaginative touch to the famous song.

16pp   Hardcover $16.99
0-525-44644-3   Dutton

POKE AND LOOK BOOKS™

Peeking through the holes is but one of the pleasures children derive from **Poke and Look Books**. Bright colors, die-cut holes, and sturdy board pages make these books much like a toy. Round safety-proof corners and educational concepts make parents happy too.

Yvonne Hooker
Illustrated by Carlo A. Michelini
ONE GREEN FROG

One of the first of the Poke and Look Books, *One Green Frog* has a big yellow hole on the cover that forms a frog's eye. Page two features two holes and two toucans, page three has three holes and three lazy jellyfish, and so on. Preschoolers will enjoy counting their animal friends.

24pp   Board Book $9.95
0-448-21031-2   Grosset

By the same author:
WHEELS GO ROUND

24pp   Board Book $9.95
0-448-21030-4   Grosset

Other Poke and Look Books:
Lisa Hopp
Illustrated by Chiara Bordoni
CIRCUS OF COLORS

24pp   Board Book $9.95
0-448-41556-9   Grosset

Wendy Lewison
Illustrated by Giulia Orecchia
NIGHTY-NIGHT

24pp   Board Book $9.95
0-448-40391-9   Grosset

The arrival of a new baby in the home is a most magical and wondrous event. For the older brother or sister it can also be a time of doubts and difficult questions. Here are a few books that will help ease the transition for your children.

FROM *Julius, the Baby of the World*

Marc Brown
ARTHUR'S BABY

In a light-hearted manner, Brown covers the range of feelings new babies cause in their older siblings. Arthur is not so happy his parents are having a baby, but his little sister D. W. is very excited. When Kate is finally born, D. W. is the little mommy, always on hand to help. But one day Kate starts to cry and nothing D. W. does will make her stop. Finally, it is Arthur who saves the day with a timely burping.

32pp   Hardcover $15.95
0-316-11123-6   Little, Brown
Paperback $5.95
0-316-11007-8   Little, Brown

Joanna Cole
Illustrated by Margaret Miller
THE NEW BABY AT YOUR HOUSE

This has long been considered the leading book on helping children cope with a new baby in their family. Photographs capture families welcoming the new baby, and run the gamut of sibling reactions from pride in helping out, anger at being left out, and jealousy—as well as love. The book, which includes a helpful introduction to parents, speaks directly to its audience without condescension.

48pp   Hardcover $16.00
0-688-13897-7   Morrow
Illustrated by Hella Hammid
Paperback $5.95
0-688-07418-9   Morrow

Kevin Henkes
JULIUS, THE BABY OF THE WORLD

Lilly the mouse is disgusted with her new baby brother Julius. While her parents sing his praises, Lilly assures him that "I am the queen." She protests her brother's existence until a cousin expresses a similar disapproval—prompting Lilly to do a complete about-face. Henkes's presentation of the universal feelings children experience when usurped by a new sibling will have readers smiling in recognition.

32pp   Hardcover $16.00
0-688-08943-7   Greenwillow
Paperback $4.95
0-688-14388-1   Mulberry

Fred Rogers
Illustrated by Jim Judkis
THE NEW BABY

In honest and supportive terms, Mr. Rogers speaks to preschoolers about how it feels to have a new brother or sister. Color photographs help foster discussion between parents and children. As usual, Mr. Rogers's underlying message to children is that they are all loved.

32pp   Paperback $6.95
0-698-11366-7   PaperStar

Harriet Ziefert
Illustrated by Emily Bolam
WAITING FOR BABY

Max can't wait for the new baby to come out. He can feel it kick when he puts his head to mommy's tummy. What's the baby waiting for? Maybe it needs a little help . . . so Max shouts to the baby, talks to it on a walkie-talkie, and plays his drum for it, but nothing seems to work. Just when Max is about to give up, the baby *finally* appears—and Max has a brand-new sister!

32pp   Hardcover   13.95
0-8050-5929-6   Henry Holt

Joanna Cole
Illustrated by Margaret Miller
YOUR NEW POTTY

This factual read-aloud opens with a six-page guide for parents. Little ones will benefit from learning what adults expect of them, and will quickly relate to the photos of children learning how to use the potty.

40pp   Paperback $5.95
0-688-08966-6   Mulberry

Alona Frankel
ONCE UPON A POTTY: HIS

Cute and to-the-point, this book has been a staple in its field since its publication in 1980. Josh was very happy to receive a potty from his grandmother, though to him it could just as well be a hat,

a cat bowl, or a flowerpot. Finally, Josh sits and sits and sits, and figures out just what it's for.

36pp   Hardcover $5.95
0-8120-5371-0   Barron's

ONCE UPON A POTTY: HERS

36pp   Hardcover $5.95
0-8120-5572-1   Barron's

Taro Gomi
EVERYONE POOPS

That's right! This very funny book confronts its subject with no fear. With simple text and hip art, Taro Gomi shows how it is natural for all animals to go to the bathroom.

28pp   Hardcover $11.95
0-916291-45-6   Kane/Miller

Bob McGrath
Illustrations by Shelley Dieterichs
UH OH! GOTTA GO! POTTY TALES FROM TODDLERS

Bob McGrath is best known as Bob from Sesame Street. Rather than prepare a "how-to" guide to toilet training, he presents brief episodes of children and their potties. This method taps a child's imagination, and opens lines of easy communication.

36pp   Hardcover $5.95
0-8120-6564-6   Barron's

Fred Rogers
Illustrated by Jim Judkis
GOING TO THE POTTY

In a clear, patient, nurturing manner, Mr. Rogers presents a guide to potty training for parents and children to read together. Mr. Rogers deals with possible mishaps in the process, and helps children feel good about themselves. His distinctive voice clearly resonates in the gentle tone of the text.

32pp   Paperback $5.99
0-698-11575-9   PaperStar

Tony Ross
I WANT MY POTTY

"The potty's the place," says the queen to the little princess. And so she learns to love the potty (even though it plays tricks on her). One day, while playing on top of the castle, the little princess is in need of her potty. The entire castle scrambles to fetch it. But it gets to her . . . a little too late. This witty storybook will let children know that it's perfectly normal—accidents *do* happen!

28pp   Hardcover $9.95
0-916-29108-1   Kane/Miller
Paperback $6.95
0-916291-14-6   Kane/Miller

Picture Books

With lavish illustrations and unforgettable characters, picture books are just right for read-alongs. One of the most popular forms of children's books, picture books are appropriate for a wide range of ages and reading levels.

Picture books come in many formats, such as:

HARDCOVER: Often jacketed, but not always

PAPERBACK: Same text, art, and size as the hardcover version

MINI-BOOK: A tiny hardcover version of the original book

BIG BOOK: Very oversized, usually paperback, often used in the classroom and at story time

BOOK & PLUSH: A book boxed with a plush character from the book

BOARD BOOK: With same illustrations and text as the original book, but with toddler-friendly board pages

Picture books have varying amounts of art and text (some are even wordless!). Some story lines are simple, while others are quite complex. Subjects can be beautiful, funny, moving, scary, or just plain silly. What is important is that you find a picture book the child in your life will relate to and enjoy.

You will recognize from your childhood many of the books listed here. Once a picture book becomes established as a classic, it stays in circulation. However, new and wonderful picture books are being written all the time, and the list of "classics" grows every year!

What to look for . . .

- Art or photography your child responds to

- Story lines that elicit questions and discussion

- Stories that develop your child's sense of humor

- Stories that help with children's issues—such as sibling rivalry, or going to school

- Stories you enjoyed as a child and would like to share with your children

- Titles recommended by reviewers and award committees

Verna Aardema
Illustrated by Leo & Diane Dillon

WHY MOSQUITOES BUZZ IN PEOPLE'S EARS: A WEST AFRICAN TALE

A mosquito tells an iguana such a preposterous tall tale that the iguana puts sticks in his ears so he won't have to hear her nonsense. This causes a chain of events that upsets *all* the animals. When King Lion calls a council to solve the problem, the animals realize the mosquito is at fault. To this day, mosquitoes whine in people's ears to ask if everyone is still angry.

32pp Hardcover $16.99 [A]
0-8037-6089-2 Dial
Paperback $5.99
0-8037-6088-4 Puffin

By the same author:
Illustrated by Beatriz Vidal

BRINGING THE RAIN TO KAPITI PLAIN: A NANDI TALE
32pp Hardcover $15.99
0-8037-0809-2 Dial
Paperback $5.99
0-14-054616-2 Puffin

Janet & Allan Ahlberg

THE JOLLY POSTMAN OR OTHER PEOPLE'S LETTERS

Join the Jolly Postman as he goes on his rounds via bicycle, delivering mail to Goldilocks, Cinderella, Jack's Giant, and other fairy-tale characters. Tucked into envelopes are actual letters for children to pluck out. Humorous and engaging, this is a perfect read over a spot of tea. *Aahhh!*

32pp Hardcover $17.95
0-316-02036-2 Little, Brown

By the same authors:

THE JOLLY POCKET POSTMAN

The third book featuring the Jolly Postman finds him in Storyland. Here, he shrinks down to size to meet Alice in Wonderland, and join Dorothy on her quest to Oz. Letters, glittery maps, and a mini magnifying glass help readers to keep an eye on the now tiny postman.

32pp Hardcover $19.95
0-316-60202-7 Little, Brown

THE JOLLY CHRISTMAS POSTMAN
32pp Hardcover $17.95
0-316-02033-8 Little, Brown

EACH PEACH PEAR PLUM

In this delightful "I Spy" storybook, nursery characters are partially hidden for eager fingers to point out. Hints in the rhyming couplet accompanying each picture guide young readers to the surprise finish. Gently amusing illustrations complement the clever text.

32pp Hardcover $12.95 [T]
0-670-28705-9 Viking
Paperback $4.99
0-14-050639-X Puffin

Jez Alborough
CUDDLY DUDLEY

Dudley the penguin is *so* adorable that his siblings won't stop cuddling him. Feeling smothered, Dudley waddles away to find some peace and quiet. Just when he thinks he has gotten what he wants—*yikes!* A scary discovery shoots him back for a cuddle with his flock of affectionate siblings.

32pp Paperback $5.99 [T]
1-56402-505-5 Candlewick

By the same author:
WHERE'S MY TEDDY?

Poor Freddy! He's lost his teddy, and he must go into the dark, scary woods to find him. But somebody *big* has lost *his* teddy too! What can Freddy do when he finds a *big* teddy? In a silly twist, toddlers get the message that being large doesn't mean being fearless.

32pp Hardcover $15.99 T
1-56402-048-7 Candlewick
Paperback $5.99
1-56402-280-3 Candlewick

IT'S THE BEAR!

In this hilarious sequel to *Where's My Teddy?* Eddie and his mom leave for a picnic in the woods—the same woods where Eddie ran into a great big bear. Eddie's mother insists no bears live in the woods, but Eddie knows better. When Eddie's mother leaves to get the blueberry pie, guess who comes out smelling good things to eat? Toddlers will enjoy the silly illustrations and minimal, rhyming text.

32pp Hardcover $15.95 T
1-56402-486-5 Candlewick
Paperback $5.99
1-56402-840-2 Candlewick

Lloyd Alexander
Illustrated by Trina Schart Hyman
THE FORTUNE-TELLERS

Tired of working with wood, a carpenter asks a fortune-teller to read his future. Much to the carpenter's delight, the fortune-teller predicts a sunny life ahead. When the carpenter returns to ask for details, the fortune-teller has disappeared—and the carpenter discovers he has a talent for an exotic new occupation. Vibrant illustrations evoke the magic of Africa in this clever folktale.

32pp Hardcover $15.99
0-525-44849-7 Dutton

Harry Allard
Illustrated by James Marshall
THE STUPIDS STEP OUT

In this first of three books about the zany Stupid family, the Stupids decide to go out—only after taking a bath with all their clothes on (and no water). With their dog Kitty driving, the Stupids visit Grandma and Grandpa Stupid, after which they enjoy a mashed potato sundae with butterscotch sauce. *Yuck!*

32pp Hardcover $14.95
0-395-18513-0 Houghton Mifflin
Paperback $5.95
0-395-25377-2 Houghton Mifflin

By the same author:
THE STUPIDS DIE

32pp Hardcover $14.95
0-395-30347-8 Houghton Mifflin
Paperback $5.95
0-395-38364-1 Houghton Mifflin

THE STUPIDS HAVE A BALL

32pp Hardcover $18.00
0-395-26497-9 Houghton Mifflin
Paperback $5.95
0-395-36169-9 Houghton Mifflin

MISS NELSON IS MISSING!

The children in Miss Nelson's class go beyond misbehaving; they are downright *terrible!* Near her wits end, Miss Nelson thinks up a brilliant plan. The next day the kids have a substitute—the nasty Viola Swamp—who loads the boys and girls with homework and *never* gives them story hour. By the time Miss Nelson finally returns, the children are so grateful they behave well. But now Viola Swamp is missing. . . .

32pp Hardcover $16.00
0-395-25296-2 Houghton Mifflin
Paperback $5.95
0-395-40146-1 Houghton Mifflin

MISS NELSON HAS A FIELD DAY
32pp Hardcover $15.00
0-395-36690-9 Houghton Mifflin
Paperback $5.95
0-395-48654-8 Houghton Mifflin

Picture Books

MISS NELSON IS BACK
32pp Hardcover $15.00
0-395-32956-6 Houghton Mifflin
Paperback $5.95
0-395-41668-X Houghton Mifflin

Mitsumasa Anno
ANNO'S COUNTING BOOK

Children will enjoy finding the additions to each picture in this clever educational book. Twelve two-page spreads illustrate months of the year, time of day, the four seasons, and a wordless story about a gradually growing town. The first number, zero, is depicted by an empty snow-covered landscape. Each page introduces a new numeral with the corresponding number of people, animals, and objects added to the scene.

32pp Hardcover $16.00 **T**
0-690-01287-X Crowell Jr.
Paperback $6.95
0-06-443123-1 HarperTrophy

By the same author:
ANNO'S JOURNEY
32pp Paperback $5.95
0-698-11433-7 PaperStar

ANNO'S MYSTERIOUS MULTIPLYING JAR
48pp Hardcover $18.95
0-399-20951-4 Philomel

FROM *Parts*

Tedd Arnold
PARTS

Oh no! A little boy discovers that his body is falling apart! Already, at age five, he finds two hairs in his comb. And the lint in his bellybutton? Certainly that means his stuffing is coming out! Perhaps if he sneezes, he will lose his head! Luckily, the boy's farfetched fears are allayed by his parents. Arnold's cartoonlike illustrations and ridiculous rhymes will have readers in stitches.

32pp Hardcover $14.99
0-8037-2040-8 Dial

By the same author:
NO JUMPING ON THE BED!
32pp Paperback $5.99
0-14-055839-X Puffin

NO MORE WATER IN THE TUB!
32pp Hardcover $14.99
0-8037-1581-1 Dial

OLLIE FORGOT
32pp Hardcover $13.99
0-8037-0485-2 Dial

Frank Asch
BEAR SHADOW

After it scares away a catch, a fishing bear tries everything he can think of to lose his pesky shadow. At high noon, Bear finally thinks he's succeeded, but then his shadow re-appears! After a lot of thought, Bear comes up with a happy solution. Asch's gentle illustrations and simple story clarify a difficult concept for young readers.

32pp Paperback $4.95 **T**
0-671-66866-8 Aladdin

By the same author:
HAPPY BIRTHDAY, MOON
32pp Hardcover $15.00 **T**
0-671-66454-9 Simon & Schuster
Paperback $4.95
0-671-66455-7 Aladdin

MOONBEAR BOOK & BEAR
16pp Board Book & Bear $16.95 **T**
0-671-89555-9 Simon & Schuster

FROM *Princess Prunella*

Margaret Atwood
Illustrated by Maryann Kovalski
PRINCESS PRUNELLA AND THE PURPLE PEANUT

Pampered, spoiled, and utterly vain, Princess Prunella cares about nothing but her pocket mirror and her peppermints. An old beggar woman, to whom Prunella is predictably rude, gives Prunella a curse: Unless the princess performs three unselfish deeds, she shall have a purple peanut on the end of her nose. By the time the peanut grows to the size of a pumpkin, Prunella is ready to change her ways. A plethora of *p*s are packed in this pleasing tale.

32pp Hardcover $13.95
0-7611-0166-7 Workman

Jim Aylesworth
Illustrated by Stephen Gammell
OLD BLACK FLY

This boisterous rhyming alphabet book begs to be sung aloud. An old black fly buzzes around and gets into everything, from an Apple pie to Mama's Yarn, until—*splat!*—this fly will Zzz no more! Stephen Gammell's messy illustrations swirl all over the page, just like a pesky fly.

32pp Hardcover $15.95 T
0-8050-1401-2 Henry Holt
Paperback $5.95
0-8050-3924-4 Henry Holt

By the same author:
Illustrated by Richard Hull
MY SISTER'S RUSTY BIKE
32pp Hardcover $16.00
0-689-31798-0 Simon & Schuster

Keith Baker
BIG FAT HEN

The familiar counting rhyme, "1, 2, buckle my shoe . . ." has been moved to the hen house in this bright oversized book. Each set of numbers is illustrated by a new hen with the requisite number of insects, eggs, and chicks. Baker's palette is warm and colorful, and he gives each hen gay plumage and a distinct personality.

32pp Hardcover $13.95 T
0-15-292869-3 Harcourt Brace
Board Book $5.95
0-15-201331-8 Harcourt Brace

By the same author:
WHO IS THE BEAST?
32pp Hardcover $14.95 T
0-15-296057-0 Harcourt Brace
Paperback $6.00
0-15-200122-0 Harcourt Brace

Molly Bang
THE PAPER CRANE

An honest and hard-working father and son own a restaurant that has fallen on hard times. One day a stranger comes to the restaurant, and though he cannot pay for his meal, he is fed like a king. In payment, the stranger gives the pair a beautifully folded white paper crane, which, at the clap of one's hands, becomes real and dances. Soon people are coming from miles around to see this remarkable bird—and to eat the good food. Bang's use of collage brings an oriental touch to this gentle fable.

32pp Hardcover $16.00
0-688-04108-6 Greenwillow
Paperback $4.95
0-688-07333-6 Mulberry

Picture Books

By the same author:
GOOSE

One stormy night, a Canada goose egg accidentally rolls into a woodchuck family's nest. When the goose hatches, she is immediately loved and the woodchucks teach her all they know. But the goose feels something lacking in her life; something she sets out to find. Bang's gem-like illustrations round out this gentle, heartwarming tale.

36pp   Hardcover $10.95
0-590-89005-0   Blue Sky

TEN, NINE, EIGHT
24pp   Hardcover $16.00
0-688-00906-9   Greenwillow
Paperback $4.95
0-688-10480-0   Mulberry
Board Book $6.95
0-688-14901-4   Morrow

T

Helen Bannerman
Illustrated by Fred Marcellino
THE STORY OF LITTLE BABAJI

Babaji goes for a walk in the jungle, proudly sporting his fine new clothes. Whom does he meet, but several hungry tigers! To avoid being eaten, Babaji convinces each tiger to take a piece of his clothing. The tale of how Babaji outwits these vain beasts, gets his clothes back, and

enjoys tiger butter with his pancake dinner has been entertaining readers since 1899. Originally titled *The Story of Little Black Sambo*, this classic is given new life by Marcellino's superb watercolors.

72pp   Hardcover $14.95
0-06-205064-8   HarperCollins

Debra & Sal Barracca
Illustrated by Mark Buehner
THE ADVENTURES OF TAXI DOG

Jim, a New York City taxi driver, rescues a stray dog and dubs his new pet Maxi. Maxi accompanies Jim in his taxi and meets all sorts

of people. With each new passenger, Maxi makes a new friend —and even helps Jim get tips! The text is written in a bouncing rhyme, and Beuhner's paintings capture Maxi's doggy personality and Jim's geniality. Can you find the cat in every picture?

32pp   Hardcover $14.99
0-8037-0671-5   Dial

By the same authors:
MAXI, THE HERO
32pp   Hardcover $14.99
0-8037-0939-0   Dial
Paperback $4.99
0-14-055497-1   Puffin

Illustrated by Alan Ayers
A TAXI DOG CHRISTMAS
32pp   Hardcover $14.99
0-8037-1360-6   Dial

Judi Barrett
Illustrated by Ron Barrett
CLOUDY WITH A CHANCE OF MEATBALLS

Grab your plates! In the land of Chewandswallow, meals—rather than rain or snow—fall from the sky. But something goes awry: the food falling from the sky gets larger and larger, causing the residents to make an escape before being squashed by giant pancakes or rolls. Ron Barrett dishes up some droll art work in this zany tall tale.

32pp   Hardcover $16.00
0-689-30647-4   Atheneum
Paperback $5.99
0-689-70749-5   Aladdin

By the same author:
ANIMALS SHOULD DEFINITELY NOT ACT LIKE PEOPLE
32pp   Paperback $4.99
0-689-71287-1   Aladdin

ANIMALS SHOULD DEFINITELY NOT WEAR CLOTHING
32pp   Hardcover $13.95
0-689-20592-9   Atheneum
Paperback $5.99
0-689-70807-6   Aladdin

FROM *Animalia*

Byron Barton
BUILDING A HOUSE

This introduction to home construction answers toddler's questions about how a house is built. The clear, simple text and bright, colorful illustrations may inspire youthful carpenters to grab a hammer and get to work!

32pp   Paperback $4.95   **T**
0-688-09356-6   Mulberry

By the same author:
DINOSAURS, DINOSAURS

Here is a nonthreatening introduction to dinosaurs. The text is clear and simple, and Barton's bright and childlike illustrations are far from scary—all the dinosaurs have eyebrows. Each dinosaur is pictured at the end, complete with name and pronunciation key.

40pp   Hardcover $10.95   **T**
0-694-00269-0   Crowell Jr.
Paperback $5.95
0-06-443298-X   HarperTrophy
Big Book $19.95
0-06-020410-9   HarperCollins
Board Book $6.95
0-694-00625-4   HarperFestival

Graeme Base
ANIMALIA

This sumptuously illustrated alphabet book is the perfect vehicle for Base's considerable talent. Each letter is pictured with an animal and a silly alliterative description. Other objects beginning with the letter are hidden in the beautifully detailed art, and readers are challenged to find as many as they can.

32pp   Oversized Hardcover $18.95
0-8109-1868-4   Abrams
Hardcover $11.95
0-8109-1939-7   Abrams
Paperback $6.99
0-14-055996-5   Puffin

By the same author:
ELEVENTH HOUR: A CURIOUS MYSTERY

32pp   Oversized Hardcover $18.95
0-8109-0851-4   Abrams
Hardcover $11.95
0-8109-3265-2   Abrams
Paperback $6.99
0-14-056160-9   Puffin

Michael Bedard
Illustrated by Barbara Cooney
EMILY

A young girl is curious about Emily, the woman who lives across the street. Why does she never leave the house? The girl's father says Emily writes poetry and always wears white. Shortly before the coming of spring, the girl's mother is invited to play piano for Emily; and when she goes, she takes the girl with her. While her mother plays, the girl sneaks upstairs. There she meets the reclusive poet Emily Dickinson, and the two new friends exchange special gifts.

40pp   Hardcover $16.95
0-385-30697-0   Doubleday

Ludwig Bemelmans
MADELINE

"In an old house in Paris that was covered with vines," lives plucky Madeline with eleven other girls under the care of the kind Miss Clavel. Madeline wakes up in the night with appendicitis and is rushed off to the hospital. The other girls visit Madeline after the operation, and see her gifts, her candy, and above all her *scar*. That night they all cry, "Boohoo, we want to have our appendix out too!" Bemelmans's drawings of Paris bring the charm of the city to young readers.

48pp   Hardcover $16.99
0-670-44580-0   Viking
Paperback $5.99
0-14-050198-3   Puffin
Big Book $17.99
0-14-054845-9   Puffin

By the same author:

MADELINE AND THE BAD HAT
56pp   Hardcover $15.99
0-670-44614-9   Viking
Paperback $5.99
0-14-050206-8   Puffin

MADELINE AND THE GYPSIES
56pp   Hardcover $19.99
0-670-44682-3   Viking
Paperback $5.99
0-14-050261-0   Puffin

MADELINE IN LONDON
56pp   Hardcover $15.99
0-670-44648-3   Viking
Paperback $5.99
0-14-050199-1   Puffin

MADELINE'S RESCUE
56pp   Hardcover $15.99
0-670-44716-1   Viking
Paperback $5.99
0-14-050207-6   Puffin

MAD ABOUT MADELINE
Fans of the little red-headed Parisian will be pleased to have all six of her adventures bound in one volume. Included are an essay by Bemelmans on how he created Madeline, sketches and photos of Bemelmans and his family, and an essay by Pulitzer Prize–winning author and journalist Anna Quindlen.

320pp   Hardcover $35.00
0-670-85187-6   Viking

Barbara Berger
GRANDFATHER TWILIGHT
Each evening Grandfather Twilight opens a chest, removes a pearl from a long string, and calls his dog for an evening stroll. As he walks, the sunset flows behind him like a beautiful robe, while in his hand the pearl grows larger. When he reaches the sea, he releases the pearl to the sky where it shines on the water below. Gentle and lulling, this book captures those serene moments that happen at twilight.

32pp   Hardcover $16.95
0-399-20996-4   Philomel
Paperback $5.95
0-698-11394-2   PaperStar

Claire Huchet Bishop
Illustrated by Kurt Wiese
THE FIVE CHINESE BROTHERS
Since 1938, this folktale about five identical Chinese brothers, each with an unusual talent, has entertained children and adults alike. When one brother is sentenced to death for a crime he could not help commit, each brother stands in for him and uses his special talent to escape the given punishment. After four tries, the judge decides the brother sentenced to death must not be guilty, and all five brothers live happily with their mother for many years.

64pp   Hardcover $12.95
0-698-20044-6   Coward
Paperback $5.95
0-698-11357-8   PaperStar

Ruth Bornstein
LITTLE GORILLA
Little Gorilla is happy because *everybody* loves him; not just his family, but green parrot, tall giraffe, red monkey, and other jungle dwellers too. One day, Little Gorilla starts to grow and GROW, until—Little Gorilla is BIG! And you know what? Everybody *still* loves him! Readers will enjoy this friendly and comforting bedtime read.

32pp   Paperback $5.95   T
0-89919-421-4   Clarion

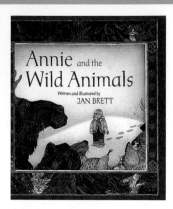

Jan Brett
ANNIE AND THE WILD ANIMALS

Annie is lonely when her cat Taffy disappears. She puts homemade corn cakes out in hopes of attracting a new friend, but each animal who comes (a moose, a bear, and a lynx) is not quite right. Finally Taffy returns, and she has a wonderful surprise! Jan Brett's detailed artwork tells stories within stories, and observant readers will discover Taffy's secret long before the end.

32pp   Hardcover $15.00
0-395-37800-1   Houghton Mifflin
Paperback $5.95
0-395-51006-6   Sandpiper

By the same author:
ARMADILLO RODEO
32pp   Hardcover $15.95
0-399-22803-9   Putnam

COMET'S NINE LIVES
32pp   Hardcover $15.95
0-399-22931-0   Putnam

FRITZ AND THE BEAUTIFUL HORSES
32pp   Hardcover $16.00
0-395-30850-X   Houghton Mifflin
Paperback $5.95
0-395-45356-9   Houghton Mifflin

THE MITTEN
32pp   Hardcover $15.95
0-399-21920-X   Putnam
Board Book $7.95
0-399-23109-9   Putnam

Marc Brown
ARTHUR'S EYES

Arthur the anteater is having trouble with his eyes—he needs glasses! When he wears glasses to school everybody teases him. He tries to lose the glasses, but this leads to some embarrassing situations—such as when he enters the girls' bathroom. Arthur decides he's better off wearing his glasses after all. This early adventure in the popular Arthur series skillfully handles a difficult situation.

32pp   Hardcover $15.95
0-316-11063-9   Joy Street
Paperback $5.95
0-316-11069-8   Little, Brown

By the same author:
ARTHUR'S BIRTHDAY
32pp   Hardcover $15.95
0-316-11073-6   Little, Brown
Paperback $5.95
0-316-11074-4   Little, Brown

ARTHUR'S NEW PUPPY
32pp   Hardcover $15.95
0-316-11355-7   Joy Street
Paperback $5.95
0-316-10921-5   Joy Street

Margaret Wise Brown
Illustrated by Clement Hurd
GOODNIGHT MOON

"In the great green room . . ." The first few words from this beloved 1947 classic are enough to start many adults reciting the rest. The story is simple: A rabbit is going to bed, and after taking stock of every item in his room, he says goodnight to each, one at a time. Brown's soothing text is complemented by Hurd's vibrant illustrations. Can you find the mouse in every colored picture?

32pp   Hardcover $13.95   **T**
0-06-020705-1   HarperCollins
Paperback $5.95
0-06-443017-0   HarperTrophy
Board Book & Bunny $24.95
0-694-00979-2   HarperCollins
Board Book $7.95
0-694-00361-1   HarperFestival

By the same author:
THE RUNAWAY BUNNY
40pp   Hardcover $14.95   **T**
0-06-020765-5   HarperCollins
Paperback $5.95
0-06-443018-9   HarperTrophy
Board Book $7.95
0-06-107429-2   HarperCollins

Caralyn Buehner
Illustrated by Mark Buehner

IT'S A SPOON, NOT A SHOVEL

Pop-eyed animals with exaggerated expressions, sly humor, and a touch of the gross are the protagonists in this book on proper etiquette. All but one of the answers to the multiple-choice questions are extremely silly, and the letters corresponding to the *correct* answers (along with a few animals) are hidden in the pictures. This is a lesson kids will hopefully bring to the table!

32pp Hardcover $14.99
0-8037-1494-7 Dial

Caralyn & Mark Buehner
Illustrated by Mark Buehner

THE ESCAPE OF MARVIN THE APE

Marvin the ape has been planning this for a long time. When no one is looking, he grabs his packed suitcase and escapes from the zoo to New York City! Two policeman cannot find Marvin, despite the banana peels he leaves in his wake. Buehner's illustrations are crammed with humorous detail. Can you find the two policemen, the ostrich, the cat, and the rabbit in each picture?

32pp Hardcover $14.99
0-8037-1123-9 Dial

By the same authors:
A JOB FOR WITTILDA

32pp Hardcover $15.99
0-8037-1149-2 Dial

John Burningham
MR. GUMPY'S OUTING

It's a pleasant day, so Mr. Gumpy decides to go for a boat ride. Each barnyard animal begs to join him, and Mr. Gumpy agrees—as long as each behaves! Two children join the fun, and as soon as the boat is launched, everyone does exactly what Mr. Gumpy asked them *not* to do. The result? *Splash!* This tale fits right into the toddler's sense of humor.

32pp Hardcover $15.95 T
0-8050-0708-3 Henry Holt
Paperback $5.95
0-8050-1315-6 Henry Holt

Virginia Lee Burton
MIKE MULLIGAN AND HIS STEAM SHOVEL

Although steam shovels are being replaced by more modern machines, Mike Mulligan refuses to consign his beloved Mary Anne to the junk heap. Desperate for work, Mike promises to dig the cellar of Popperville's new town hall in just one day—or go without pay. All the townsfolk gather to watch Mike and Mary Anne in their race against the sun. They win, but in his haste, Mike forgets a very important detail. First published in 1939, this classic is full of informative illustrations, including a diagram of a steam shovel.

52pp Hardcover $14.95
0-395-16961-5 Houghton Mifflin
Paperback $5.95
0-395-25939-8 Houghton Mifflin

By the same author:
CHOO CHOO

48pp Hardcover $16.00
0-395-17684-0 Houghton Mifflin
Paperback $5.95
0-395-47942-8 Houghton Mifflin

KATY AND THE BIG SNOW

40pp Hardcover $15.00
0-395-18155-0 Houghton Mifflin
Paperback $6.95
0-395-18562-9 Houghton Mifflin

THE LITTLE HOUSE

40pp Hardcover $14.95 A
0-395-18156-9 Houghton Mifflin
Paperback $5.95
0-395-25938-X Houghton Mifflin

FROM *Stellaluna*

Janell Cannon
STELLALUNA

Stellaluna, a little brown bat, is accidentally dropped by her mother. The helpless baby falls smack into a nest of bird fledglings, and is immediately accepted as one of the family. Stellaluna tries to fit in, but keeps acting unbirdlike; hanging upside down and wanting to fly at night. By chance Stellaluna is reunited with her mother and finally learns to be a proper bat. Cannon's breathtaking illustrations make this a gift-giving favorite.

48pp   Hardcover $16.00
0-15-280217-7   Harcourt Brace
Hardcover & Finger Puppet $21.00
0-15-201302-4   Harcourt Brace

Eric Carle
THE VERY HUNGRY CATERPILLAR

A caterpillar hatches out of his egg and is very hungry. On his first day, he eats through one piece of food; on his second, two, and so on. Little holes cut in the

pages allow toddlers to wiggle their fingers through the food, just like the caterpillar. Vivid and colorful illustrations and ingeniously layered pages help preschoolers learn the days of the week, how to count, and how a caterpillar turns into a butterfly. This picture book is considered a must for every toddler's library.

32pp   Hardcover $19.95   T
0-399-20853-4   Philomel
Mini-hardcover $5.95
0-399-21301-5   Philomel
Board Book $9.95
0-399-22690-7   Philomel

By the same author:
THE VERY QUIET CRICKET

A little cricket hatches out of an egg eager to respond to the friendly greetings of everyone he meets. From dawn to dusk, the cricket tries to chirp back to a variety of insects—a locust, a praying mantis, and a spittlebug, among others—but every time he rubs his legs together, nothing happens. When night falls, he

meets a female cricket who is also quiet. This time, when the cricket rubs his legs together, a computer chip plays his beautiful song.

32pp   Hardcover $21.99   T
0-399-21885-8   Philomel

THE GROUCHY LADYBUG

48pp   Hardcover $15.95   T
0-06-027087-X   HarperCollins
Paperback $6.95
0-06-443450-8   HarperTrophy

THE VERY BUSY SPIDER

24pp   Hardcover $19.95   T
0-399-21166-7   Philomel
Board Book $9.95
0-399-22919-1   Philomel

THE VERY LONELY FIREFLY

32pp   Hardcover $19.95   T
0-399-22774-1   Philomel

Nancy White Carlstrom
Illustrated by Bruce Degen
JESSE BEAR, WHAT WILL YOU WEAR?

This lilting poem follows Jesse Bear and the things that he wears throughout the day. In the morning, he dons "My shirt of red / Pulled over my head," while at noon his apparel is "carrots and peas / And a little more please." Night time brings "sleep in my eyes / And stars in the skies / Moon on my bed / And dreams in my head." Degen's cheerful illustrations help capture the playful interaction between toddler and parent.

32pp   Hardcover $15.00   T
0-02-717350-X   Macmillan
Paperback $5.99
0-689-80623-X   Aladdin
Board Book $6.99
0-689-80930-1   Simon & Schuster

By the same author:
**BETTER NOT GET WET,
JESSE BEAR**
32pp   Hardcover $15.00   `T`
0-02-717280-5   Macmillan

HAPPY BIRTHDAY, JESSE BEAR!
32pp   Hardcover $15.00   `T`
0-02-717277-5   Macmillan

**HOW DO YOU SAY IT TODAY,
JESSE BEAR?**
32pp   Hardcover $15.00   `T`
0-02-717276-7   Macmillan

**LET'S COUNT IT OUT,
JESSE BEAR**
32pp   Hardcover $15.00   `T`
0-689-80478-4   Simon & Schuster

Lynne Cherry
THE GREAT KAPOK TREE

A man walks into a lush rain
forest and starts chopping down a
huge kapok tree. Lulled by the
heat, he sits down and soon falls
asleep. The forest dwellers
approach, each pleading in his ear
a reason to keep the tree standing.
Suddenly, the man wakes up, and
for the first time notices the

beauty all around him. Will he
still chop down the tree? The
beauty of Cherry's art helps to
convey an important message in
this environmental tale.

32pp   Hardcover $16.00
0-15-200520-X   Gulliver Green

By the same author:
**THE ARMADILLO FROM
AMARILLO**
40pp   Hardcover $16.00
0-15-200359-2   Gulliver Green

Barbara Cooney
MISS RUMPHIUS

As a child, Miss Rumphius
dreams of traveling to faraway
places. Her grandfather assures
her that this is possible, but also
advises her to do something to
make the world more beautiful.
As an old lady, Miss Rumphius
returns to her home by the sea,
but realizes she has yet to fulfill
her grandfather's wish. Inspired
by her garden, Miss Rumphius
creates a world of loveliness for
those who live nearby.

32pp   Hardcover $15.99
0-670-47958-6   Viking
Paperback $5.99
0-14-050539-3   Puffin

By the same author:
HATTIE AND THE WILD WAVES
40pp   Hardcover $14.95
0-670-83056-9   Viking
Paperback $5.99
0-14-054193-4   Puffin

Jamie Lee Curtis
Illustrated by Laura Cornell
**TELL ME AGAIN ABOUT THE
NIGHT I WAS BORN**

A young girl asks her parents to
repeat the cherished tale she
knows so well about her birth
and adoption. Told from the
child's point of view, the story
and pictures are full of fun
details. On the plane down to get
her, "there was no movie, only
peanuts." When carrying her
home, her parents "glared at
anyone who sneezed." Under the
silliness in both the text and
illustrations, there lies a strong
message of the parents' love for
this new baby girl.

32pp   Hardcover $14.95
0-06-024528-X   HarperCollins

By the same author:
**WHEN I WAS LITTLE:
A FOUR-YEAR-OLD'S MEMOIR
OF HER YOUTH**
32pp   Hardcover $14.95
0-06-021078-8   HarperCollins
Paperback $4.95
0-06-443423-0   HarperTrophy

Picture Books

Alexandra Day
GOOD DOG, CARL

Mother needs to go out for a while, but Carl, the family Rottweiler, will watch the baby while she is gone. As soon as mother leaves, Carl wastes no time in helping the baby have fun! They jump on the bed, try on Mother's jewelry, slide down the laundry chute, and swim in the fish tank. The exquisite illustrations in this nearly wordless book will have readers of all ages gleefully cheering for Carl and baby.

36pp   Hardcover $12.00   T
0-671-75204-9   Simon & Schuster

By the same author:
CARL GOES SHOPPING
32pp   Hardcover $12.95   T
0-374-31110-2   FSG

CARL GOES TO DAYCARE
32pp   Hardcover $12.95   T
0-374-31093-9   FSG
Board Book $5.95
0-374-31145-5   FSG

CARL'S AFTERNOON IN THE PARK
32pp   Hardcover $12.95   T
0-374-31109-9   FSG

CARL'S BIRTHDAY
32pp   Hardcover $12.95   T
0-374-31144-7   FSG

Hans de Beer
LITTLE POLAR BEAR

Lars, an endearing young polar bear, wakes up to find that the ice he was sleeping on is floating south. He reaches a tropical land with no snow or ice, but amazing new animals and exciting new colors! Though there is much to see and do, Lars gets homesick. His new friends arrange to get Lars back home, where he is happily reunited with his anxious parents.

32pp   Hardcover $15.95
1-55858-028-X   North-South
Paperback $6.95
1-55858-358-0   North-South

By the same author:
AHOY THERE, LITTLE POLAR BEAR
32pp   Hardcover $13.95
1-55858-028-X   North-South
Paperback $6.95
1-55858-389-0   North-South

LITTLE POLAR BEAR FINDS A FRIEND
32pp   Hardcover $13.95
1-55858-092-1   North-South
Paperback $6.95
1-55858-607-5   North-South

LITTLE POLAR BEAR, TAKE ME HOME!
32pp   Hardcover $15.95
1-55858-630-X   North-South

Jean de Brunhoff
THE STORY OF BABAR

This first of the Babar adventures tells how the little elephant is rescued by a rich old lady in Paris after his mother is killed by a hunter. In Paris, Babar is educated and taught to be a gentleman. Though happy with the old lady, he misses his friends. When Babar's cousins Arthur and Celeste find him, Babar bids his old lady a fond farewell and the three elephants return to the forest. Home at last, Babar is crowned king and Celeste is crowned queen. Since 1931, Babar has charmed young audiences all over the world.

48pp   Hardcover $13.00
0-394-80575-5   Random House

By the same author:
BABAR AND HIS CHILDREN
40pp   Hardcover $14.00
0-394-80577-1   Random House

BABAR THE KING
48pp   Hardcover $14.00
0-394-80580-1   Random House

THE TRAVELS OF BABAR
48pp Hardcover $14.00
0-394-80576-3 Random House

Tomie de Paola
STREGA NONA

Strega Nona (Italian for "Grandma Witch") warns foolish Big Anthony *never* to touch her pasta pot. One day, Big Anthony sees Strega Nona sing to it, and the pot magically fills with spaghetti. What Anthony *doesn't* see is the three kisses Strega Nona blows to make the pot stop. Left alone for the day, Big Anthony excitedly uses the pot to feed the whole town, but is helpless when pasta flows *everywhere*. Strega Nona returns, stops the pot—and punishes Big Anthony by handing him a fork!

32pp Paperback $6.95
0-671-66606-1 Aladdin

By the same author:
BIG ANTHONY AND THE MAGIC RING
32pp Hardcover $16.00
0-15-207124-5 Harcourt Brace
Paperback $6.00
0-15-611907-2 Harcourt Brace

BILL AND PETE
32pp Paperback $5.95
0-698-11400-0 PaperStar

STREGA NONA: HER STORY
32pp Hardcover $15.95
0-399-22818-7 Putnam

STREGA NONA'S MAGIC LESSONS
32pp Hardcover $15.00
0-15-281785-9 Harcourt Brace
Paperback $7.00
0-15-281786-7 Harcourt Brace

FROM *Aunt Isabel Tells a Good One*

Kate Duke
AUNT ISABEL TELLS A GOOD ONE

When Penelope asks her Aunt Isabel (both are mice) to tell her a story, Aunt Isabel agrees, but only if Penelope helps her. What develops is a wonderful collaboration between the two: they tell a story with all the required ingredients—a prince, a heroine, some villains, an adventure, and romance. Readers will be touched by the special bond between niece and aunt.

32pp Hardcover $14.99
0-525-44835-7 Dutton
Paperback $5.99
0-14-050534-2 Puffin

By the same author:
AUNT ISABEL MAKES TROUBLE
32pp Hardcover $13.99
0-525-45496-9 Dutton

Lois Ehlert
PLANTING A RAINBOW

Ehlert's simple text and bright, graphic art introduce children to colors, flowers, and gardening in this cheerful concept book. Seeds, bulbs, and corms—all labeled— are planted in the ground and blossom into gay flowers. Following is a series of cleverly layered pages: each is edged with a color of the rainbow, and conceals flowers of the next color on the spectrum. Readers will be dazzled by their bright array!

32pp Hardcover $16.00 **T**
0-15-262609-3 Harcourt Brace
Paperback $6.00
0-15-262610-7 Harcourt Brace

By the same author:
EATING THE ALPHABET: FRUITS AND VEGETABLES FROM A TO Z
32pp Hardcover $15.00 **T**
0-15-224435-2 Harcourt Brace
Paperback $7.00
0-15-224436-0 Harcourt Brace

FISH EYES: A BOOK YOU CAN COUNT ON

32pp   Hardcover $14.95   ▧
0-15-228050-2   Harcourt Brace
Paperback $6.00
0-15-228051-0   Harcourt Brace

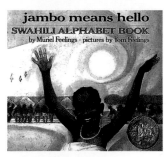

Muriel Feelings
Illustrated by Tom Feelings

JAMBO MEANS HELLO: SWAHILI ALPHABET BOOK

Here is an introduction not only to the letters of the alphabet, but also to another language and culture. Each of the twenty-four letters (there are no *q* or *x* sounds in Swahili) is represented by a Swahili word, a clear phonetic pronunciation guide, and an explanation of how the word fits into African life. Gorgeous pencil and ink illustrations help give young African-Americans a glimpse of their heritage.

60pp   Hardcover $16.99
0-8037-4346-7   Dial
Paperback $5.99
0-14-054652-9   Puffin

By the same author:

MOJA MEANS ONE: SWAHILI COUNTING BOOK

32pp   Paperback $5.99
0-14-054662-6   Dial

Marjorie Flack
ASK MR. BEAR

Danny doesn't know what to give his mother for her birthday. The barnyard animals each make a suggestion, but they are all things Danny's mother already has—such as eggs from the chicken, feathers from the goose, and milk from the cow. Finally, the cow advises Danny to ask Mr. Bear. Off Danny goes to the forest, and Mr. Bear comes up with the perfect gift suggestion! Wonderful illustrations and an unusual layout make this classic, first published in 1932, a super read-aloud.

32pp   Hardcover $14.00   ▧
0-02-735390-7   Macmillan
Paperback $4.95
0-02-043090-6   Aladdin

By the same author:
Illustrated by Kurt Wiese

THE STORY ABOUT PING

This classic story about a duckling who lives on a boat on the Yangtze River has charmed readers since 1933. When the owner calls for the ducks to come home, Ping, the smallest duck, tries not to be the last up the gangplank—for the last duck counted gets a spank on the back. One evening Ping misses the call to come home and stays out all night. His harrowing adventures the following day send him paddling back, only to be last again. Poor Ping!

32pp   Hardcover $14.99
0-670-67223-8   Viking
Paperback $5.99
0-14-050241-6   Puffin

Denise Fleming
IN THE SMALL, SMALL POND

Follow a frog in this colorful portrayal of the circle of life around a small pond. In the spring, the frog leaps into the water where "wiggle, jiggle, tadpoles wriggle." As the seasons pass, herons plunge, turtles doze, and minnows scatter. Finally, when snow starts to fall, the frog digs himself into the mud to sleep until the following spring. Fleming's vibrant art and energetic, rhyming text bring a toddler closer to the world of nature. Readers will enjoy finding the frog in each picture.

32pp   Hardcover $15.95   ▧
0-8050-2264-3   Henry Holt

By the same author:

IN THE TALL, TALL GRASS

32pp   Hardcover $15.95   ▧
0-8050-1635-X   Henry Holt
Paperback $5.95
0-8050-3941-4   Henry Holt

WHERE ONCE THERE WAS A WOOD

32pp   Hardcover $15.95   ▧
0-8050-3761-6   Henry Holt

Picture Books

Mem Fox
Illustrated by Patricia Mullins

HATTIE AND THE FOX

"Goodness gracious me!" exclaims Hattie, a splendid black hen, "I can see a nose in the bushes!" The other animals in the yard only answer with boredom and disdain. Hattie continues to warn the others as, bit by bit, a fox emerges. When it pounces, Hattie flies up a tree, but all the other animals are thrown into confusion—except the cow, who gives such a mighty MOO! that the fox is frightened away. The animals' languid indifference and the silly illustrations make this an extremely enjoyable read-aloud.

32pp   Hardcover $16.00   **T**
0-02-735470-9   Simon & Schuster
Paperback $5.99
0-689-71611-7   Simon & Schuster

By the same author:
Illustrated by Jane Dyer

TIME FOR BED

As night falls, all sorts of animals are putting their babies to bed. Lavish illustrations show dogs, cats, sheep—and even fish, bees, and snakes—crooning soothing rhymes about sleep to their babies. At last a small child is shown tucked snugly into bed. Like a lullaby, this gentle and loving goodnight book will send children off to sleep feeling comforted and serene.

32pp   Hardcover $15.00   **T**
0-15-288183-2   Gulliver

FROM *Corduroy*

Illustrated by Julie Vivas

WILFRID GORDON MCDONALD PARTRIDGE

Wilfrid Gordon McDonald Partridge is a small boy who lives next to a home for old people, all of whom are his friends. His favorite is Nancy Alison Delacourt Cooper, because she has four names too. Wilfrid is worried when he hears his parents mention that Miss Nancy has lost her memory. He asks the old people what a memory is, and all of their answers inspire him to fill a basket with objects. When this small boy presents the basket to Miss Nancy, each object sparks a special memory from her childhood.

32pp   Hardcover $13.95
0-916291-04-9   Kane-Miller
Paperback $7.95
0-916291-26-X   Kane-Miller
Big Book $19.95
0-916291-56-1   Kane-Miller

Illustrated by Pamela Lofts

KOALA LOU

32pp   Hardcover $13.95
0-15-200502-1   Harcourt Brace
Paperback $6.00
0-15-200076-3   Gulliver

Don Freeman

CORDUROY

Corduroy the stuffed bear has always wanted a home. Lisa wants to buy him, but her mother points out that the little bear's green overalls are missing a button! Corduroy tries to pull a button off a mattress, but the noise he makes alerts a night guard who puts Corduroy back on his shelf. The next day Lisa buys Corduroy, takes him to her room, and sews a new button on his pants. Now Corduroy has a home *and* a friend!

32pp   Hardcover $14.99
0-670-24133-4   Viking
Paperback $5.99
0-14-050173-8   Puffin

Picture Books

By the same author:
DANDELION

Dandelion the lion feels he should look snazzy for a party, so he opts for the latest in fashion: a curled mane, a spiffy new sport coat, and a hat with a cane. When Dandelion arrives, the hostess doesn't recognize her friend, and closes the door in his face! After a storm reduces Dandelion to his former scruffy self, he is welcomed to the party, and everyone, including Dandelion, laughs when they realize that *he* was that silly looking dandy!

48pp Hardcover $14.99
0-670-25532-7 Viking
Paperback $5.99
0-14-050218-1 Puffin

BEADY BEAR
48pp Paperback $4.99
0-14-050197-5 Puffin

BEARYMORE
40pp Paperback $4.99
0-14-050279-3 Puffin

NORMAN THE DOORMAN
64pp Paperback $5.99
0-14-050288-2 Puffin

Wanda Gág
MILLIONS OF CATS

An old couple is lonely—if only they had a pretty white cat! The old man finds a hill *covered* with cats and brings them home. His wife points out that they cannot possibly keep them *all*. The cats get in a fight over who gets to stay, and the couple is left with a scrawny little kitten. With love, the kitten becomes the most beautiful cat in the world. This classic is as popular now as it was when it was first published in 1928.

32pp Hardcover $11.95
0-698-20091-8 Coward
Paperback $4.95
0-698-11363-2 PaperStar

Patricia Lee Gauch
Illustrated by Satomi Ichikawa
DANCE, TANYA

As Tanya's older sister Elise practices ballet, Tanya performs plié's, arabesques, and jeté's right alongside her, but Tanya is too little to take ballet lessons. After the whole family attends Elise's dance recital, Tanya's mother puts on the music to *Swan Lake*, and an inspired Tanya gives a recital all her own. Ichikawa's soft pictures capture Tanya's innocence and joy.

32pp Hardcover $15.95
0-399-21521-2 Philomel
Paperback $5.95
0-698-11378-0 PaperStar

By the same author:
BRAVO, TANYA
40pp Hardcover $15.95
0-399-22145-X Philomel
Paperback $5.95
0-698-11391-8 PaperStar

TANYA AND EMILY IN A DANCE FOR TWO
40pp Hardcover $15.95
0-399-22688-5 Philomel

Mirra Ginsburg
Illustrated by Byron Barton
GOOD MORNING, CHICK

The playful refrain "like this," makes Ginsburg's simple story one children will love reading with their parents. A "little house, white and smooth" cracks open, revealing a plump yellow chick. His mother, Speckled Hen, takes good care of him by chasing away a troublesome cat and teaching him to peck in the dirt. Toddlers will identify with the chick when he tries to crow like the rooster, but all that comes out is a tiny "peep peep." Barton's sunny, childlike pictures enliven Ginsburg's tale.

32pp Hardcover $18.95
0-688-15391-7 Mulberry
Paperback $4.95
0-688-08741-8 Mulberry

By the same author:
Illustrated by Jose Aruego and Ariane Dewey
MUSHROOM IN THE RAIN
32pp Paperback $5.99
0-689-71441-6 Aladdin

Paul Goble
THE GIRL WHO LOVED WILD HORSES

A Native American girl loves horses and spends all her free time with them. When a storm hits, she and her horses are forced to flee and they end up lost, but a handsome stallion, the leader of the wild horses, welcomes her to live with them. Gradually the girl relinquishes her life with her people, and, years later, turns into a beautiful mare herself. Goble writes exclusively about Native Americans, and his art reflects their culture and customs.

32pp Hardcover $16.00
0-02-736570-0 Bradbury
Paperback $5.99
0-689-71696-6 Aladdin

By the same author:
GIFT OF THE SACRED DOG
32pp Hardcover $15.00
0-02-736560-3 Bradbury
Paperback $4.95
0-02-043280-1 Macmillan

Peter Golenbock
TEAMMATES

In the 1940s, segregation and racial discrimination were rampant, and in order to play professional baseball, blacks had to form their own league. Branch Rickey, the owner of the Brooklyn Dodgers, thought this was unfair, and signed Jackie Robinson to be the first black man in the all-white Majors. Robinson was severely taunted and even suffered threats to his life. During one such ugly moment, one of his teammates—the legendary Pee Wee Reese—had courage enough to defend him.

32pp Hardcover $16.00
0-15-200603-6 Gulliver
Paperback $6.00
0-15-284286-1 Gulliver

Hardie Gramatky
LITTLE TOOT

Little Toot is a sturdy little tugboat who loves to chug on the river, puffing out silly little smoke clouds as he goes. Little Toot is happy except for one thing: afraid of the rough ocean, he hates to work. The other tugs complain that Little Toot only gets in the way and call him a sissy. One stormy day, Little Toot's smoke clouds help out in a courageous rescue, and he becomes a hero. First published in 1939, Little Toot still captivates young readers.

96pp Hardcover $16.95
0-399-22419-X Putnam
Paperback $5.95
0-698-11576-7 PaperStar

Bill Grossman
Illustrated by Kevin Hawkes
MY LITTLE SISTER ATE ONE HARE

Written in the spirit of "I Know an Old Lady Who Swallowed a Fly," this counting book is certain to be a hit with the age group that finds bodily functions hilarious. A girl with a cast-iron stomach manages to put away a wide variety of creatures: one hare, two snakes, three ants *(and their underpants)*, four shrews (along with their smelly socks and shoes) . . . all the way up to ten green peas—whoops, too healthy! Kevin Hawkes's clever illustrations show the little sister swallowing her fare with great gusto.

32pp Hardcover $17.00
0-517-59600-8 Crown

Deborah Guarino
Illustrated by Steven Kellogg
IS YOUR MAMA A LLAMA?

A young llama is curious—are all his friends' mamas llamas? Each animal tells Lloyd facts about its mother, and Lloyd—along with young readers—guesses what kind of animal each mother is. The rhyming text and illustrations give hints, and preschoolers will enjoy yelling out the answers, which are revealed by turning the page.

32pp Hardcover $15.95
0-590-41387-2 Scholastic [T]
Paperback $4.95
0-590-44725-4 Blue Ribbon

Brenda Z. Guiberson
Illustrated by Megan Lloyd
CACTUS HOTEL

The saguaro cactus is born when a seed is dropped in the shade of a tree. In the one hundred fifty years it takes to reach its full height, it becomes a "hotel" for desert wildlife. When it is two hundred years old, the fifty-foot cactus topples and supplies shelter for ground dwellers. Guiberson has a talent for writing factual picture books that read like stories, and the vivid, colorful pictures bring this fascinating topic to life.

32pp   Hardcover $15.95
0-8050-1333-4   Henry Holt
Paperback $5.95
0-8050-2960-5   Henry Holt

By the same author:
Illustrated by Alix Berenzy
INTO THE SEA
32pp   Hardcover $15.95
0-8050-2263-5   Henry Holt

Fred Gwynne
A CHOCOLATE MOOSE FOR DINNER

A young girl tries to figure out what her parents are talking about; Mommy said she had a chocolate moose for dinner, and afterward, she toasted Daddy—*yikes!* Pictured also are the new wing on the house, Daddy playing the piano by ear, the arms race, and car pools. Older kids and adults will find Gwynne's deadpan humor hilarious, while younger readers may learn what those idioms actually mean.

48pp   Paperback $6.99
0-671-66741-6   Aladdin

By the same author:
THE KING WHO RAINED
48pp   Paperback $5.95
0-671-66744-0   Aladdin

A LITTLE PIGEON TOAD
48pp   Paperback $6.99
0-671-69444-8   Aladdin

Kevin Henkes
LILLY'S PURPLE PLASTIC PURSE

Lilly the mouse adores her teacher Mr. Slinger—until he takes away the purple plastic purse she was proudly showing off to her class. Lilly is so angry she draws a nasty picture of Mr. Slinger and slips it in his bag. At the end of the day, Lilly gets her purse back, and inside is a sympathetic note and a bag of treats. As in all his other books, Henkes shows an incredible sensitivity to children's feelings.

32pp   Hardcover $15.00
0-688-12897-1   Greenwillow

By the same author:
CHRYSANTHEMUM
32pp   Hardcover $16.00
0-688-09699-9   Greenwillow
Paperback $4.95
0-688-14732-1   Mulberry

SHEILA RAE, THE BRAVE
32pp   Hardcover $16.00
0-688-07155-4   Greenwillow
Paperback $4.95
0-688-14738-0   Mulberry

James Herriot
Illustrated by Ruth Brown and Peter Barrett
JAMES HERRIOT'S TREASURY FOR CHILDREN

Adults who have enjoyed the heartwarming stories of this Yorkshire veterinarian can now experience them again through the eyes of children. Selections of Herriot's amusing tales have been adapted into eight lavishly illustrated picture books, all gathered in this one gift volume. Young readers are introduced to such delightfully unusual animals as Oscar, a cat who enjoys public functions, Gyp, a sheepdog who never barks, and Smudge, a lamb who seeks adventure away from his field.

260pp   Hardcover $19.95
0-312-08512-5   St. Martin's Press

By the same author:
Illustrated by Peter Barrett
MOSES THE KITTEN
32pp   Paperback $6.95
0-312-06419-5   St. Martin's Press

ONLY ONE WOOF
32pp   Paperback $6.95
0-312-09129-X   St. Martin's Press

Illustrated by Ruth Brown

OSCAR, CAT-ABOUT-TOWN

32pp   Hardcover $13.00
0-312-05137-9   St. Martin's Press
Paperback $6.95
0-312-09130-3   St. Martin's Press

Russell Hoban
Illustrated by Lillian Hoban

BREAD AND JAM FOR FRANCES

Frances knows what she likes—jam spread on bread. In fact, this is all Frances wants to eat, so her wise mother gives her just that for breakfast, lunch, snack, *and* dinner. Finally, one evening when everyone else gets spaghetti and meatballs, Frances starts to cry and declares that she would like spaghetti and meatballs too! In the end, Frances enjoys a wonderful lunch at school, filled with a variety of foods—but *no* bread and jam!

32pp   Hardcover $15.00
0-06-022359-6   HarperCollins
Paperback $5.95
0-06-443096-0   HarperTrophy

By the same author:

A BABY SISTER FOR FRANCES

32pp   Hardcover $15.00
0-06-022335-9   HarperCollins
Paperback $5.95
0-06-443006-5   HarperTrophy

A BARGAIN FOR FRANCES

64pp   Hardcover $14.95
0-06-022329-4   HarperCollins
Paperback $3.75
0-06-444001-X   HarperTrophy

BEST FRIENDS FOR FRANCES

32pp   Hardcover $15.00
0-06-022327-8   HarperCollins
Paperback $5.95
0-06-443008-1   HarperTrophy

Illustrated by Garth Williams

BEDTIME FOR FRANCES

32pp   Hardcover $14.95
0-06-027106-X   HarperCollins

Mary Ann Hoberman
Illustrated by Betty Fraser

A HOUSE IS A HOUSE FOR ME

In a rollicking rhyme, the author introduces us to all types of homes for both people and animals. The poem engages in flights of fancy—what about a husk being a house for an ear of corn, or a throat being a house for a hum? "And once you get started in thinking this way, / It seems that whatever you see / Is

either a house or it lives in a house, / And a house is a house for me!" Whimsical drawings color the imaginative text.

48pp   Hardcover $16.99
0-670-38016-4   Viking
Paperback $4.99
0-14-050394-3   Puffin

Mary Hoffman
Illustrated by Caroline Binch

AMAZING GRACE

Grace loves stories, and with a boundless imagination she acts them all out. One day, her teacher asks who would like to play the lead in the play Peter Pan. Grace eagerly raises her hand, but Raj tells her she can't play the part because she isn't a boy, and Natalie tells her she can't because she is black. Nana sets Grace straight: she can do anything she sets her mind to! Grace's talent bursts forth, and she wins the audition hands down. Binch's radiant illustrations add to this inspiring story.

32pp   Hardcover $15.99
0-8037-1040-2   Dial

By the same author:

BOUNDLESS GRACE

32pp   Hardcover $14.99
0-8037-1715-6   Dial

Picture Books

FROM *Angelina Ballerina*

Katharine Holabird
Illustrated by Helen Craig
ANGELINA BALLERINA

Angelina is a little mouse who *loves* dancing. She dances down the stairs, in the kitchen, all the way to school, and even on her bed. After Angelina's arabesque knocks over a plate of her mother's best cheddar cheese pies, her parents enroll Angelina in ballet school. She works so hard she becomes a great ballerina. Craig's charming and humorous illustrations are a perfect match to this sweet and very popular story.

24pp   Hardcover $16.00
0-517-55083-0   Clarkson Potter
Paperback $5.99
0-517-57668-6   Clarkson Potter
Mini-hardcover & Doll $30.00
0-517-57089-0   Clarkson Potter

By the same author:
ANGELINA AND ALICE
24pp   Hardcover $16.00
0-517-56074-7   Clarkson Potter

ANGELINA AND THE PRINCESS
24pp   Hardcover $16.00
0-517-55273-6   Clarkson Potter

ANGELINA ON STAGE
24pp   Hardcover $16.00
0-517-56073-9   Clarkson Potter

ANGELINA'S BABY SISTER
32pp   Hardcover $16.00
0-517-58600-2   Clarkson Potter

**ANGELINA'S BIRTHDAY
SURPRISE**
32pp   Hardcover $15.00
0-517-57325-3   Clarkson Potter

James Howe
Illustrated by Ed Young
I WISH I WERE A BUTTERFLY

The littlest cricket is sad. The frog told him he is the ugliest creature around the pond. How he wishes he were a beautiful butterfly! All the other insects offer advice, but only his friend the spider knows how to help. She reassures cricket that he is beautiful to her because he is her friend. Feeling better, cricket begins to sing, just as a butterfly floats overhead. "What beautiful music," thinks the butterfly, "I wish I were a cricket!" Young's illustrations add a stunning insect-eye view of nature to the parable.

32pp   Hardcover $17.00
0-15-200470-X   Gulliver
Paperback $7.00
0-15-238013-2   Voyager

By the same author:
Illustrated by Lillian Hoban
**THE DAY THE TEACHER WENT
BANANAS**
32pp   Paperback $4.99
0-14-054744-4   Puffin

Shirley Hughes
DOGGER

David is inconsolable when he loses his precious stuffed dog Dogger. Even the neighborhood fair can't cheer him up. When his sister Bella wins a huge teddy bear, David wanders off to a used toy stall—where whom does he see, but Dogger! David runs to find his parents, but can only find Bella. They rush back to the stall but when they get there, a little girl has bought Dogger and won't sell him back. With sisterly love, Bella trades her new teddy for Dogger, and Dogger is reunited with David. Hughes's scruffy illustrations capture a child's world perfectly.

32pp   Paperback $4.95
0-688-11704-X   Mulberry

Picture Books

Pat Hutchins
THE DOORBELL RANG

Ma makes some freshly baked chocolate chip cookies, and her two kids sit down to eat them when *ding dong!* the doorbell rings! More kids arrive to share the cookies, but just when they sit down, *ding dong!* Finally, when there is only one cookie for each child, the doorbell rings again. Who is it? Grandma, with a new tray of fresh baked cookies! And no one bakes cookies as good as Grandma's! Hutchins sneaks a bit of math into this funny tale.

24pp   Hardcover $16.00
0-688-05251-7   Greenwillow
Paperback $3.95
0-688-09234-9   Mulberry

By the same author:
DON'T FORGET THE BACON!
32pp   Paperback $4.95
0-688-08743-4   Mulberry

Susan Jeffers
BROTHER EAGLE, SISTER SKY: A MESSAGE FROM CHIEF SEATTLE

During the 1850s, the white man negotiated to buy some land from the Northwest Nations. Chief Seattle, head of the Suquamish and Duwamish Indians, spoke to the white man in his native tongue about the importance of preserving the earth. His speech, translated here and lushly illustrated by Susan Jeffers, eloquently conveys the message that we must respect the earth and all it has on it. This speech has been the cornerstone for many environmental movements.

32pp   Hardcover $16.99
0-8037-0969-2   Dial

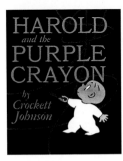

Crockett Johnson
HAROLD AND THE PURPLE CRAYON

Harold's wonderful purple crayon makes everything he draws become real. One evening, Harold draws a path and a moon and goes for a walk—and the moon comes too. After many adventures, Harold gets tired and can't find his bedroom. Finally, he remembers that the moon always shines through his bedroom window. He draws a window around the moon, draws himself a bed, and "the purple crayon dropped on the floor, and Harold dropped off to sleep." This little gem is filled with visual and written puns.

64pp   Hardcover $12.95
0-06-022935-7   HarperCollins
Paperback $5.95
0-06-443022-7   HarperTrophy

By the same author:
HAROLD'S ABC
64pp   Paperback $5.95
0-06-443023-5   HarperTrophy

HAROLD'S CIRCUS
64pp   Paperback $5.95
0-06-443024-3   HarperTrophy

Barbara M. Joosse
Illustrated by Mary Whyte
I LOVE YOU THE PURPLEST

Two brothers and their mother spend the day fishing on a lake. The two boys are eager to find out which of them she loves the best. For all of their questions, the mother comes up with answers that compliment them both. She ultimately tells one she loves him the reddest and the other she loves him the bluest— each for his own special self. This heartwarming book will bring comfort and security to young listeners.

32pp   Hardcover $14.95
0-8118-0718-5   Chronicle

By the same author:
Illustrated by Barbara Lavallee
MAMA, DO YOU LOVE ME?
32pp   Hardcover $13.95
0-87701-759-X   Chronicle

William Joyce
GEORGE SHRINKS

George wakes up one morning to find he's shrunk during the night. With a new pint-sized perspective, mundane chores are more exciting—washing dishes becomes a skiing expedition and the bathtub is as big as an ocean. The only drawback is the family cat becomes very interested in tiny George. Joyce's retro-illustrations add a lot of humor to this fun tale.

32pp Hardcover $15.00
0-06-023070-3 HarperFestival
Paperback $4.95
0-06-443129-0 HarperFestival
Mini-hardcover $3.95
0-06-023299-4 HarperFestival

By the same author:
DINOSAUR BOB
48pp Hardcover $15.00
0-06-021074-5 HarperCollins
Paperback $4.95
0-06-443247-5 HarperTrophy

Maira Kalman
OOH-LA-LA (MAX IN LOVE)

Max Stravinsky, poet-beagle, has gone to Paris in the springtime. The city of love is buzzing with the news of his arrival, and Pierre Potpourri of the Crazy Wolf Nightclub asks Max to perform. The show opens with the divine Dalmatian Crêpes Suzette playing the piano, and—*ooh-la-la*, Max is smitten! Crammed with visual allusions, Kalman's busy pictures bring to mind Paris at its artistic heyday, and her witty text is filled with French wordplay. *C'est magnifique!*

32pp Hardcover $16.99
0-670-84163-3 Viking

By the same author:
MAX IN HOLLYWOOD, BABY
32pp Hardcover $16.99
0-670-84479-9 Viking

MAX MAKES A MILLION
32pp Hardcover $17.00
0-670-83545-5 Viking

Ezra Jack Keats
THE SNOWY DAY

Peter wakes up to find the world covered in snow—crisp, clean, and white. Excitedly, Peter ventures out to play. His feet make a variety of tracks, and when he hits a snow-laden tree with a stick, the snow falls off—*plop!* onto his head. Keats's sparse collage illustrations capture the wonder and beauty a snowy day can bring to a small child.

40pp Hardcover $15.99
0-670-65400-0 Viking
Paperback $5.99
0-14-050182-7 Puffin
Board Book $6.99
0-670-86733-0 Viking

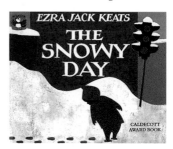

By the same author:
GOGGLES!
40pp Hardcover $15.99
0-670-88062-0 Viking

HI, CAT!
40pp Paperback $5.99
0-689-71258-8 Aladdin

JENNIE'S HAT
32pp Paperback $6.95
0-06-443072-3 HarperTrophy

PET SHOW!
40pp Paperback $5.99
0-689-71159-X Aladdin

Picture Books

Steven Kellogg
JOHNNY APPLESEED

John Chapman, born in
Massachusetts in 1774, loved
animals and nature so much that
he left home to live in the
wilderness. Wherever he roamed,
he cleared the land to plant apple
trees. He gave the trees to settlers
who followed, thus earning the
fond name "Johnny Appleseed."
Kellogg combines history with
some of the legends surrounding
this popular figure.

48pp   Hardcover $16.00
0-688-06417-5   Morrow

By the same author:
PAUL BUNYAN
48pp   Paperback $5.95
0-688-05800-0   Mulberry
Big Book $18.95
0-688-12610-3   Mulberry

PECOS BILL
32pp   Hardcover $16.00
0-688-05871-X   Morrow
Paperback $5.95
0-688-09924-6   Morrow

David Kirk
MISS SPIDER'S NEW CAR

The spider with the long
eyelashes is looking for a new car,
and a fetching turbo-bumbled
power mobile with two-stem
engine is among her colorful
choices. Kirk's vivid illustrations
will send children's imaginations
zooming!

32pp   Hardcover $16.95
0-590-30713-4   Scholastic

By the same author:
MISS SPIDER'S TEA PARTY
32pp   Hardcover $15.95
0-590-47724-2   Scholastic

MISS SPIDER'S WEDDING
40pp   Hardcover $15.95
0-590-56866-3   Scholastic

Ruth Krauss
Illustrated by Crockett Johnson
THE CARROT SEED

A small boy plants a carrot seed,
only to be told by his family
members that it won't grow. The
little boy ignores the family,
continues to tend his seed, and is
rewarded one day with a HUGE

carrot. This story about belief in
oneself has been enjoyed by
children for more than two
decades. Johnson's flat and
cartoonlike illustrations match
Krauss's simple text perfectly.

32pp   Hardcover $13.95   T
0-06-023350-8   HarperCollins
Paperback $4.95
0-06-443210-6   HarperTrophy
Board Book $6.95
0-694-00492-8   HarperFestival

By the same author:
Illustrated by Maurice Sendak
A HOLE IS TO DIG: A BOOK OF FIRST DEFINITIONS

Krauss has brought together
many whimsical definitions made
by small children; such as "dogs
are to kiss people" and "a face is
something to have on the front of
your head." Humorous and
cheerful, this 1952 classic inspires
giggles from all readers. Sendak's
illustrations capture the essence
of a child's world.

48pp   Hardcover $14.95   T
0-06-023405-9   HarperCollins
Paperback $4.95
0-06-443205-X   HarperTrophy

Karla Kuskin
Illustrated by Marc Simont
THE PHILHARMONIC GETS DRESSED

From taking showers and putting on underwear to donning tuxedos or black dresses, Kuskin and Simont reveal step-by-step how one hundred five people get dressed for work on a Friday night in winter. The text is surrounded by wonderfully humorous illustrations, some showing only feet or torsos peeking from the page edges. This brilliant work shows the glamorous world of musicians from a perspective familiar to all.

48pp Hardcover $14.95
0-06-023622-1 HarperCollins
Paperback $4.95
0-06-443124-X HarperTrophy

By the same author:
THE DALLAS TITANS GET READY FOR BED
48pp Paperback $4.95
0-06-443180-0 HarperTrophy

Munro Leaf
Illustrated by Robert Lawson
THE STORY OF FERDINAND

Ferdinand, a peaceful bull who loves to sit and smell flowers, is mistakenly carted off to a bullfight in Madrid, where he is believed to be the fiercest bull around. Ferdinand trots into the ring, only to sit and smell the flowers in the ladies hair. No matter what the frustrated matador and his helpers do, they cannot get Ferdinand to fight. Lawson's memorable black-and-white pictures speak volumes in this childhood classic.

72pp Hardcover $16.99
0-670-67424-9 Viking
Paperback $5.99
0-14-050234-3 Puffin

Helen Lester
Illustrated by Lynn Munsinger
TACKY THE PENGUIN

Tacky the penguin defines the word *tacky*—he dresses in Hawaiian shirts, greets friends with a slap on the back, and sings *dreadfully!* All the other penguins are put off by Tacky's behavior, but when some rough hunters come by, Tacky's manners send *them* packing too! Tacky may be odd, but he sure is a good penguin to have around!

32pp Hardcover $15.00
0-395-45536-7 Houghton Mifflin
Paperback $5.95
0-395-56233-3 Houghton Mifflin

By the same author:
ME FIRST
32pp Hardcover $15.00
0-395-58706-9 Houghton Mifflin
Paperback $5.95
0-395-72022-2 Houghton Mifflin

Julius Lester
Illustrated by Jerry Pinkney
SAM AND THE TIGERS

In this retelling of *The Story of Little Black Sambo*—the tale of a boy who outwits a group of tigers—Sam is a boy in the land of Sam-sam-sa-mara, where everyone is named Sam and animals live and work among people. Lester uses a black southern storytelling voice, which, together with Pinkney's magnificent illustrations, make this much maligned classic a tale all races can enjoy.

40pp Hardcover $16.99
0-8037-2028-9 Dial

By the same author:
JOHN HENRY
40pp Hardcover $16.99
0-8037-1606-0 Dial

Leo Lionni
LITTLE BLUE AND LITTLE YELLOW

Little Blue and Little Yellow are so happy to see each other that they hug and hug until they are united into one green mass. When they return home, nobody recognizes them, but when they begin to cry, their tears separate them back into their original selves. Their parents are so relieved that they all hug big green hugs. This gentle parable offers simple lessons in color, friendship, and acceptance.

48pp Hardcover $14.95 T
0-8392-3018-4 Astor-Honor
Paperback $4.95
0-688-13285-5 Mulberry

By the same author:

SWIMMY

Swimmy is a happy black fish who lives in a school of red fish until a big tuna eats all of his brothers and sisters. Lonely and sad, Swimmy searches the sea and finally finds another school of red fish. These fish are too frightened to swim in the ocean, so Swimmy comes up with a plan: all the red fish swim close together in the shape of one giant fish, and black Swimmy is the eye!

32pp Hardcover $16.00
0-394-81713-3 Knopf
Paperback $5.99
0-394-82620-5 Knopf

FREDERICK
32pp Hardcover $16.00
0-394-81040-6 Knopf
Paperback $5.99
0-394-82614-0 Knopf

FREDERICK'S FABLES: A TREASURY OF 16 FAVORITE LEO LIONNI STORIES
164pp Hardcover $29.00
0-679-88826-8 Knopf

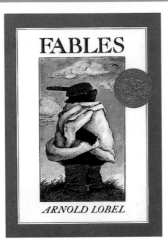

Arnold Lobel
FABLES

Lobel follows in Aesop's footsteps with this collection of fables. Many of life's hard lessons are brought forth, but they are softened with humor and sometimes downright silliness. The stories can be enjoyed on a basic level by young readers and on a more sophisticated level by older ones.

48pp Hardcover $15.00 A
0-06-023973-5 HarperCollins
Paperback $5.95
0-06-443046-4 HarperTrophy

Jonathan London
Illustrated by Frank Remkiewicz
FROGGY GETS DRESSED

Froggy wakes up while it's snowing and gets dressed to go out and play. Each time Froggy gets outside, his mother calls "Frrrooggyy!" to remind him of something he forgot to wear. Froggy hops back into the house, gets undressed, redresses with the missing article of clothing, then hops back outside. After his mother calls to tell him he forgot his *underwear*, Froggy is so exhausted that he climbs back into bed to sleep for the rest of winter. The silly sounds punctuating Froggy getting dressed will have toddlers in stitches.

32pp Hardcover $14.99 T
0-670-84249-4 Viking
Paperback $4.99
0-14-054457-7 Puffin
Big Book $18.99
0-14-055378-9 Puffin

By the same author:

FROGGY GOES TO SCHOOL
32pp Hardcover $13.99
0-670-86726-8 Viking

FROGGY LEARNS TO SWIM
32pp Hardcover $15.99
0-670-85551-0 Viking
Paperback $5.99
0-14-055312-6 Puffin

LET'S GO, FROGGY!
32pp Hardcover $14.99
0-670-85055-1 Viking
Paperback $5.99
0-14-054991-9 Puffin

Picture Books

James Marshall
GEORGE AND MARTHA

These five short stories, starring two huge hippos with buckteeth and pin-dot eyes, show what friendship is all about. Covering topics such as privacy, vanity, and honesty, all are told with a dry but gentle humor. Marshall knows just how much *not* to say, and his pictures convey volumes.

48pp   Hardcover $16.00
0-395-16619-5   Houghton Mifflin
Paperback $6.95
0-395-19972-7   Houghton Mifflin

By the same author:
GEORGE AND MARTHA
BACK IN TOWN

32pp   Hardcover $16.00
0-395-35386-6   Houghton Mifflin
Paperback $6.95
0-395-47946-0   Sandpiper

GEORGE AND MARTHA:
THE COMPLETE STORIES OF TWO
BEST FRIENDS

340pp   Hardcover $25.00
0-395-85158-0   Houghton Mifflin

GEORGE AND MARTHA ENCORE

48pp   Hardcover $15.95
0-395-17512-7   Houghton Mifflin
Paperback $6.95
0-395-25379-9   Houghton Mifflin

GEORGE AND MARTHA
ONE FINE DAY

48pp   Paperback $6.95
0-395-32921-3   Houghton Mifflin

GEORGE AND MARTHA
RISE AND SHINE

48pp   Paperback $6.95
0-395-28006-0   Houghton Mifflin

GEORGE AND MARTHA
TONS OF FUN

48pp   Hardcover $16.00
0-395-29524-6   Houghton Mifflin
Paperback $6.95
0-395-42646-4   Houghton Mifflin

Bill Martin Jr.
Illustrated by Eric Carle
BROWN BEAR, BROWN BEAR,
WHAT DO YOU SEE?

Eric Carle's double-page tissue collages and Bill Martin's friendly chant unite to create this vibrant introduction to colors. The first line of the book is the title, to which a big brown bear responds, "I see a redbird looking at me." The redbird responds with another animal and so on, until a mother (or a teacher, depending on the edition) asks a group of children what *they* see. A wonderful read-aloud for either a group or individuals, this book is a favorite for teachers.

32pp   Hardcover $15.95 **T**
0-8050-0201-4   Henry Holt
(original edition, with mother)
Hardcover $15.95
0-8050-1744-5   Henry Holt
(25th anniversary edition, with teacher)
Board Book $6.95
0-8050-4790-5   Henry Holt

By the same author:
POLAR BEAR, POLAR BEAR,
WHAT DO YOU HEAR?

32pp   Hardcover $15.95 **T**
0-8050-1759-3   Henry Holt
Board Book $6.95
0-8050-5388-3   Henry Holt

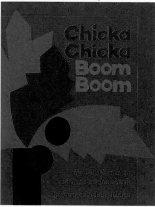

Bill Martin Jr. and John Archambault
Illustrated by Lois Ehlert
CHICKA CHICKA BOOM BOOM

"**A** told **B**, / and **B** told **C**, / I'll meet you at the top of the coconut tree." Rascally **A** entices the whole alphabet up the tree, but the tree cannot handle the weight. All the lowercase letters come crashing to the ground, "Chicka chicka . . . BOOM! BOOM!" Uppercase letters rush in to comfort the little ones, and all is well—for a while—in this irresistible alphabet book. Ehlert's bright, graphic illustrations join the jazzy foot-tapping rhyme. Watch out for that imp, **A**!

40pp   Hardcover $15.00 **T**
0-671-67949-X   Simon & Schuster

By the same author:

CHICKA CHICKA ABC

14pp   Board Book $4.95   T
0-671-87893-X   Simon & Schuster

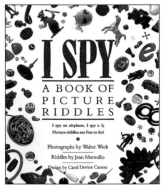

Jean Marzollo
Illustrated by Walter Wick

I SPY: A BOOK OF PICTURE RIDDLES

A treat for the eyes, this oversized book features riddle rhymes, whose answers readers are challenged to find in the accompanying photographs. Without seeming cluttered, each two-page thematic photo is crammed with objects. Those wishing for more "I Spying" will find additional riddle rhymes at the end of the book. Happy hunting!

40pp   Hardcover $12.95
0-590-45087-5   Scholastic

By the same author:

I SPY FANTASY: A BOOK OF PICTURE RIDDLES

40pp   Hardcover $12.95
0-590-46295-4   Cartwheel

I SPY FUN HOUSE: A PICTURE BOOK OF RIDDLES

40pp   Hardcover $12.95
0-590-46293-8   Cartwheel

I SPY MYSTERY: A BOOK OF PICTURE RIDDLES

40pp   Hardcover $12.95
0-590-46294-6   Cartwheel

I SPY SCHOOL DAYS: A BOOK OF PICTURE RIDDLES

40pp   Hardcover $12.95
0-590-48135-5   Cartwheel

Mercer Mayer

THERE'S A NIGHTMARE IN MY CLOSET

A little boy anxiously awaits a nightmare he knows lives in his closet. When it finally appears, the little boy shoots it with his popgun. Looking more sheepish than terrifying, the nightmare starts to blubber, and the little boy realizes the nightmare isn't scary at all. He takes the nightmare by the hand and tucks it into bed. Silly and comforting, this is the perfect book to get rid of those bedtime bogeys.

32pp   Hardcover $15.99
0-8037-8682-4   Dial
Paperback $5.99
0-14-054712-6   Puffin

By the same author:

THERE'S AN ALLIGATOR UNDER MY BED

32pp   Hardcover $14.99
0-8037-0374-0   Dial

THERE'S SOMETHING IN MY ATTIC

32pp   Hardcover $11.95
0-8037-0414-3   Dial
Paperback $5.99
0-14-054813-0   Puffin

Sam McBratney
Illustrated by Anita Jeram

GUESS HOW MUCH I LOVE YOU

Little Nutbrown Hare is trying to tell Big Nutbrown Hare just how much he loves him, but each time Big Nutbrown Hare's love seems to be bigger. Indeed, there is no way to measure the love, and Little Nutbrown Hare can finally only express it by saying his love is as far as the moon. After Big Nutbrown Hare kisses Little Nutbrown Hare goodnight, he whispers that his love is as far as the moon *and* back. This loving goodnight book has expressive and lively illustrations.

32pp   Hardcover $15.99   T
1-56402-473-3   Candlewick
Board Book & Bunny $15.99
0-7636-0164-0   Candlewick
24pp   Board Book $6.99
0-7636-0013-X   Candlewick

Robert McCloskey
MAKE WAY FOR DUCKLINGS

This classic about Mr. and Mrs. Mallard and their brood of ducklings has been a favorite since 1941. When Mrs. Mallard and her eight ducklings are stuck at a busy street in downtown Boston, their policeman friend Michael rushes in to stop traffic and make way for them. McCloskey's sepia illustrations are priceless, and a statue of Mrs. Mallard and her ducklings can be found in Boston Commons today.

68pp   Hardcover $15.99   A
0-670-45149-5   Viking
Paperback $4.99
0-14-050171-1   Puffin
Big Book $20.99
0-14-054434-8   Puffin

By the same author:
BLUEBERRIES FOR SAL

56pp   Hardcover $15.99   T
0-670-17591-9   Viking
Paperback $5.99
0-14-050169-X   Puffin

ONE MORNING IN MAINE

64pp   Hardcover $16.99
0-670-52627-4   Viking
Paperback $5.99
0-14-050174-6   Puffin

TIME OF WONDER

64pp   Hardcover $16.99   A
0-670-71512-3   Viking
Paperback $5.99
0-14-050201-7   Puffin

Susan Meddaugh
MARTHA SPEAKS

Martha is just an ordinary dog until the day she eats a bowl of alphabet soup. Something goes haywire, and the letters, instead of going to her stomach, head straight for her brain. The result? Martha speaks! She ends up yakking *so* much, that her family, initially proud of their talented pet, tells her to SHUT UP! Martha is so wounded that she stops speaking and refuses to eat more soup, that is, until one fateful night!

32pp   Hardcover $15.00
0-395-63313-3   Houghton Mifflin
Paperback $5.95
0-395-72952-1   Houghton Mifflin

By the same author:
MARTHA BLAH BLAH

32pp   Hardcover $14.95
0-395-79755-1   Houghton Mifflin

MARTHA CALLING

32pp   Hardcover $14.95
0-395-69825-1   Houghton Mifflin
Paperback $5.95
0-395-82741-8   Houghton Mifflin

Laura Krauss Melmed
Illustrated by Jim LaMarche
THE RAINBABIES

An old couple's wish for children is unexpectedly granted when, one rainy night under a full moon, they find twelve tiny babies. In the next few days, the couple risk their lives as the babies are subjected to fantastic dangers. The fourth evening, a stranger offers to buy the babies. When the couple refuse, the stranger reveals herself to be the babies' mother, Mother Moonshower. In exchange for taking her babies back, she gives the deserving pair a child of their own. Breathtaking illustrations accompany this moving tale.

32pp   Hardcover $16.00
0-688-10755-9   Lothrop

Ken Mochizuki
Illustrated by Dom Lee
BASEBALL SAVED US

When a Japanese-American boy and his family are interned in a camp during WWII, they decide to combat their depression by building a baseball field. During a game the boy channels his humiliation—both from being a prisoner and from being a bad player—to anger, giving him the strength to hit a game-winning home run.

32pp Hardcover $15.95
1-880000-01-6 Lee & Low
Paperback $6.95
1-880000-19-9 Lee & Low

Inga Moore
SIX-DINNER SID

Unbeknownst to each of his owners, Sid the cat lives with six different people on the same street. By doing so, he's able to get six different dinners every night! He also answers to six names, sleeps in six beds, and maintains six different personalities. All is perfect for Sid—until the day he catches a dreadful cough. Then it is off to the vet not once, but *six* times! Moore's humorous illustrations capture Sid's sly nature.

32pp Hardcover $15.00
0-671-73199-8 Simon & Schuster
Paperback $5.95
0-671-79613-5 Aladdin

Bernard Most
IF THE DINOSAURS CAME BACK

What would the world be like if the dinosaurs came back? Well, just *think* of all the useful things they could do! They could reach books from tall shelves, cut down trees, mow lawns, give giraffes someone to look up to—and, most of all, be pets for those who love dinosaurs! Most's whimsical first book, illustrated with simple, childlike drawings, is a springboard for discussion with young dinosaur lovers.

32pp Hardcover $15.00
0-15-238020-5 Harcourt Brace
Paperback $6.00
0-15-238021-3 Harcourt Brace
Big Book $23.95
0-15-238022-1 Harcourt Brace

By the same author:
HOW BIG WERE THE DINOSAURS?
24pp Hardcover $16.00
0-15-236800-0 Harcourt Brace
Paperback $6.00
0-15-200852-7 Voyager

WHATEVER HAPPENED TO THE DINOSAURS?
32pp Hardcover $16.00
0-15-295295-0 Harcourt Brace
Paperback $4.95
0-15-295296-9 Harcourt Brace

Robert Munsch
Illustrated by Michael Martchenko
THE PAPER BAG PRINCESS

Before pretty Princess Elizabeth can marry handsome Prince Ronald, a dragon burns down the castle and carries Ronald off. Dressed in a paper bag, the brave princess heroically finds the dragon's cave, tricks the dragon into exhausting itself, and rescues Ronald while the dragon is sleeping. Ronald then has only one thing to say to Elizabeth—that she is a mess! Elizabeth quickly realizes that she is better off without this ungrateful bum. Young feminists, here is a book for you!

32pp Hardcover $14.95
0-920236-82-0 Annick
Paperback $5.95
0-920236-16-2 Annick
Mini-paperback $.99
0-920236-25-1 Annick

By the same author:
I HAVE TO GO!
24pp Hardcover $14.95
0-920303-77-3 Annick
Paperback $5.95
0-920303-74-9 Annick

JONATHAN CLEANED UP: THEN HE HEARD A SOUND
32pp Hardcover $14.95
0-920236-22-7 Annick
Paperback $4.95
0-920236-20-0 Annick

STEPHANIE'S PONYTAIL
24pp   Hardcover $16.95
1-55037-485-0   Annick
Paperback $5.95
1-55037-484-2   Annick

Trinka Hakes Noble
Illustrated by Steven Kellogg
THE DAY JIMMY'S BOA ATE THE WASH

A little girl tells her mother (in true elementary school style) about her boring class field trip to the farm. Indeed, it *seems* boring until Jimmy pulls out his pet boa constrictor to meet all the animals. A kid's free-for-all ensues—eggs are thrown, pigs brought on to the bus, a cow cries, and the boa eats the laundry off the line—making this far from a typical class field trip. Kellogg's illustrations of friendly animals, gleeful kids, and distraught adults are right on the mark.

32pp   Hardcover $15.99
0-8037-1723-7   Dial
Paperback $5.99
0-14-054623-5   Puffin

By the same author:
JIMMY'S BOA AND THE BIG SPLASH BIRTHDAY BASH
32pp   Hardcover $13.95
0-8037-0539-5   Dial
Paperback $5.99
0-14-054921-8   Dial

JIMMY'S BOA BOUNCES BACK
32pp   Paperback $4.99
0-14-054654-5   Dial

Laura Joffe Numeroff
Illustrated by Felicia Bond
IF YOU GIVE A MOUSE A COOKIE

What happens if you give a mouse a cookie? Why, he'll need a glass of milk to go with it! He'll also need a straw, a napkin, a mirror—each item prompts the need for another. When the mouse is hanging a picture from a refrigerator (how did he get there?), he's reminded that he's *thirsty* and needs a glass of milk (uh-oh). With this milk, it's absolutely necessary to have—a cookie, of course! Bond's wonderful illustrations enliven this modern day classic.

32pp   Hardcover $13.95
0-06-024586-7   HarperCollins
Big Book $19.95
0-06-443409-5   HarperTrophy

By the same author:
Illustrated by Joe Mathieu
CHIMPS DON'T WEAR GLASSES
32pp   Hardcover $14.00
0-689-80150-5   Simon & Schuster

DOGS DON'T WEAR SNEAKERS
40pp   Hardcover $15.00
0-671-79525-2   Simon & Schuster

Illustrated by Felicia Bond
IF YOU GIVE A MOOSE A MUFFIN
32pp   Hardcover $14.95
0-06-024405-4   HarperCollins
Big Book $19.95
0-06-443366-8   HarperCollins

Jerry Pallotta
Illustrated by Ralph Masiello
THE ICKY BUG ALPHABET BOOK

Pallotta breaks all stereotypes in this unusual alphabet book. Masiello's smooth, realistic paintings and a frequently humorous text, which incorporates many scientifically accurate facts, make it the bee's buzz!

32pp   Hardcover $15.95
0-88106-456-4   Charlesbridge
Paperback $6.95
0-88106-450-5   Charlesbridge

By the same author:
THE DINOSAUR ALPHABET BOOK
32pp   Hardcover $15.95
0-88106-467-X   Charlesbridge
Paperback $6.95
0-88106-466-1   Charlesbridge

THE YUCKY REPTILE ALPHABET BOOK
32pp   Hardcover $15.95
0-88106-460-2   Charlesbridge
Paperback $6.95
0-88106-454-8   Charlesbridge

Illustrated by Edgar Stewart
THE BIRD ALPHABET BOOK
32pp   Hardcover $15.95
0-88106-457-2   Charlesbridge
Paperback $6.95
0-88106-451-3   Charlesbridge

THE FURRY ALPHABET BOOK
32pp Hardcover $15.95
0-88106-465-3 Charlesbridge
Paperback $6.95
0-88106-464-5 Charlesbridge

Illustrated by Leslie Evans
THE FLOWER ALPHABET BOOK
32pp Hardcover $14.95
0-88106-459-9 Charlesbridge
Paperback $6.95
0-88106-453-X Charlesbridge

THE SPICE ALPHABET BOOK
32pp Hardcover $14.95
0-88106-898-5 Charlesbridge
Paperback $6.95
0-88106-897-7 Charlesbridge

Marcus Pfister
THE RAINBOW FISH

Shining from Rainbow Fish's multicolored body are several shimmering silver scales. All the other fish in the ocean admire him and want to play, but Rainbow Fish is too proud to play with *them;* nor will he share his sparkling scales. Alone and friendless, Rainbow Fish soon learns that generosity is far more rewarding than vanity. Pfister makes novel use of rainbow-colored foil to create Rainbow Fish's scales.

32pp Hardcover $18.95
1-55858-009-3 North-South
Big Book $25.00
1-55858-441-2 North-South

By the same author:
DAZZLE THE DINOSAUR
32pp Hardcover $18.95
1-55858-337-8 North-South

RAINBOW FISH TO THE RESCUE!
32pp Hardcover $18.95
1-55858-486-2 North-South

Dav Pilkey
DOG BREATH: THE HORRIBLE TROUBLE WITH HALLY TOSIS

Hally is a happy dog, a member of the Tosis family. Unfortunately, Hally has such *horrible* breath that the parents decide he must get new owners. Desperate to keep her, the children try everything to rid Hally of her rancid breath, but ultimately it is two burglars who ensure that Hally will stay! As in all of Pilkey's books, wacky illustrations and horrible puns abound.

32pp Hardcover $12.95
0-590-47466-9 Blue Sky

By the same author:
DOGZILLA
32pp Hardcover $12.00
0-15-223944-8 Harcourt Brace
Paperback $7.00
0-15-223944-8 Harcourt Brace

KAT KONG
32pp Hardcover $10.95
0-15-242036-3 Harcourt Brace
Paperback $7.00
0-15-242037-1 Harcourt Brace

Patricia Polacco
PINK AND SAY

There are few picture books written about the Civil War, and none are as powerful as this one. This story about how a young black soldier rescues a white soldier opens young readers' eyes to the injustices of slavery and the senselessness of war. Highly charged emotionally, this masterful retelling of a true story, narrated through the white soldier's eyes, is made all the more powerful when it is revealed that the soldier was the author's great-great-grandfather.

48pp Hardcover $15.95
0-399-22671-0 Philomel

By the same author:
BABUSHKA BABA YAGA
32pp Hardcover $15.95
0-399-22531-5 Philomel
Paperback $5.99
0-689-11633-X PaperStar

BABUSHKA'S DOLL
40pp Hardcover $16.00
0-671-68343-8 Simon & Schuster
Paperback $6.95
0-689-80255-2 Aladdin

JUST PLAIN FANCY
32pp Paperback $5.99
0-440-40937-3 Yearling

THE KEEPING QUILT
32pp Hardcover $16.00
0-671-64963-9 Simon & Schuster

Beatrix Potter

Since the early 1900s, Beatrix Potter's twenty-three little volumes featuring rabbits, mice, frogs, and other creatures have delighted children. Her first story, *The Tale of Peter Rabbit*, was an instant success. While Potter's clothed animals appear precious, the characters are in fact quite mischievous and get into scrapes that children can easily identify with. The timeless quality of Potter's stories ensures that her books will entertain generations of readers to come.

THE COMPLETE TALES
400pp   Hardcover $35.00
0-7232-4404-9   Warne

THE TALE OF BENJAMIN BUNNY
60pp   Hardcover $5.95
0-7232-3463-9   Warne
Paperback $3.99
0-14-054300-7   Puffin

THE TALE OF PETER RABBIT
60pp   Hardcover $5.95
0-7232-3460-4   Warne
Paperback $3.99
0-14-054497-6   Puffin
Paperback $2.25
0-7232-3485-X   Warne
Big Book $18.99
0-7232-4029-9   Warne

THE TALE OF SQUIRREL NUTKIN
60pp   Hardcover $5.95
0-7232-3461-2   Warne

THE TALE OF TOM KITTEN
60pp   Hardcover $5.95
0-7232-3467-1   Warne
Paperback $2.25
0-7232-3492-2 Warne

THE TALE OF TWO BAD MICE
60pp   Hardcover $5.95
0-7232-3464-7   Warne

FROM *The Tale of Benjamin Bunny*

FROM *The Tale of Tom Kitten*

THE TALE OF PETER RABBIT

THE TALE OF TWO BAD MICE

BEATRIX POTTER
THE ORIGINAL AND AUTHORIZED EDITION
New colour reproductions
F. WARNE & Co

FROM *Curious George*

H. A. Rey
CURIOUS GEORGE

The first adventure in this highly popular series tells how the little monkey Curious George, caught in the jungle and brought back to the city by a man in a yellow hat, can't help being interested in all the new things around him. Though well meaning, George's curiosity *always* gets him into trouble. Young readers can easily relate, and Rey's cheerful illustrations celebrate Curious George's innocence.

56pp   Hardcover $14.95
0-395-15993-8   Houghton Mifflin
48pp   Paperback $5.95
0-395-15023-X   Sandpiper

By the same author:
THE ADVENTURES OF CURIOUS GEORGE
3 Book Boxed Set $12.00
0-395-73518-1   Houghton Mifflin

CURIOUS GEORGE GETS A MEDAL
48pp   Hardcover $14.95
0-395-16973-9   Houghton Mifflin
Paperback $6.95
0-395-18559-9   Sandpiper

CURIOUS GEORGE LEARNS THE ALPHABET
72pp   Hardcover $14.95
0-395-16031-6   Houghton Mifflin
Paperback $5.95
0-395-13718-7   Sandpiper

CURIOUS GEORGE RIDES A BIKE
48pp   Hardcover $14.95
0-395-16964-X   Houghton Mifflin
Paperback $5.95
0-395-17444-9   Sandpiper

CURIOUS GEORGE TAKES A JOB
48pp   Hardcover $14.95
0-395-15086-8   Houghton Mifflin
Paperback $5.95
0-395-18649-8   Sandpiper

Peggy Rathmann
GOOD NIGHT, GORILLA

Unaware that a gorilla has stolen his keys, a zookeeper wishes all the animals goodnight and sets off for home. A troupe of newly freed beasts follow the sleepy keeper back to his house and into his bed. When the keeper's wife wakes to wish her husband good-night, many good-night wishes come back to her from out of the dark!

36pp   Hardcover $14.95   T
0-399-22445-9   Putnam
Board Book $6.95
0-399-23003-3   Putnam

By the same author:
OFFICER BUCKLE AND GLORIA

None of the children listen when Officer Buckle gives his talk about safety tips. But when Gloria the police dog accompanies Officer Buckle, his speech is suddenly in huge demand. When the talk is videotaped, Officer Buckle discovers the real secret to his popularity—Gloria's slapstick enactment of what happens when you *don't* follow the tips. Rathmann's humorous illustrations contain a lot of feeling, and her portrayal of the earnest Officer Buckle and the expressive yet well-meaning Gloria is priceless.

32pp   Hardcover $15.95   A
0-399-22616-8   Putnam

RUBY THE COPYCAT
32pp   Hardcover $9.95
0-590-76715-1   Scholastic
Paperback $4.95
0-590-47423-5   Blue Ribbon

Margret & H. A. Rey
Illustrated by H. A. Rey
THE COMPLETE ADVENTURES OF CURIOUS GEORGE
416pp   Hardcover $29.95
0-395-75410-0   Houghton Mifflin

CURIOUS GEORGE FLIES A KITE
80pp   Hardcover $14.95
0-395-16965-8   Houghton Mifflin
Paperback $5.95
0-395-25937-1   Sandpiper

CURIOUS GEORGE GOES TO THE HOSPITAL
48pp   Hardcover $14.95
0-395-18158-5   Houghton Mifflin
Paperback $5.95
0-395-07062-7   Houghton Mifflin

Faith Ringgold
AUNT HARRIET'S UNDERGROUND RAILROAD IN THE SKY
A young African-American girl and her brother meet the spirit of Harriet Tubman at her train to freedom in the sky. There, Tubman tells them of the horrors of slavery, and sends Cassie to follow the same terrifying and arduous path her ancestors took to gain freedom. Ringgold weaves facts into her dreamlike story and succeeds in vividly portraying to young readers slavery's hardships. A biographic sketch of Tubman, suggestions for further reading, and a map of the Underground Railroad are included.

32pp   Paperback $6.99
0-517-88543-3   Dragonfly

By the same author:
DINNER AT AUNT CONNIE'S HOUSE
32pp   Hardcover $15.95
1-56282-425-2   Hyperion
Paperback $4.95
0-7868-1150-1   Hyperion

FROM *Aunt Harriet's Underground Railroad in the Sky*

MY DREAM OF MARTIN LUTHER KING
32pp   Hardcover $18.00
0-517-59976-7   Crown

TAR BEACH
32pp   Hardcover $18.00
0-517-58030-6   Crown
Paperback $6.99
0-517-88544-1   Dragonfly

A

Cynthia Rylant
Illustrated by Stephen Gammell
THE RELATIVES CAME
When the relatives come bumping up from Virginia, the house fills with people and hugs. There are so many people that meals have to be eaten in rotation, and arms and legs get tangled at bedtime! When summer ends and the relatives leave, beds feel "too big and too quiet," yet we know that the relatives will return next summer. Gammell's scratchy, messy illustrations capture the family's boisterous and loving togetherness.

32pp   Hardcover $16.00
0-02-777220-9   Simon & Schuster
Paperback $5.99
0-689-71738-5   Aladdin

By the same author:
Illustrated by Cynthia Rylant
THE BOOKSHOP DOG
40pp   Hardcover $14.95
0-590-54331-8   Blue Sky

DOG HEAVEN
32pp   Hardcover $14.95
0-590-41701-0   Blue Sky

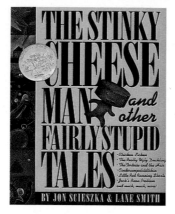

Allen Say
GRANDFATHER'S JOURNEY

This autobiographical reminiscence describes the wanderlust of the author's grandfather, who is torn between love for his native Japan and for California. Missing one place while in the other, the grandfather is always longing to be where he isn't. The grandson inherits his grandfather's love of travel, and, like him, longs to be in both places at the same time. Soft-hued paintings decorate this quiet testament of love for both family and place.

32pp   Hardcover $16.95
0-395-57035-2   Houghton Mifflin A

By the same author:
THE BICYCLE MAN

40pp   Hardcover $14.95
0-395-32254-5   Houghton Mifflin
Paperback $5.95
0-395-50652-2   Houghton Mifflin

EMMA'S RUG

32pp   Hardcover $16.95
0-395-74294-3   Houghton Mifflin

Jon Scieszka
Illustrated by Lane Smith
THE STINKY CHEESE MAN AND OTHER FAIRLY STUPID TALES

Ten wildly hilarious mixed-up fairy tales with wacky illustrations are gathered in this zany book. Not only are the stories silly ("Cinderumpelstiltskin," "Little Red Running Shorts," and "The Princess and the Bowling Ball" among them), but the variety of type-faces and layout add to the general mayhem. It is a challenge for readers of all ages to keep a straight face while reading this irreverent collection, and *The Gingerbread Man* will never be the same!

56pp   Hardcover $16.99
0-670-84487-X   Viking

By the same author:
MATH CURSE

Arrgh! Does tunafish plus tunafish equal *fournafish?* A girl finds herself trapped in a math curse when her teacher tells the class they can think of almost anything as a math problem. Soon she sees math *everywhere*.

Scieszka and Smith join forces again to create another lunatic masterpiece, and adults will writhe in sympathy as they remember their own math curses.

32pp   Hardcover $16.99
0-670-86194-4   Viking

THE TRUE STORY OF THE 3 LITTLE PIGS!

32pp   Hardcover $15.99
0-670-82759-2   Viking
Paperback $5.99
0-14-054451-8   Puffin

Illustrated by Steve Johnson
THE FROG PRINCE CONTINUED

32pp   Hardcover $14.95
0-670-83421-1   Viking
Paperback $5.99
0-14-054285-X   Puffin

FROM *Where the Wild Things Are*

Maurice Sendak
WHERE THE WILD THINGS ARE

Max is being so terrible that his mother sends him to his room without supper. But Max doesn't care—he sails off to the land of the Wild Things, and they make him his king. There, Max can be as terrible as he pleases, and the Wild Things join in the rumpus. Finally, Max is tired of being wild, and yearns to go home. Marvelous pictures and the superb story combine to make this a quintessential picture book. In it, readers will recognize their own wild sides.

48pp   Hardcover $16.95
0-06-025492-0   HarperCollins
Paperback $5.95
0-06-443178-9   HarperTrophy

By the same author:
ALLIGATORS ALL AROUND: AN ALPHABET

32pp   Paperback $4.95
0-06-443254-8   HarperTrophy

CHICKEN SOUP WITH RICE: A BOOK OF MONTHS

32pp   Paperback $4.95
0-06-443253-X   HarperTrophy

ONE WAS JOHNNY: A COUNTING BOOK

48pp   Paperback $4.95
0-06-443251-3   HarperTrophy

PIERRE: A CAUTIONARY TALE IN FIVE CHAPTERS AND A PROLOGUE

48pp   Paperback $4.95
0-06-443252-1   HarperTrophy

NUTSHELL LIBRARY 4 BOOK BOXED SET

Hardcover $15.95
0-06-025500-5   HarperCollins

IN THE NIGHT KITCHEN

48pp   Hardcover $15.95
0-06-026668-6   HarperCollins
Paperback $5.95
0-06-443436-2   HarperTrophy

> "Each word has been carefully chosen and the simplicity of the language is quite deceptive."
>
> —*School Library Journal*

Dr. Seuss

Dr. Seuss, pseudonym for Theodor Seuss Geisel, is world renowned for his inventiveness and wit. His stories are instantly recognizable by their use of fantastic words, clever rhymes, and unusual creatures—drawn in his distinctive style. His first book, *And to Think That I Saw It on Mulberry Street* (1937), a fanciful tale, was followed by several others equally so. His fame took off after the publication of *The Cat in the Hat* (1957), written to replace the dull reading primers in schools. Using a limited vocabulary and incorporating juicy bits of misbehavior, Seuss managed to tell a story children could easily and readily respond to. Best of all, his book was *funny*. Seventeen other beginning reader books were written, among them *Green Eggs and Ham* (1960), *One Fish, Two Fish, Red Fish, Blue Fish* (1960), and *Hop on Pop* (1963) [these can be found in the "Early Readers" section of this book]. His later stories contain more contemporary themes, such as the protection of the environment in *The Lorax* (1971) and a call for nuclear disarmament in *The Butter Battle Book* (1984). Translated into many languages, his books have brought universal joy and opened the world of reading to millions.

And the Grinch, with his grinch-feet ice-cold in the snow,
Stood puzzling and puzzling: "How *could* it be so?
"It came without ribbons! It came without tags!
"It came without packages, boxes or bags!"
And he puzzled three hours, till his puzzler was sore.
Then the Grinch thought of something he hadn't before!
"Maybe Christmas," he thought, *doesn't* come from a store.
"Maybe Christmas . . . perhaps . . . means a little bit more!"

— *HOW THE GRINCH STOLE CHRISTMAS*

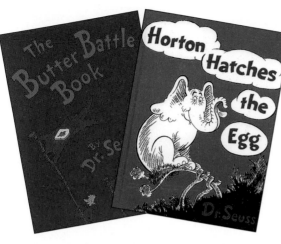

THE 500 HATS OF BARTHOLOMEW CUBBINS
48pp   Hardcover $14.00
0-394-84484-X   Random House

AND TO THINK THAT I SAW IT ON MULBERRY STREET
32pp   Hardcover $14.00
0-394-84494-7   Random House

THE BUTTER BATTLE BOOK
48pp   Hardcover $14.00
0-394-86580-4   Random House

HORTON HATCHES THE EGG
56pp   Hardcover $14.00
0-394-80077-X   Random House

HOW THE GRINCH STOLE CHRISTMAS!
56pp   Hardcover $14.00
0-394-80079-6   Random House

THE LORAX
64pp   Hardcover $14.00
0-394-82337-0   Random House

OH, THE PLACES YOU'LL GO!
48pp   Hardcover $17.00
0-679-80527-3   Random House
Deluxe Slip Case $25.00
0-679-84736-7   Random House

YERTLE THE TURTLE AND OTHER STORIES
96pp   Hardcover $14.00
0-394-80087-7   Random House

Nancy Shaw
Illustrated by Margot Apple
SHEEP IN A JEEP

Using very few words (sheep, jeep, thud, mud, heap, jeep, cheap), a tableau unfolds in which five silly yet distinctive sheep futilely attempt to ride in their jeep. Amusing details—such as tattoos on pigs' arms—abound in the pictures. Apple's expressive illustrations and Shaw's minimal text make this an extremely clever read-aloud.

32pp Hardcover $14.00 T
0-395-41105-X Houghton Mifflin
Paperback $4.95
0-395-47030-7 Houghton Mifflin

By the same author:
SHEEP IN A SHOP
32pp Hardcover $14.00 T
0-395-53681-2 Houghton Mifflin
Paperback $4.95
0-395-70672-6 Sandpiper

SHEEP ON A SHIP
32pp Hardcover $13.95 T
0-395-48160-0 Houghton Mifflin
Paperback $4.95
0-395-64376-7 Houghton Mifflin

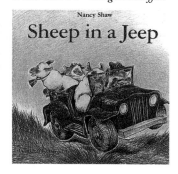

Shel Silverstein
THE GIVING TREE

A little boy befriends a tree. Loving and generous, the tree provides everything she can for him—fruit, shade, a place for a swing—throughout the boy's life. He, in turn, takes from the tree without noticing the sacrifices she makes. It isn't until he's old and infirm and gratefully rests on her stump that he understands all she has done. This powerful parable is fitting for all age groups.

56pp Hardcover $14.95
0-06-025665-6 HarperCollins

By the same author:
A GIRAFFE AND A HALF
48pp Hardcover $14.95
0-06-025655-9 HarperCollins

THE MISSING PIECE
112pp Hardcover $14.95
0-06-025671-0 HarperCollins

THE MISSING PIECE MEETS THE BIG O
112pp Hardcover $13.95
0-06-025657-5 HarperCollins

Peter Sís
STARRY MESSENGER: GALILEO GALILEI

Using his dual talents as illustrator and storyteller, Sís pays homage to Galileo, the great seventeenth-century mathematician and astronomer. Sís's extraordinary maps and vistas of Renaissance times, together with artistically rendered quotes from the astronomer and other famous scholars, powerfully evoke Galileo's world.

36pp Hardcover $16.00
0-374-37191-1 FSG

Esphyr Slobodkina
CAPS FOR SALE: A TALE OF A PEDDLER, SOME MONKEYS AND THEIR MONKEY BUSINESS

A cap peddler wakes from a nap to find all his caps are gone—a bunch of naughty monkeys have taken them up a tree. Angrily shaking his finger at the monkeys, the peddler demands his caps back, but the monkeys only shake *their* fingers and say, "Tsz, tsz, tsz." No matter what the peddler does, the monkeys only imitate him. Finally, the peddler is so enraged he throws his cap on the ground— and all the monkeys follow suit!

48pp Hardcover $13.95 T
0-201-09147-X HarperCollins
Paperback $4.95
0-06-443143-6 HarperTrophy

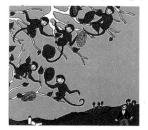

Peter Spier
PEOPLE

In this encyclopedic picture book, Spier celebrates humankind in all its diversity—how we are similar and how we are different; in what we wear, eat, play, and how we worship. Small vignettes fill each page, illustrating the wonderful variety that exists among peoples of different cultures and races.

48pp   Hardcover $16.95
0-385-13181-X   Doubleday
Paperback $10.95
0-385-24469-X   Doubleday

By the same author:
NOAH'S ARK
44pp   Hardcover $16.95
0-385-09473-6   Doubleday
Paperback $6.99
0-440-40693-5   Yearling

William Steig
DOCTOR DESOTO

Doctor DeSoto and his wife, both mice, assist animals large and small with their dental needs—that is, all animals except cats and foxes! One day a fox comes to them in such great pain that they agree to treat his rotten tooth. When it becomes clear the fox intends to eat them when the job is done, the DeSotos come up with a brilliant plan. As usual, Steig combines elegant writing with amusing and sophisticated illustrations.

32pp   Hardcover $16.00
0-374-31803-4   FSG
Paperback $4.95
0-374-41810-1   FSG

From *Dinosaur Roar*

By the same author:
SYLVESTER AND THE MAGIC PEBBLE

While hurrying home to show his parents a wish-granting pebble, Sylvester the donkey is startled by a hungry lion emerging from the bushes. Flustered, Sylvester wishes he were a rock, and is immediately transformed. A year later, Sylvester's grieving parents go for a picnic and choose the rock that is Sylvester as their table. Sylvester's father happens to find the magic pebble and places it on the table, just as Sylvester wishes he were himself again. With great joy, the family is reunited.

32pp   Hardcover $16.00
0-671-66154-X   Simon & Schuster
Paperback $5.95
0-671-66269-4   Aladdin

THE AMAZING BONE
32pp   Hardcover $17.00
0-374-30248-0   FSG
Paperback $5.95
0-374-40358-9   Sunburst

BRAVE IRENE
32pp   Hardcover $17.00
0-374-30947-7   FSG
Paperback $5.95
0-374-40927-7   Sunburst

SPINKY SULKS
32pp   Paperback $4.95
0-374-46990-3   Sunburst

THE TOY BROTHER
32pp   Hardcover $14.95
0-06-205078-8   HarperCollins

Henrietta Stickland
Illustrated by Paul Stickland
DINOSAUR ROAR!

This simple book of opposites uses dinosaurs to reach its audience. The clever rhyming text ("dinosaur sweet, dinosaur grumpy, dinosaur spiky and dinosaur lumpy") speaks directly to toddlers, and Stickland uses bright swirls of color to illustrate his friendly and expressive dinosaurs. Put it all together, and you have one catchy reptilian romp.

32pp   Hardcover $12.99
0-525-45276-1   Dutton
Board Book $6.99
0-525-45834-4   Dutton

By the same author:
DINOSAUR STOMP!
32pp   Hardcover $15.99
0-525-45591-4   Dutton   T

Mark Teague
THE SECRET SHORTCUT
Wendell and Floyd are
continually late to school because
something—such as pirates
stalking the streets, or a plague of
frogs—always delays them. When
their teacher gives them a final
warning about being late, Wendell
and Floyd use a secret shortcut.
After meandering through jungles
and quicksand, swinging from
vines and landing in mud, the
two finally make it to school—
and on time! What a shortcut!
32pp   Hardcover $14.95
0-590-67714-4   Scholastic

By the same author:
PIGSTY
32pp   Hardcover $14.95
0-590-45915-5   Scholastic

FROM *Eloise*

Kay Thompson
Illustrated by Hilary Knight
ELOISE
Meet Eloise, the irrepressible six-
year-old who lives with her
British nanny, her dog Weenie,
and her turtle Skipperdee in New
York City's Plaza Hotel. Eloise
makes a nuisance of herself—
riding elevators, dragging sticks
along the walls as she roller-
skates down the corridors, and
"helping" the staff prepare rooms
for official functions. Told from
Eloise's perspective, readers will
recognize the naughty impulses
they always wanted to satisfy.
Room service, anyone?
64pp   Hardcover $17.00
0-671-22350-X   Simon & Schuster

James Thurber
Illustrated by Marc Simont
MANY MOONS
Princess Lenore is ill, and won't
get well until she owns the moon.
The King summons all his wise
men—the Lord Chamberlain,
the Royal Wizard, and the Royal
Mathematician—but none of

them knows how to get the
moon for his daughter. Finally,
the most unlikely of figures—the
Court Jester—sorts out what to
do. First published in 1943, this
edition has fresh new pictures by
artist Marc Simont.
48pp   Hardcover $14.95
0-15-251872-X   Harcourt Brace

By the same author:
Illustrated by Louis Slobodkin
MANY MOONS
48pp   Hardcover $16.00   A
0-15-251873-8   Harcourt Brace
Paperback $7.00
0-15-656980-9   Harcourt Brace

Illustrated by Steven Kellogg
THE GREAT QUILLOW
56pp   Hardcover $17.95
0-15-232544-1   Harcourt Brace

Alvin Tresselt
Illustrated by Yaroslava
THE MITTEN
A little boy, gathering kindling in
the snow, doesn't notice when his
furry mitten falls off. A mouse
finds the mitten and decides to
make it a cozy home. Just as the

mouse gets comfortable, other forest dwellers, including a big brown bear, ask to squeeze in. Alas, when a little cricket wants in too, the mitten finally bursts, and the animals tumble out onto the snow. The animals' clothing reflects the Ukrainian origin of the story.

30pp   Paperback $4.95   **T**
0-688-09238-1   Mulberry

By the same author:
Illustrated by Roger Duvoisin
WHITE SNOW, BRIGHT SNOW
32pp   Hardcover $16.00   **A, T**
0-688-41161-4   Lothrop
Paperback $4.95
0-688-08294-7   Mulberry

Chris Van Allsburg
JUMANJI
When Judy and Peter find a board game under a tree in the park, it looks like just another boring game. But Jumanji has more thrills than even a child could wish for. Imagine a lion, a python, and stampeding rhinos in your living room! The surreal story is enhanced by Van Allsburg's incredible artwork.

32pp   Hardcover $17.95   **A**
0-395-30448-2   Houghton Mifflin

By the same author:
BAD DAY AT RIVERBEND
32pp   Hardcover $17.95
0-395-67347-X   Houghton Mifflin

THE GARDEN OF ABDUL GASAZI
32pp   Hardcover $17.95
0-395-27804-X   Houghton Mifflin

THE POLAR EXPRESS
32pp   Hardcover $18.95   **A**
0-395-38949-6   Houghton Mifflin

FROM *Jumanji*

TWO BAD ANTS
32pp   Hardcover $17.95
0-395-48668-8   Houghton Mifflin

THE WIDOW'S BROOM
32pp   Hardcover $17.95
0-395-64051-2   Houghton Mifflin

Nancy Van Laan
Illustrated by George Booth
POSSUM COME A-KNOCKIN'
That rascally possum is the kind of critter that knocks on the door and then hides! Granny is a-rockin', Pappy is a-whittlin' and Ma's a-cookin' taters when that possum comes a-knockin' at the door. That sets Coon-dawg a-growlin' and Tom-cat a-sniffin', but nobody believes the little girl when she says she sees that ol' possum! Van Laan's rollicking rhyme reads like a rap song, and George Booth is at his comic best.

32pp   Paperback $7.99
0-679-83468-0   Dragonfly

By the same author:
Illustrated by Beatriz Vidal
RAINBOW CROW
40pp   Paperback $5.99
0-679-81942-8   Knopf

Picture Books

Judith Viorst
Illustrated by Ray Cruz
ALEXANDER AND THE TERRIBLE, HORRIBLE, NO GOOD, VERY BAD DAY

From the moment Alexander wakes up and finds gum in his hair, everything goes wrong! His brothers both get prizes in *their* cereal boxes, his best friend demotes him to third-best friend, there are lima beans for dinner, and there is kissing on TV. *All* kids experience this type of day, and will be glad to find they are not alone!

32pp   Hardcover $14.00
0-689-30072-7   Atheneum
Paperback $4.99
0-689-71173-5   Aladdin

By the same author:
ALEXANDER, WHO USED TO BE RICH LAST SUNDAY
32pp   Hardcover $15.00
0-689-30602-4   Atheneum
Paperback $3.95
0-689-71199-9   Aladdin

Illustrated by Robin Preiss Glasser
ALEXANDER, WHO'S NOT (DO YOU HEAR ME? I MEAN IT!) GOING TO MOVE
32pp   Hardcover $15.00
0-689-31958-4   Atheneum

Illustrated by Kay Chorao
MY MAMA SAYS THERE AREN'T ANY ZOMBIES, GHOSTS, VAMPIRES, CREATURES, DEMONS, MONSTERS, FIENDS, GOBLINS OR THINGS
48pp   Hardcover $16.00
0-689-30102-2   Atheneum
Paperback $5.99
0-689-71204-9   Aladdin

Bernard Waber
LYLE, LYLE, CROCODILE

Lyle, the caviar-eating crocodile who lives with the Primm family on East 88th Street, is loved by the whole neighborhood—except for Mr. Grumps and his cat, Loretta. Mr. Grumps manages to get Lyle sent to the zoo, but Lyle escapes, just in time to save Mr. Grumps and Loretta from a fire.

48pp   Hardcover $14.95
0-395-16995-X   Houghton Mifflin
Paperback $5.95
0-395-13720-9   Houghton Mifflin

By the same author:
FUNNY, FUNNY LYLE
40pp   Hardcover $16.00
0-395-43619-2   Houghton Mifflin
Paperback $5.95
0-395-60287-4   Houghton Mifflin

THE HOUSE ON EAST 88TH STREET
48pp   Hardcover $14.95
0-395-18157-7   Houghton Mifflin
Paperback $5.95
0-395-19970-0   Sandpiper

LOVABLE LYLE
48pp   Hardcover $16.00
0-395-19858-5   Houghton Mifflin
Paperback $5.95
0-395-25378-0   Houghton Mifflin

IRA SLEEPS OVER

Ira is excited—he's going to sleep over at a friend's house for the very first time! His sister puts a damper on things by reminding Ira about the teddy bear he always sleeps with. What should Ira do? He can't sleep without Tah Tah, but his friend Reggie will laugh if he brings him. Finally, Ira decides to leave his bear behind, but gets a big surprise when the lights go out!

48pp   Hardcover $15.00
0-395-13893-0   Houghton Mifflin
Paperback $5.95
0-395-20503-4   Houghton Mifflin

IRA SAYS GOODBYE
40pp   Hardcover $15.00
0-395-48315-8   Houghton Mifflin
Paperback $5.95
0-395-58413-2   Houghton Mifflin

Martin Waddell
Illustrated by Barbara Firth

CAN'T YOU SLEEP, LITTLE BEAR?

Afraid of the dark, Little Bear has trouble sleeping in his cave. Big Bear brings him a teeny-weeny lantern to chase the dark away. When that doesn't work, Big Bear brings a medium-size lantern, then the Biggest Lantern of Them All. Little Bear insists the dark is *still* there. Big Bear takes him outside to show him the moon, and Little Bear falls asleep snug in Big Bear's arms. Firth's illustrations add humor to this cozy bedtime story.

32pp   Hardcover $15.99   T
1-56402-007-X   Candlewick
Paperback $5.99
1-56402-262-5   Candlewick

By the same author:
LET'S GO HOME, LITTLE BEAR

32pp   Hardcover $15.99   T
1-56402-131-9   Candlewick
Paperback $5.99
1-56402-447-4   Candlewick

YOU AND ME, LITTLE BEAR

32pp   Hardcover $15.99   T
1-56402-879-8   Candlewick

Illustrated by Helen Oxenbury
FARMER DUCK

40pp   Hardcover $15.99
1-56402-009-6   Candlewick
Paperback $4.99
1-56402-596-9   Candlewick

William Wegman
ABC

Famous in the art world for his photographs of weimaraners, Wegman has expanded his scope to include children's books. In this innovative alphabet book, the dogs are photographed with props to highlight words beginning with each letter. Tongue-in-cheek captions accompany the witty pictures. Lying together, the dogs also form the shape of the letters and spell out the words. Sophisticated yet silly, this is not just for learning your ABC's!

64pp   Hardcover $17.95   T
1-56282-696-4   Hyperion

By the same author:
CINDERELLA

40pp   Hardcover $16.95
1-56282-348-5   Hyperion

LITTLE RED RIDING HOOD

40pp   Hardcover $16.95
1-56282-416-3   Hyperion

WILLIAM WEGMAN'S MOTHER GOOSE

40pp   Hardcover $17.95   T
0-7868-0218-9   Hyperion

Rosemary Wells
Illustrated by Susan Jeffers
LASSIE COME-HOME

Wells and Jeffers have made Eric Knight's 1938 classic accessible to younger readers by adapting it into picture book format. The story about the collie who travels a thousand miles through Scotland and England to be with the boy she loves has none of the saccharinity of the television series; rather, it is full of hardship, devotion, and courage. Poignant yet stirring, this is a perfect family read-aloud.

48pp   Hardcover $16.95
0-8050-3794-2   Henry Holt

FROM *Tuesday*

Rosemary Wells
SHY CHARLES

Charles is painfully shy. He won't speak to Wanda Sue, or go anywhere near the phone. On trips to town, he is too overcome with bashfulness to say thank you or goodbye. Charles's parents hope to make him more outgoing by sending him to ballet school and then football practice, but both are disasters. One fateful night the baby-sitter falls down the stairs. Charles jumps into action and calls for help. "He saved my life," moans the baby-sitter. All give Charles a resounding "Thank you." But of course, Charles is too shy to say . . . anything. The expressive faces and beautifully crafted story of Charles captures a situation that many families face.

32pp Paperback $4.99
0-14-054537-9 Puffin

By the same author:
FRITZ AND THE MESS FAIRY
32pp Hardcover $14.00
0-8037-0981-1 Dial
Paperback $5.99
0-14-055681-8 Puffin

HAZEL'S AMAZING MOTHER
32pp Paperback $5.99
0-14-054911-0 Puffin

David Wiesner
TUESDAY

It's Tuesday night, and a large bullfrog suddenly wakes up to discover he and his lily pad are floating in the air! Soon the sky is *filled* with flying frogs, careening on their pads and having a whale of a time. At dawn, they all come crashing to the ground, and return to their now boring life at the pond. Whatever will *next* Tuesday bring? Wiesner uses his considerable artistic talents to weave humor and the surreal into this nearly wordless tale.

32pp Hardcover $15.95 **A**
0-395-55113-7 Clarion
Paperback $5.95
0-395-87082-8 Clarion

By the same author:
FREE FALL
32pp Hardcover $16.00
0-688-05583-4 Lothrop
Paperback $4.95
0-688-10990-X Mulberry

HURRICANE
32pp Hardcover $16.00
0-395-54382-7 Clarion
Paperback $5.95
0-395-62974-8 Clarion

JUNE 29, 1999
32pp Hardcover $15.95
0-395-59762-5 Clarion

Sue Williams
Illustrated by Julie Vivas
I WENT WALKING

A little girl goes for a walk and encounters, one by one, several familiar friendly animals. Toddlers can try to identify each partially shown animal every time the book asks, "What did you see?" Each animal joins the girl and her walk ends in a joyous romp. Vivas's soft watercolors enrich this pleasingly repetitious tale.

32pp Hardcover $16.00 **T**
0-15-200471-8 Gulliver
Paperback $7.00
0-15-238011-6 Voyager
Board Book $6.00
0-15-200771-7 Red Wagon

Vera B. Williams

"MORE MORE MORE," SAID THE BABY: 3 LOVE STORIES

Williams uses vibrant colors and hand-painted rainbow letters to tell story-poems about three children: Little Guy, Little Pumpkin, and Little Bird. In each story, the child is chased and caught by a loving parent or grandparent, and readers can practically hear the squeals of delight as the children clamor for "more, more, more!" Many grownups have played similar games of love with their children, and the whole book feels like one giant hug.

32pp   Hardcover $16.00   [T]
0-688-09173-3   Greenwillow
Paperback $4.95
0-688-14736-4   Mulberry

By the same author:

A CHAIR FOR MY MOTHER

32pp   Hardcover $16.00
0-688-00914-X   Greenwillow
Paperback $4.95
0-688-04074-8   Mulberry

CHERRIES AND CHERRY PITS

32pp   Hardcover $16.00
0-688-05145-6   Greenwillow
Paperback $4.95
0-688-10478-9   Mulberry

THREE DAYS ON A RIVER IN A RED CANOE

32pp   Hardcover $16.00
0-688-80307-5   Greenwillow
Paperback $5.95
0-688-04072-1   Mulberry

Audrey Wood
Illustrated by Don Wood

THE NAPPING HOUSE

It's a rainy night, and granny is snoring on her bed. A sleepy boy plops on top of her, then a dog crawls up and dozes off on top of him. Next, a cat leaps up and settles for a snooze, and a teeny mouse jumps to the tippy top of the slumbering pile. All sleep happily, until a wakeful flea bites the mouse . . . *ouch!!!* Wood uses gradual changes in color and perspective, and her gleeful cumulative tale ends in sunshine and play.

32pp   Hardcover $15.00   [T]
0-15-256708-9   Harcourt Brace

By the same author:

HECKEDY PEG

32pp   Hardcover $16.00
0-15-233678-8   Harcourt Brace
Paperback $6.00
0-15-233679-6   Harcourt Brace

Illustrated by David Shannon

THE BUNYANS

32pp   Hardcover $15.95
0-590-48089-8   Blue Sky

Illustrated by Mark Teague

THE FLYING DRAGON ROOM

32pp   Hardcover $14.95
0-590-48193-2   Blue Sky

Don & Audrey Wood
Illustrated by Don Wood

THE BIG HUNGRY BEAR

A hungry mouse is all set to pick a plump red strawberry when the narrator warns him of the big hungry bear! This bear *loves* strawberries; *nothing* will prevent him from getting one, especially one that's just been picked. The only way the mouse can save his strawberry is to cut it in two, and share half with the narrator. Don Wood's exaggerated art style is perfect for this silly tale. *Mmm, good!*

32pp   Hardcover $13.99   [T]
0-85953-182-1   Child's Play

Picture Books

By the same authors:
QUICK AS A CRICKET
32pp   Hardcover $13.99
0-85953-151-1   Child's Play **T**

Douglas Wood
Illustrated by Cheng-Khee Chee
OLD TURTLE

In the time that animals could talk to one another, a great argument took place. Each animal insisted that God was in *his* image. The argument grew and grew until Old Turtle spoke. He told the animals that people would come, made in the image of God, and would act as keepers of the earth. But over the years the people forgot—until Old Turtle's message rang from the earth. Chee's watercolors adorn this gentle parable.

48pp   Hardcover $17.95
0-938586-48-3   Pfeifer-Hamilton

HARRY
THE DIRTY DOG

by Gene Zion
pictures by Margaret Bloy Graham

Gene Zion
Illustrated by Margaret Bloy Graham
HARRY THE DIRTY DOG

Harry, a white dog with black spots, hates baths so much that when he hears his bathwater running he buries his scrub brush and runs away. Harry has a great time getting filthy in the dirt but soon is tired and hungry. He returns home, only to find his family doesn't recognize him, even after he performs all the tricks he knows. Finally, Harry tries a new trick—he begs for a bath, and once clean, is recognized at last.

32pp   Hardcover $15.00
0-06-026865-4   HarperCollins
Paperback $5.95
0-06-443009-X   HarperTrophy

By the same author:
HARRY BY THE SEA
32pp   Paperback $5.95
0-06-443010-3   HarperTrophy

NO ROSES FOR HARRY!
32pp   Paperback $5.95
0-06-443011-1   HarperTrophy

Charlotte Zolotow
Illustrated by William Pène du Bois
WILLIAM'S DOLL

William is a happy little boy who wants only one thing: a doll. His brother calls him a sissy, and his father buys him "boy" toys to try to get him to change. When William's understanding grand-mother learns what William wants, she takes him to the store and chooses a doll for him. She knows that William needs the doll to cuddle and love, and to help him become a caring father one day.

32pp   Hardcover $14.95
0-06-027047-0   HarperCollins
Paperback $4.95
0-06-443067-7   HarperTrophy

By the same author:
Illustrated by Martha Alexander
BIG SISTER AND LITTLE SISTER
32pp   Paperback $5.95
0-06-443217-3   HarperTrophy

Illustrated by Stefano Vitale
WHEN THE WIND STOPS
32pp   Paperback $4.95
0-06-443472-9   HarperTrophy

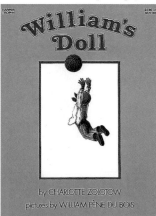

William's Doll

by CHARLOTTE ZOLOTOW
pictures by WILLIAM PÈNE DU BOIS

Poetry and Anthology

POETRY ANTHOLOGIES

Children become familiar with rhymes during their earliest experiences at home, in school, and on the playground. For parent and child, making the transition from jump-rope rhymes to more traditional poems is easy and immensely fun.

Books such as *Ride a Purple Pelican* (Jack Prelutsky) and *Where the Sidewalk Ends* (Shel Silverstein) make it easy for children to enjoy the written word. These and other poetry books will become a staple of your library of children's books. Read along and share the humor, spirit, whimsy, and innocence of poetry for children.

OTHER ANTHOLOGIES

The other anthologies we present combine many stories, fables, folktales, and poems in one volume. They cover a wide age range and make wonderful gift books that can be used by the entire family for generations.

Toot! Toot!

A peanut sat on a railroad track,
His heart was all a-flutter;
The five-fifteen came rushing by—
Toot! toot! peanut butter!

Anonymous

What to look for . . .

- A book the whole family can enjoy. Many of these books are ageless.

- Books that appeal to the sense of humor your child is developing

- Story collections covering your child's interests

- Books that encourage your child to seek out other stories and poems

- Illustrations that engage your child

- Books that encourage discussion

ELETELEPHONY

Once there was an elephant
Who tried to use the telephant—
No! No! I mean an elephone
Who tried to use the telephone—
(Dear me! I am not certain quite
That even now I've got it right.)

Howe'er it was, he got his trunk
Entangled in the telephunk;
The more he tried to get it free,
The louder buzzed the telephee—
(I fear I'd better drop the song
Of elephop and telephong!)

—Laura E. Richards

Selected by Beatrice Schenk de Regniers, Eva Moore, Mary Michaels White, and Jan Carr
Illustrated by nine Caldecott Medalists

SING A SONG OF POPCORN: EVERY CHILD'S BOOK OF POEMS

A. A. Milne, Robert Louis Stevenson, Shel Silverstein, Carl Sandburg, and Langston Hughes are among the contributors to this splendid collection. The one hundred twenty-eight poems are divided into nine thematic sections, each illustrated by a Caldecott Medalist. Originally intended for classroom use, the editors were careful to choose poems that would instill in children a love for poetry.

160pp   Hardcover $18.95
0-590-43974-X   Scholastic

Selected by Helen Ferris
Illustrated by Leonard Weisgard

FAVORITE POEMS OLD AND NEW

This comprehensive introduction to poetry, filled with over seven hundred poems, is a valuable source for both the novice and the poetry lover. The compendium covers a wide range of periods and styles: psalms from the Bible, sonnets from Shakespeare, classic poems, and works by both familiar and lesser-known poets. Eighteen thematic sections cover a broader range of subjects than those usually found in poetry collections, ensuring something for everyone.

598pp   Hardcover $23.95
0-385-07696-7   Doubleday

THE PURPLE COW

I never saw a purple cow,
I never hope to see one;
But I can tell you, anyhow,
I'd rather see than be one!

—Gelett Burgess

Selected by X. J. Kennedy & Dorothy M. Kennedy
Illustrated by Jane Dyer

TALKING LIKE THE RAIN: A FIRST BOOK OF POEMS

More than one hundred old favorites and lesser-known gems, all copiously illustrated by Jane Dyer's soft watercolors, grace this oversized gift collection. Poems are divided into subjects familiar to children, such as birds and beasts, weather, seasons of the year, and play and families.

96pp   Hardcover $19.95
0-316-48889-5   Little, Brown

By the same authors:
Illustrated by Karen Ann Weinhaus

KNOCK AT A STAR: A CHILD'S INTRODUCTION TO POETRY

160pp   Paperback $10.95
0-316-48854-2   Little, Brown

Selected and Introduced by
Kenneth Koch and
Kate Farrell
Illustrated with reproductions from
the Metropolitan Museum of Art

TALKING TO THE SUN: AN ILLUSTRATED ANTHOLOGY OF POEMS FOR YOUNG PEOPLE

A treat for the eyes as well as the ears, this diverse selection of poetry is matched with works of art culled from New York City's Metropolitan Museum of Art. The art, like the poetry, spans many time periods and genres, making this a true "museum" for all ages.

112pp   Hardcover $26.95
0-8050-0144-1   Henry Holt

Jeff Moss
Illustrated by Chris Demarest

THE BUTTERFLY JAR

Jeff Moss, one of the original creators of Sesame Street, wrote many of the show's stories and songs, including the hit "Rubber Duckie." Collected here are eighty-nine of his poems, which humorously depict the trials and tribulations of everyday life.

128pp   Hardcover $16.95
0-553-05704-9   Bantam

Jack Prelutsky
Illustrated by James Stevenson

THE NEW KID ON THE BLOCK

Prelutsky is a prolific writer of humorous poetry for children, and this is one of his most popular collections. The concerns of school-aged kids, especially children eight to twelve years old, are captured perfectly in these

Ride a purple pelican,
ride a silver stork,
ride them from Seattle
to the city of New York,
soar above the buildings,
bobble like a cork,
ride a purple pelican,
ride a silver stork.

FROM Ride a Purple Pelican

hilarious rhymes. This is poetry at its most fun, and kids will gobble it up like candy.

160pp   Hardcover $17.95
0-688-02271-5   Greenwillow

By the same author:

A PIZZA THE SIZE OF THE SUN

160pp   Hardcover $18.00
0-688-13235-9   Greenwillow

SOMETHING BIG HAS BEEN HERE

160pp   Hardcover $17.95
0-688-06434-5   Greenwillow

Illustrated by Garth Williams

RIDE A PURPLE PELICAN

Twenty-eight rollicking rhymes are paired with bright, sunny artwork in this collaboration between two children's books celebrities. Many of Prelutsky's catchy poems mention cities in North America, and Williams's full-page illustrations accent their whimsy.

64pp   Hardcover $17.95   **T**
0-688-04031-4   Greenwillow

Poetry

BENEATH A BLUE UMBRELLA
64pp   Hardcover $15.95   [T]
0-688-06429-9   Greenwillow

Jack Prelutsky, editor
Illustrated by Marc Brown
READ-ALOUD RHYMES FOR THE VERY YOUNG
112pp   Hardcover $20.00   [T]
0-394-87218-5   Knopf

Selected by Jack Prelutsky
Illustrated by Arnold Lobel
THE RANDOM HOUSE BOOK OF POETRY FOR CHILDREN: A TREASURY OF 572 POEMS FOR TODAY'S CHILD

This deceptively slender volume contains a treasure-trove of poems. Each page is crammed with verse and illustrations by Caldecott Medalist Arnold Lobel. Everyone's favorite poems are complemented by fresh new voices and organized into such unusual themes as food, the city, spooky poems, and word play.

248pp   Hardcover $20.00
0-394-85010-6   Random House

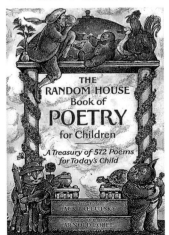

HUG O' WAR

I will not play at tug o' war.
I'd rather play at hug o' war,
Where everyone hugs
Instead of tugs,
Where everyone giggles
And rolls on the rug,
Where everyone kisses,
And everyone grins,
And everyone cuddles,
And everyone wins.

FROM *Where the Sidewalk Ends*

Michael Rosen, editor
Illustrated by Alice Englander
THE KINGFISHER BOOK OF CHILDREN'S POETRY

The two hundred fifty poems in this collection deal with contemporary issues that speak directly to today's children. Though many of the poems are British in tone, they work well on this side of the Atlantic. Aimed at a more sophisticated audience, this is a fine anthology for English-speaking readers everywhere.

256pp   Hardcover $16.95
1-85697-910-5   Kingfisher
Paperback $11.95
1-85697-909-1   Kingfisher

Shel Silverstein
WHERE THE SIDEWALK ENDS: THE POEMS & DRAWINGS OF SHEL SILVERSTEIN

Irreverent, hilarious, and wildly popular, Silverstein's collection of verse is hard to put down. His black pen drawings are an integral part of the poems, which range from funny and gross to introspective or tender. Silverstein is a master at tickling the funny bone, and his book is definitely not just for kids!

176pp   Hardcover $16.95
0-06-025667-2   HarperCollins

By the same author:
FALLING UP
176pp   Hardcover $16.95
0-06-024802-5   HarperCollins

A LIGHT IN THE ATTIC
176pp   Hardcover $16.95
0-06-025673-7   HarperCollins

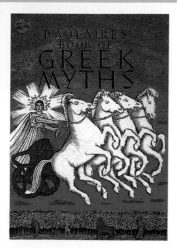

Ingri & Edgar Parin D'Aulaire

D'AULAIRES' BOOK OF GREEK MYTHS

Oversized and lavishly illustrated, this definitive volume of Greek mythology introduces readers to all the major and lesser gods and goddesses as well as the mortal descendants of Zeus. The thrilling tales, along with the vivid artwork, bring the gods and such heroes as Hercules, Theseus, and Jason to life. A family tree, a map of the constellations, and a chart showing both the Greek and Roman names of the major gods are also included.

192pp   Hardcover $29.95
0-385-01583-6   Doubleday
Paperback $18.95
0-440-40694-3   Doubleday

Jane Dyer, illustrator

THE RANDOM HOUSE BOOK OF BEDTIME STORIES

What more pleasant way to say goodnight to your child than by sharing a story? Here are twenty-one tales to snuggle up with, many of them old favorites—such as *Goldilocks and the Three Bears*, *Snow White and Rose Red*, and *The Tale of Peter Rabbit*. All are amply illustrated with full-color watercolors.

160pp   Hardcover $19.00
0-679-80832-9   Random House

Josephine Evetts-Secker, reteller
Illustrated by Helen Cann

MOTHER AND DAUGHTER TALES

Gathered from around the world, these ten tales celebrate the special relationship between mothers and daughters. While the stories come from a wide variety of cultures and time periods, such themes as honesty, independence, and love act as a common thread. Water-color illustrations light up this unusual collection.

80pp   Hardcover $19.95
0-7892-0281-6   Abrams

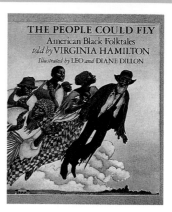

Virginia Hamilton, reteller
Illustrated by Leo & Diane Dillon

THE PEOPLE COULD FLY: AMERICAN BLACK FOLKTALES

Many of the stories in this collection were told among slaves as they dreamt of freedom or remembered their lives in Africa. Hamilton focuses on several themes—animal tales, magical and supernatural tales, and tales of freedom—and following each story is a note explaining its history and meaning. Black-and-white illustrations by Caldecott Medalists Leo and Diane Dillon round out this important book.

192pp   Paperback $14.00 Ⓐ
0-679-84336-1   Knopf

By the same author:
Illustrated by Barry Moser

IN THE BEGINNING: CREATION STORIES FROM AROUND THE WORLD

176pp   Hardcover $25.00
0-15-238740-4   Harcourt Brace
Paperback $18.00
0-15-238742-0   Harcourt Brace

Anthology

Julius Lester, reteller
Illustrated by Jerry Pinkney

THE TALES OF UNCLE REMUS: THE ADVENTURES OF BRER RABBIT

Originally told by Southern slaves, these animal tales were collected by Joel Chandler Harris and published between 1896 and 1918. Lester has selected and rewritten forty-eight of the stories featuring Brer Rabbit, adapting the language and setting for modern-day audiences. This important volume, steeped in black history, is decorated with both full-color and black-and-white illustrations.

176pp Hardcover $19.99
0-8037-0271-X Dial

By the same author:

MORE TALES OF UNCLE REMUS: FURTHER ADVENTURES OF BRER RABBIT, HIS FRIENDS, ENEMIES, AND OTHERS

160pp Hardcover $18.99
0-8037-0419-4 Dial

FURTHER TALES OF UNCLE REMUS: THE MISADVENTURES OF BRER RABBIT, BRER FOX, BRER WOLF, THE DOODANG, AND OTHER CREATURES

160pp Hardcover $18.99
0-8037-0610-3 Dial

THE LAST TALES OF UNCLE REMUS

176pp Hardcover $18.99
0-8037-1303-7 Dial

FROM *The Random House Book of Stories from the Ballet*

Margaret Mayo, reteller
Illustrated by Jane Ray

MAGICAL TALES FROM MANY LANDS

Fourteen magical tales from all over the world are gathered in this volume. Although the stories are of many different origins—Zulu, Arabic, Japanese, Inca, Australian, and Chinese, to name a few—the themes of the stories are universal. Jane Ray's gemlike illustrations are warmed with gold, making this an enchanting collection.

128pp Hardcover $19.99
0-525-45017-3 Dutton

Geraldine McCaughrean, reteller
Illustrated by Angela Barrett

THE RANDOM HOUSE BOOK OF STORIES FROM THE BALLET

Here are the stories of the ten most popular ballets, including *Swan Lake*, *Giselle*, *Petrouchka*, and *Romeo and Juliet*. Reading like a collection of fairy tales, this beautifully illustrated treasury will be valued by all balletomanes.

112pp Hardcover $20.00
0-679-87125-X Random House

A. A. Milne
Illustrated by Ernest H. Shepard

POOH'S BEDTIME BOOK

Complete in one volume is a selection of five poems and three chapters from the original Winnie-the-Pooh books by A. A. Milne. The stories show this beloved stuffed bear trying to get honey from some bees, being introduced to the bouncy tiger Tigger, and joining Piglet and friends in search for the North Pole. The original line drawings by Shepard have been colored, making this bedtime favorite cheery throughout.

48pp Hardcover $13.99
0-525-44895-0 Dutton

By the same author:

THE POOH STORY BOOK

80pp Hardcover $13.99
0-525-37546-5 Dutton
Paperback $5.99
0-14-038168-6 Puffin

Iona & Peter Opie, *editors*
Illustrated by Maurice Sendak
I SAW ESAU: THE SCHOOLCHILD'S POCKET BOOK

Renowned for their collections of children's rhymes, the Opies have gathered here a sophisticated anthology of comebacks, riddles, and joke poems—all decorated with Sendak's wickedly humorous illustrations. Appropriate for adults as well as children, this saucy handbook is invaluable for use in the schoolyard, especially for those who tend to be shy, or for those seeking recognition for being clever.

160pp   Hardcover $19.95
1-56402-046-0   Candlewick

Mary Pope Osborne, *reteller*
Illustrated by Michael McCurdy
AMERICAN TALL TALES

A little exaggeration makes legends from simple historical characters, legends that help form the fabric of our culture. In this volume, the tales of nine folk heroes are related—humorous and very tall indeed! Meet Paul Bunyan, Johnny Appleseed, Sally Ann Thunder, Ann Whirlwind, John Henry, and more, and celebrate the riches this country has to offer.

128pp   Hardcover $22.00
0-679-80089-1   Knopf

Molly Perham, *reteller*
Illustrated by Julek Heller
KING ARTHUR & THE LEGENDS OF CAMELOT

The heroic adventures of King Arthur and his knights, which have captivated readers for centuries, have been retold for today's audiences in this over-sized gift collection. These exciting tales of valor, coupled with Heller's stunning illustrations, are sure to keep young readers on the edge of their seats.

176pp   Hardcover $22.00
0-670-84990-1   Viking

Janet Schulman, *editor*
Illustrated by various artists
THE RANDOM HOUSE BOOK OF EASY-TO-READ STORIES

This bright and sunny collection features eleven complete stories and five selections from previously published works. Featured are such authors and illustrators as Dr. Seuss, Stan and Jan Berenstain, P. D. Eastman, Richard Scarry, and Tomie de Paola.

256pp   Hardcover $18.00
0-679-83438-9   Random House

Alvin Schwartz, *editor*
Illustrated by Stephen Gammell
SCARY STORIES TO TELL IN THE DARK: COLLECTED FROM AMERICAN FOLKLORE

This collection of scary stories has scared the pants off of many an eager reader. Gathered here are many frightening tales along with a few gruesome ones with funny endings. Stephen Gammell's scratchy black-and-white drawings add to the appeal of the popular book.

128pp   Hardcover $14.95
0-397-31926-6   HarperCollins
Paperback $3.95
0-06-440170-7   HarperTrophy

By the same author:

MORE SCARY STORIES TO TELL IN THE DARK: COLLECTED AND RETOLD FROM FOLKLORE
128pp   Hardcover $14.95
0-397-32081-7   HarperCollins
Paperback $4.95
0-06-440177-4   HarperTrophy

SCARY STORIES 3: MORE TALES TO CHILL YOUR BONES
128pp   Hardcover $14.95
0-06-021794-4   HarperCollins
Paperback $3.95
0-06-440418-8   HarperTrophy

SCARY STORIES BOXED SET
Paperback $11.85
0-06-440465-X   HarperTrophy

Early Readers

THE BOOKS IN THIS SECTION are designed to supplement your child's reading program at school. As with picture books, early readers cover a wide variety of subjects. They are illustrated, though the emphasis is more on text than on illustrations. Early readers are targeted towards specific reading levels, ordered by grade. As every child is different, you may wish to judge on your own which reading level is appropriate. The books in this section are alphabetized by series. Look for subjects that will inspire a continued interest in reading.

What to look for . . .

- A reading level that will challenge but will not intimidate your child

- Clear text. The print size varies with reading levels.

- A topic that will stimulate further interest in reading

- Favorite artists your child has enjoyed at an earlier level of reading

- Nonfiction subjects your child enjoys, such as sports, history, or adventure

- New subjects to introduce your child to, such as fantasy and folklore

ALL ABOARD READING™

The **All Aboard Reading** series features stories that capture beginning readers' imagination while developing their vocabulary and reading comprehension. **The Picture Readers**, appropriate for pre-schoolers, combine a very simple text with rebuses. Flash cards bound in the book help make the transition from the rebus to the printed word. As the levels progress, the stories get longer, and the print size gets smaller, preparing readers for longer books with chapters. All the books are illustrated in full color, and engage a child's curiosity with a range of topics from science to sports, history, and fantasy.

PICTURE READERS: PRESCHOOL–GRADE 1

Jennifer Dussling
Illustrated by Davy Jones
IN A DARK, DARK HOUSE

One night, a boy goes into a dark, dark house, up the dark, dark stairs, through a dark, dark door, where he finds a dark, dark trunk and *EEK!* Inside the trunk is a truly scary monster! Here the refrain of "Was I scared? No!" changes to an emphatic "Was I scared? Yes!" The boy races out of the house with the monster in pursuit and finds safety in a tree. This book is only meant for youngsters who like a good scare.

32pp   Paperback $3.95
0-448-40970-4   Grosset

In the same series:
Cathy East Dubowski
Illustrated by Mark Dubowski
PICKY NICKY
32pp   Paperback $3.95
0-448-41295-0   Grosset

LEVEL 1: PRESCHOOL–GRADE 1

Patricia Demuth
Illustrated by Michael Montgomery
JOHNNY APPLESEED

One of America's legendary heroes is introduced to beginning readers in this highly accessible tale. Full-page illustrations show Johnny, pot on head, tramping across a young United States, sowing apple trees as he goes.

32pp   Paperback $3.99
0-448-41130-X   Grosset

Gail Herman
Illustrated by Norman Gorbaty
WHAT A HUNGRY PUPPY!

Lucky is a hungry puppy, so off he goes in search of a bone. He digs up several little treasures— an old shoe, a smelly sock, a jump rope—but none of them will do.

Finally he finds a bone, but finds the bone's large *owner* as well! Lucky runs, but the big dog chases him all the way to his house. Lucky is relieved when he realizes the big dog only wants to be friends, and is even more relieved when dinner is finally served! What a hungry puppy!

32pp   Paperback $3.95
0-448-40536-9   Grosset

By the same author in this series:
Illustrated by Jerry Smath
DOUBLE-HEADER
32pp   Paperback $3.95
0-448-40157-6   Grosset

Judith Moffatt
WHO STOLE THE COOKIES?

Bright and colorful collages illustrate this popular rhyme about missing cookies from the cookie jar. A girl, a bird, a cat, a dog, and a mouse—each accused in turn ("Who, me?") as the cookie thief—follow a trail of crumbs to a cave where they discover the *real* culprit. Then it's back home to make a new batch for everyone!

32pp   Paperback $3.95
0-448-41127-X   Grosset

Early Readers

Jane O'Connor
Illustrated by I DiSalvo-Ryan

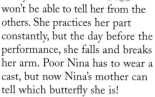

NINA, NINA BALLERINA

Nina is thrille[d] ballet class is [going to] put on a recit[al] everyone will [be a] butterfly. Her [only] worry is her m[other] won't be able to tell her from the others. She practices her part constantly, but the day before the performance, she falls and breaks her arm. Poor Nina has to wear a cast, but now Nina's mother can tell which butterfly she is!

32pp   Paperback $3.99
0-448-40511-3   Grosset

By the same author in this series:
KATE SKATES
32pp   Paperback $3.95
0-448-40935-6   Grosset

NINA, NINA STAR BALLERINA
32pp   Paperback $3.95
0-448-41492-9   Grosset

LEVEL 2: GRADES 1–3

Patricia Demuth
Illustrated by Jim Deal
WAY DOWN DEEP: STRANGE OCEAN CREATURES

Giant squid, sea cucumbers, and fish with huge jaws, sharp teeth, and lights on their bodies are among the unusual creatures that make the ocean floor their home. Beginning readers will get a glimpse of these fascinating animals (still only partially accessible to humans), along with a lesson on the ocean floor's

geography and the methods scientists are using to explore the murky depths.

48pp   Paperback $3.95
0-448-40851-1   Grosset

By the same author in this series:
Illustrated by Paul Lopez
GORILLAS
48pp   Paperback $3.95
0-448-40217-3   Grosset

Illustrated by Judith Moffatt
SNAKES
48pp   Paperback $3.95
0-448-40513-X   Grosset

Cathy East Dubowski
Illustrated by Mark Dubowski
PIRATE SCHOOL

Every day, Pete goes to his school, P.S.1—the P.S. stands for *Pirate School!* There, Pete learns everything about being a good pirate. His only problem is Grimy, the class bully. One day, the class splits up on Skull Island to find a buried treasure. Pete and Grimy find the treasure—and fall into an old abandoned ship. Can enemies become friends in a time of need?

48pp   Paperback $3.95
0-448-41132-6   Grosset

Pete learned to add by adding up gold coins.

Joyce Milton
Illustrated by Silvia Duran
BIG CATS

Fascinating facts about the large cats of the world are presented in this easy-to-read science book. The big cats—cougars, jaguars, leopards, cheetahs, lions, and tigers—are shown in their natural habitats, and their behavior is compared with that of domestic cats. Did you know that lions and tigers *purr* when they are happy?

48pp   Paperback $4.95
0-448-40564-4   Grosset

By the same author in this series:
Illustrated by Judith Moffatt
BATS: CREATURES OF THE NIGHT
48pp   Paperback $3.95
0-448-40193-2   Grosset

Illustrated by Susan Swan
MUMMIES
48pp   Paperback $3.95
0-448-41325-6   Grosset

Nicholas Nirgiotis
Illustrated by Michael Radencich
VOLCANOES: MOUNTAINS THAT BLOW THEIR TOPS

What young reader can resist the allure of a volcano? The how and why of volcanoes is made perfectly clear by an easy-to-understand text that combines scientific facts with a history of volcanic eruptions. Crisp cut-paper illustrations round out this informative book.

48pp   Paperback $3.95
0-448-41143-1   Grosset

LEVEL 3: GRADES 2–4

Dana del Prado
Illustrated by Stephen Marchesi

TERROR BELOW! TRUE SHARK STORIES

Did you know that more people die of bee stings each year than from shark attacks? The true stories of three men who had rare but terrifying close-call encounters with sharks are interspersed with facts about these scary fish.

48pp   Paperback $3.95
0-448-41124-5   Grosset

Joan Elste
Illustrated by DyAnne DiSalvo-Ryan

TRUE BLUE

J. D.'s dog, Blue, has the best nose in the county. Blue's best friend is the neighbor's old dog, Molasses, and when the two dogs are suddenly missing, J. D. is frightened—poachers have been shooting at anything that moves. She searches for Blue and finally finds him, but Blue won't come home. Instead, he leads her to Molasses, who has been wounded by the poachers. Luckily, J. D. and her father get Molasses home, and he is saved—saved by his *true blue* friend, Blue!

48pp   Paperback $3.95
0-448-41264-0   Grosset

Jean Fritz
Illustrated by DyAnne DiSalvo-Ryan

GEORGE WASHINGTON'S MOTHER

There have been many books about George Washington, but not many about his mother! Mary Washington worries a lot about her son. If only he would stop gallivanting around in the army and take care of *her!* This stubborn old lady hates to dress in fancy garb and refuses to see company—she prefers to dress in old clothes, work in her garden, and occasionally smoke a pipe. I cannot tell a lie: this humorous peek into the past will make readers grin.

48pp   Paperback $3.95
0-448-40384-6   Grosset

By the same author in this series:
Illustrated by Charles Robinson

JUST A FEW WORDS, MR. LINCOLN: THE STORY OF THE GETTYSBURG ADDRESS

48pp   Paperback $3.99
0-448-40170-3   Grosset

Deborah Hautzig, adapter
Illustrated by Natalie Carabetta

FRANCES HODGSON BURNETT'S THE SECRET GARDEN

Frances Hodgson Burnett's beloved classic is adapted for beginning readers in this colorfully illustrated version. The spoiled orphan Mary Lennox leaves India to live with her cold uncle in his dreary mansion in England. When Mary hears of a secret garden kept locked for ten years, she is determined to find it and tend it back to life. With the help of her uncle's sickly son and a boy who knows all about nature, Mary secretly transforms the garden—and all of their lives.

48pp   Paperback $3.95
0-448-40736-1   Grosset

By the same author in this series:

FRANCES HODGSON BURNETT'S A LITTLE PRINCESS

48pp   Paperback $3.95
0-448-41327-2   Grosset

S. A. Kramer
Illustrated by Mitchell Heinze

HOOP STARS

Fans will enjoy these biographies of basketball's superstars Hakeem Olajuwon, Charles Barkley, Shaquille O'Neal, and David Robinson. The book shows the hard work and perseverance that led them into the NBA, and illustrates each player's unique and fantastic playing ability with highlights from specific games.

48pp   Paperback $3.95
0-448-40943-7   Grosset

By the same author in this series:
Illustrated by Jim Campbell

FOOTBALL STARS

48pp   Paperback $3.95
0-448-41591-7   Grosset

BEGINNER BOOKS ®

Back in 1957, Theodor Geisel responded to an article in *Life* magazine that lamented the use of boring reading primers in schools. Using the pseudonym of "Dr. Seuss" (Seuss was Geisel's middle name) and only two hundred twenty-three words, Geisel created a replacement for those dull primers: *The Cat in the Hat*. The instant success of the book prompted Geisel and his wife to found **Beginner Books**, and Geisel wrote many popular books in this series, including *Hop on Pop*, *Fox in Socks*, and *Green Eggs and Ham*. Other favorite titles in this series are *Go, Dog, Go!* and *Are You My Mother?* by P. D. Eastman, *A Fly Went By*, by Mike McClintock, and *Put Me in the Zoo*, by Robert Lopshire. These affordable hardcover books combine large print, easy vocabulary, and large, bright illustrations in stories kids will want to read again and again.

GRADES 1–2

Marc Brown
SPOOKY RIDDLES

"How does a witch tell time? With a witchwatch!" This and many other silly riddles about witches, ghosts, mummies, and vampires make this easy-to-read book perfect for Halloween. Humorous full-page color illustrations take the scare out of the subject, making it a perfect match for this age group.

48pp   Hardcover $7.99
0-394-86093-4   Random House

P. D. Eastman
ARE YOU MY MOTHER?

A mother bird leaves her egg in the nest to go look for some food. While she's gone, the egg hatches, and the baby bird sets off to find his mother—but he doesn't know what she looks like. His search leads him to ask a variety of animals and machines, "Are you my mother?" Finally, a crane deposits him back in his nest, where his mother is waiting. Just the right amount of tension and the happy and secure ending make this an extremely popular story.

64pp   Hardcover $7.99
0-394-80018-4   Random House

Look at those dogs go.
Go, dogs. Go!

By the same author in this series:
GO, DOG. GO!

Dogs in all shapes, sizes, and colors—black, white, yellow, green, blue, pink and red—star in this wonderfully goofy book. Floppy-eared canines zooming around in cars, riding a Ferris wheel, and generally having a marvelous time illustrate simple concepts in single- and two-page vignettes. Recurring through the book is a disagreement about hats—a disagreement that is finally resolved at the great dog party high in the top of a tree.

64pp   Hardcover $7.99
0-394-80020-6   Random House

THE BEST NEST
72pp   Hardcover $7.99
0-394-80051-6   Random House

SAM AND THE FIREFLY
72pp   Hardcover $7.99
0-394-80006-0   Random House

Mike McClintock
Illustrated by Fritz Siebel
A FLY WENT BY

A boy's peaceful reverie by a lake is interrupted when a fly, fleeing from a frog, zooms by. When the boy scolds the frog for chasing the fly, the frog tells him that he's only fleeing from a cat. Each ensuing animal claims its running from something else, until a man claims he's running from a monster—which turns out to be only a lamb with its foot stuck in a bucket! The boy sets everyone straight, and returns to the peace and quiet by the lake.

72pp   Hardcover $7.99
0-394-80003-6   Random House

Helen Palmer
Illustrated by P. D. Eastman
A FISH OUT OF WATER

When a boy feeds his new fish Otto too much food, disaster strikes! Otto grows and grows, and the boy can't find a bowl big enough for him. The police and the firemen can't help—even the town pool is too small for Otto! Finally, out of desperation, the boy calls the pet store owner, who magically restores Otto to his proper size.

72pp   Hardcover $7.99
0-394-80023-0   Random House

It did not take P. J. very long to find out that he did not like living with the skunks.

Marilyn Sadler
Illustrated by Roger Bollen
IT'S NOT EASY BEING A BUNNY

P. J. Funnybunny has had it with being a bunny. He has too many brothers and sisters, he's tired of eating carrots, and his ears are too big. P. J. decides to run away and live with a different animal. Unfortunately, every animal he goes to live with has very *un*-bunny-like characteristics—the bears sleep too much, the pigs like to lie in the mud, the beavers are too busy, and the skunks . . . well, that's pretty obvious. P. J. finally decides that home with the bunnies is where he belongs.

48pp   Hardcover $7.99
0-394-86102-7   Random House

By the same author in this series:
HONEY BUNNY FUNNYBUNNY
36pp   Hardcover $7.99
0-679-88181-6   Random House

Dr. Seuss
THE CAT IN THE HAT

One wet, rainy day while mother is out, a boy and a girl sit dejectedly in their chairs, watching the rain beat against the window. They're bored. Suddenly, in bursts a large cat in a tall striped hat, ready to play— and not just ordinary games, *oh no!* This cat likes to create mischief and mayhem, and to aid him, he brings Thing One and Thing Two. These two small fuzzy blue imps race around the house, wreaking havoc. Who's going to clean up this mess? This most famous of all the Beginner Books has been beloved by readers young and old since 1957.

72pp   Hardcover $7.99
0-394-80001-X   Random House

By the same author in this series:
THE CAT IN THE HAT COMES BACK
72pp   Hardcover $7.99
0-394-80002-8   Random House

I do not like them,
Sam-I-am.
I do not like
green eggs and ham.

GREEN EGGS AND HAM

Sam-I-am won't give up! He keeps trying to get the grumpy grownup in the story to taste green eggs and ham. No matter how Sam-I-am presents the green eggs and ham (in a box, with a fox, in the rain, on a train), the curmudgeon refuses to try them. Finally, Sam-I-am's pesky persistence pays off. A crowd of open-mouthed onlookers watch in suspense as the old grouch takes a bite. And? . . . SAY! The old sourpuss's face is wreathed in smiles as he gratefully acknowledges, "I do so like green eggs and ham. Thank you, thank you, Sam-I-am!"

72pp   Hardcover $7.99
0-394-80016-8   Random House

HOP ON POP

Subtitled "The Simplest Seuss for Youngest Use," this book is perfect for teaching the rudiments of reading. Simple rhyming words, such as PUP and UP, are stacked one over the other in large capitals, so that readers see that "up" is contained in the word "pup." Sentences using these words are accompanied by humorous illustrations to complete the playful reading lesson.

72pp   Hardcover $7.99
0-394-80029-X   Random House

I CAN READ WITH MY EYES SHUT!

48pp   Hardcover $7.99
0-394-83912-9   Random House

ONE FISH TWO FISH RED FISH BLUE FISH

This nonsensical romp through a gallery of imaginary creatures introduces beginning readers to a variety of rhyming letter combinations. Meet the Yink, who likes to wink and drink pink ink. Or the Yop, who hops from finger top to finger top. Then there is morose Ned who doesn't like his little bed. The short anecdotal poems have just the right combination of humor and the fantastic to enrapture readers.

72pp   Hardcover $7.99
0-394-80013-3   Random House

FOX IN SOCKS

72pp   Hardcover $7.99
0-394-80038-9   Random House

OH, THE THINGS YOU CAN THINK!

48pp   Hardcover $7.99
0-394-83129-2   Random House

This one has
a little star.

This one has a little car.
Say! what a lot
of fish there are.

BOB BOOKS ®

What can be more satisfying to a child than to close a book and say, "I read it all by myself!" This series of books for the very beginner has children beaming with pride. Instead of relying on large print and pictures to teach children to read, **Bob Books** employs one of the oldest methods around: phonics. Each book focuses on a few vowel or consonant sounds and limits the story to just a few words. For example, in Book 1, *Mat*, the only words used are "Mat," "Sam," "on," "cat," and "sat." In this way, the novice learns—and remembers—a few sounds at a time. To reinforce these sounds, each book starts with a guide showing the letters that will be introduced with an accompanying word example and cheerful picture. All the **Bob Books** are illustrated with humorous line drawings that beg to be colored. Included also is a guide to parents and teachers, plus two easy-to-assemble finger puppets and a cardboard stage, for readers to act out the stories they just read—all on their own. The silly stories, gentle pace, and overall friendliness of the **Bob Books** help make reading a happy pastime.

Cat sat on Sam.

Bobby Lynn Maslen
Illustrated by John R. Maslen
BOB BOOKS® FOR BEGINNING READERS (SET 1): PRESCHOOL— GRADE 1
144pp   Paperback $14.95
0-590-20373-8   Scholastic

MORE BOB BOOKS® FOR YOUNG READERS (SET 2): PRESCHOOL—GRADE 1
144pp   Paperback $14.95
0-590-20374-6   Scholastic

EVEN MORE BOB BOOKS® FOR YOUNG READERS (SET 3): PRESCHOOL—GRADE 1
144pp   Paperback $15.95
0-590-20375-4   Scholastic

BOB BOOKS® PLUS: PRESCHOOL—GRADE 1
160pp   Paperback $15.95
0-590-92171-1   Scholastic

Mat sat on Sam.

BRIGHT & EARLY BOOKS ®

Like the parent **Beginner Books**, **Bright & Early Books** feature the same affordable hardcover format, imaginative stories, and colorful pictures. Geared for a younger audience, these books use simple words, repetition, and pictures that act as clues to the text. Contributors include Dr. Seuss (*Mr. Brown Can Moo! Can You?*, *There's a Wocket in My Pocket!*, *The Nose Book*), Stan and Jan Berenstain (*Inside, Outside, Upside Down*; *Bears on Wheels*), Al Perkins (*Hand, Hand, Fingers, Thumb*) and Michael Frith (*I'll Teach My Dog 100 Words*).

PRESCHOOL–GRADE 1

Stan & Jan Berenstain
OLD HAT NEW HAT

With a minimum of rhyming words, the Berenstains have created a silly story for early readers to enjoy. A bear with an saggy beat-up hat goes into a store to buy a new one. But nothing the increasingly grumpy sales clerk shows him is right— the hats are "Too big. Too small. Too flat. Too tall." The hats and the refusals get sillier and sillier, and by the time the clerk is bringing in hats by the wheelbarrow, the little bear decides his old hat is "just right!"

36pp   Hardcover $7.99
0-394-80669-7   Random House

By the same authors in this series:
HE BEAR SHE BEAR
48pp   Hardcover $7.99
0-394-82997-2   Random House

INSIDE OUTSIDE UPSIDE DOWN
36pp   Hardcover $7.99
0-394-81142-9   Random House

Al Perkins
Illustrated by Eric Gurney
HAND, HAND, FINGERS, THUMB

A monkey uses its fingers and hands to beat on a drum, "dum ditty, dum ditty, dum, dum dum!" More monkeys come and join in the fun, drumming, picking fruit, shaking hands, and strumming banjoes. The catchy rhythm of this rhyming text sweeps the reader along, creating an infectious and riotous romp.

36pp   Hardcover $7.99
0-394-81076-7   Random House

By the same author in this series:
Illustrated by Bill O'Brian
THE EAR BOOK
36pp   Hardcover $7.99
0-394-81199-2   Random House

Illustrated by Roy McKie
THE NOSE BOOK
36pp   Hardcover $7.99
0-394-80623-9   Random House

BOOM BOOM BOOM
Mr. Brown is a wonder!
BOOM BOOM BOOM
Mr. Brown makes thunder!

Dr. Seuss
MR. BROWN CAN MOO! CAN YOU? DR. SEUSS'S BOOK OF WONDERFUL NOISES

The talented Mr. Brown displays his virtuoso art through a variety of noises. Not only can he moo like a cow, but he can blurp like a horn, sizzle like an egg in a frying pan, pop like a cork , eek eek like a creaky shoe, and even imitate the sound of a hippopotamus chewing gum (grum, grum, grum)! The silly rhyming text makes this a wonderful book to read aloud and giggle along with the listeners!

36pp   Hardcover $7.99
0-394-80622-0   Random House
Board Book $4.99
0-679-88282-0   Random House

By the same author in this series:
MARVIN K. MOONEY WILL YOU PLEASE GO NOW!
36pp   Hardcover $7.99
0-394-82490-3   Random House

THERE'S A WOCKET IN MY POCKET!
36pp   Hardcover $7.99
0-394-82920-4   Random House

HELLO MATH READER™

Combining two concepts into one, Scholastic came up with a new twist to their **Hello Reader!** beginning reader line. The innovative **Hello Math Reader** series combines simple math concepts in an easy-to-read story plus six pages of math activities for parents and children to enjoy together.

LEVEL 1: PRESCHOOL–GRADE 1

Teddy Slater
Math Activities by Marilyn Burns
Illustrated by Gioia Fiammenghi
STAY IN LINE

In a bouncing rhyme, simple math concepts are woven into a story about twelve kids and their trip to the zoo. How many different ways can a dozen children be grouped? Follow the class and find out! Can you see who pulls one little girl's pigtail?

32pp   Paperback $3.50
0-590-22713-0   Cartwheel

LEVEL 2: KINDERGARTEN –GRADE 2

Anne Schreiber
Math Activities by Marilyn Burns
Illustrated by Larry Daste
SLOWER THAN A SNAIL

A little girl, accused by her older brother of being slower than a snail, proceeds to set him straight with a plethora of comparisons. She is wider than a string bean, longer than a noodle, shorter than a skyscraper, and heavier than a duck. She tells him this and more, and when she whizzes past him, she declares the one thing she is *not* is slower than a snail!

32pp   Paperback $3.50
0-590-18074-6   Cartwheel

LEVEL 3: GRADES 1–2

Caren Holtzman
Math Activities by Marilyn Burns
Illustrated by Betsy Day
A QUARTER FROM THE TOOTH FAIRY

A boy who gets a quarter from the tooth fairy just can't figure out how to spend it. Whatever he buys he ends up returning, and each time he gets his 25¢ back in different coins than he had before. Finally, when he trades twenty-five pennies back to a quarter, he uses his money in an unusual way—he buys his tooth back!

40pp   Paperback $3.99
0-590-26598-9   Cartwheel

LEVEL 4: GRADES 2–3

Joanne Rocklin
Illustrated by Meredith Johnson
HOW MUCH IS THAT GUINEA PIG IN THE WINDOW?

When a class earns $50 from a bake sale, their teacher says they can use the money to buy a class pet. But first they must find a pet they can afford and raise money to buy its food. Many math concepts come into play as competing teams raise money by recycling bottles and cans. Complicating the story is a reluctant boy who doesn't want a class pet at all.

48pp   Paperback $3.50
0-590-22716-5   Cartwheel

HELLO READER! ®

With inspiring and educational stories, Scholastic's **Hello Reader!** series caters to the spectrum of reading abilities among beginning readers. **My First Hello Reader!** books use basic words to reinforce phonics and sight vocabulary. They offer punch-out flash cards plus six additional pages of skill-building activities. Levels 1–4 combine a greater vocabulary and longer sentence length. Each book has an introductory letter from an education specialist guiding parents on how to help their children learn to read.

MY FIRST HELLO READER!™: PRESCHOOL– KINDERGARTEN

Nancy Christensen
Illustrated by Rowan Barnes-Murphy
WHO AM I?

Hardly any preschooler can resist a riddle, and this book is no exception. The title asks the riddle, and the rhyming text describes characteristics that do *not* fit the animal in question. Cartoonlike illustrations show animals who fit the description, while showing only part of the mystery creature. The last page reveals the answer, as a bow-tied cat springs from a tree. Silly, indeed!

32pp plus flash cards
Paperback $3.99
0-590-46192-3   Cartwheel

Paul Fehlner
Illustrated by Laura Rader
NO WAY!

A little girl never wants to do what her parents ask her. "No way!" she replies to their requests. But who always gets their way? Her parents—that is, until they all go visit Grandma!

32pp plus flash cards
Paperback $3.99
0-590-48514-8   Cartwheel

Kirsten Hall
Illustrated by Laura Rader
A BAD, BAD DAY

Oh, it's hard to get up, especially when everything goes wrong! Young readers (and older ones!) will empathize with the boy in this light verse as the morning fills with mishaps. He bumps his head, gets toothpaste on his shirt, spills his cereal, and misses the bus. *Oh, what a bad day*—until he gets his paper back in school! *Hooray!*

32pp plus flash cards
Paperback $3.99
0-590-25496-0   Cartwheel

Wendy Cheyette Lewison
Illustrated by Hans Wilhelm
BUZZ SAID THE BEE

The farm animals are all in a tizzy—a bee sits on the tail of a duck and won't scat! The duck then sits on a hen, who sits on a pig, who sits on a cow, who sits on a sleeping sheep . . . *Eek!* The piled up animals fall, one by one, uttering their quacks, clucks, oinks, moos, and baas. Last is the bee who says *"Buzz!"* and *all* the animals scat! The repetitive rhyme is paired with expressive illustrations—perfect for this silly barnyard romp.

32pp   Paperback $3.50
0-590-44185-X   Cartwheel

Mary Packard
Illustrated by Dee de Rosa
I KNOW KARATE

An enthusiastic karate student shows readers what he has learned in class: his kick, his chop, and his bow. He has learned so much that he can scare away monsters. But what is that scary, hairy shadow—oh, it's only his dog, Hairy! Karate fans will enjoy the simple rhyming text and see the moves they know shown clearly in the realistic, full-page illustrations.

32pp plus flash cards
Paperback $3.99
0-590-25498-7   Cartwheel

LEVEL 1: PRESCHOOL–GRADE 1

Gail Herman
Illustrated by Doug Cushman
TEDDY BEAR FOR SALE

None of the children want the teddy bear in the toy shop, so the bear decides to run away. He jumps into a toy car, drives off, then sails a boat, conducts a train, and rides a roller-skate. Then . . . *whee!* It's down a slide—but *whoops!* He lands on a trampoline, flies through the air, and lands *plop!* onto the counter, where an admiring boy buys him and takes him home.

32pp   Paperback $3.50
0-590-25943-1   Cartwheel

Grace Maccarone
Illustrated by Betsy Lewin

THE CLASSROOM PET

It's time for Christmas vacation, and Sam is elated because he gets to take home Star, the classroom hermit crab. Sam lets her out for a walk, and when he turns his back for a second, Star disappears! He searches everywhere but cannot find her. *Wait!*—what is that hanging from the Christmas tree like an ornament? What a story to tell the rest of the class!

32pp   Paperback $3.50
0-590-26264-5   Cartwheel

By the same author in this series:

ITCHY, ITCHY CHICKEN POX

What are these spots? *Oh no!* Chicken pox! In catchy rhyme, a boy describes being sick with this itchy disease. Spots are everywhere and it's hard not to scratch, but an oatmeal bath and lotion take away some of the itchiness. The days go by, and the spots go away. At last the spots are gone, and he feels better. *Hooray!* It's back to school again!

32pp   Paperback $3.50
0-590-44948-6   Cartwheel

THE LUNCH BOX SURPRISE

Everyone in the class has a yummy lunch today, but when Sam opens his lunch box, he gets an awful surprise—it's empty! Feeling sorry for him, Sam's classmates share their lunches. Soon Sam goes from having no lunch to having the best lunch ever!

32pp   Paperback $3.50
0-590-26267-X   Cartwheel

Jean Marzollo
Illustrated by Judith Moffatt

I'M A SEED

Two seeds in the soil are speaking to each other. "I'm a seed!" they both say. One knows it's a marigold, but the other doesn't know what it is. Each plant grows leaves, then flowers, and when the mystery seed grows big and round and orange, the riddle is solved. The clever text weaves facts about plants into the story, and the beautiful collages show a host of wildlife for readers to identify. This is a wonderful introduction to a plant's life cycle.

32pp   Paperback $3.50
0-590-26586-5   Cartwheel

**LEVEL 2:
PRESCHOOL–GRADE 2**

Patience Brewster
TOO MANY PUPPIES

Milly is going to have puppies, and her little girl owner wants to keep them *all*. "Too many puppies," says Mommy. When the seven puppies are born, they are sweet and fluffy, and the little girl *still* wants to keep them all—until the puppies turn mischievous, chewing up her toys, all barking at once, and *always* begging for food! Maybe it's better to keep only one—Milly, the *grown-up* puppy!

32pp   Paperback $3.50
0-590-60276-4   Cartwheel

Sheri Brownrigg
Illustrated by Meredith Johnson

BEST FRIENDS WEAR PINK TUTUS

Emily and Amanda are best friends, and wear their pink tutus everywhere. Today, their ballet teacher is going to decide who will play the lead in a performance of *The Nutcracker*. Both girls want to play the lead—but neither wants to make the other sad! What a relief when they are both chosen to be snowflakes! And guess what? The snowflakes wear pink tutus!

32pp   Paperback $3.50
0-590-46437-X   Cartwheel

By the same author in this series:

ALL TUTUS SHOULD BE PINK
32pp Paperback $3.50
0-590-43904-9 Cartwheel

Rita Golden Gelman
Illustrated by Mort Gerberg

MORE SPAGHETTI, I SAY!

Mmmm! Spaghetti! Minnie the monkey can't get enough! Poor Freddy wants to play with her, but Minnie won't stop eating spaghetti! She could eat it all day—by itself, or with other foods. She could eat it by the truck-full, ski on it, hide in it . . . *uh oh!* Minnie feels sick! She ate too much! Freddy takes the bowl away, and—what's this? Now *Freddy* is eating spaghetti and won't play with Minnie!

32pp Paperback $3.50
0-590-45783-7 Cartwheel

LEVEL 3: KINDERGARTEN –GRADE 2

Karen Backstein
Illustrated by Annie Mitra

THE BLIND MEN AND THE ELEPHANT

Six blind men have learned about the world through sound and touch. When the prince gets a new elephant, the men decide to go to the palace and touch it. Each man feels only a part of the elephant—its side, its trunk, its tusk, its ear, its tail, and its leg—and gets a different impression of what an elephant looks like. They argue among themselves about it, until the wise prince kindly tells them that they are *all* right—they just need to put all the parts together!

48pp Paperback $3.50
0-590-45813-2 Cartwheel

Joanna Cole
Illustrated by Jared Lee

MONSTER MANNERS

Rosie the monster can't seem to master monster manners. No matter how hard she tries, she just cannot growl into the telephone; she always answers politely. Nor can she chew her rocks without flossing, or forget *not* to say "please." Poor Rosie! Her parents are beside themselves. But when an emergency occurs, Rosie's "bad" manners come to the rescue!

48pp Paperback $3.99
0-590-53951-5 Cartwheel

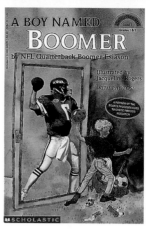

Boomer Esiason
Illustrated by Jacqueline Rogers

A BOY NAMED BOOMER

Former football star Boomer Esiason recalls different episodes from his childhood for each month of the year. The famous left-handed quarterback had the same kinds of adventures as most kids, and readers will be inspired by this to set their own goals for greatness. Eleven biographical pages about Boomer's football career are included, as well as an autographed photo.

48pp Paperback $3.99
0-590-52835-1 Cartwheel

Margo Lundell
Illustrated by Irene Trivas

A GIRL NAMED HELEN KELLER

The Kellers are devastated to discover that their two-year-old girl is both blind and deaf after a severe illness. Determined to help her live like other children, the Kellers hire Anne Sullivan, a teacher from a school for the blind. Miss Sullivan first has to tame the wild and spoiled Helen,

Early Readers

then spend hours working with her, trying to get her to understand her surroundings. Finally, and against all odds, Anne's diligence pays off: Helen's world suddenly opens up. Helen later writes about this miraculous moment, "my heart began to sing!"

48pp   Paperback $3.99
0-590-47963-6   Cartwheel

LEVEL 4: GRADES 2–4

Robert D. Ballard with Nan Froman
Illustrated by Ken Marschall
FINDING THE TITANIC

The great ship *Titanic* sank in April 1912, and for almost seventy-five years lay unfound on the ocean floor. Scientist Robert Ballard dreamt of finding the lost ship, and this is the thrilling account of how he made this dream come true. Interspersed in the narrative is the story of the sinking itself, as told through the eyes of a twelve-year-old girl, one of the fortunate survivors. The you-are-there narrative, photos, and drawings add to the excitement, and help readers to understand the magnitude of this great tragedy.

48pp   Paperback $3.99
0-590-47230-5   Cartwheel

Wade Hudson
Illustrated by Ron Garnett
GREAT BLACK HEROES: FIVE NOTABLE INVENTORS

The names of these inventors are unknown to most people, yet their inventions have changed the lives of millions. Inventions such as the stoplight, the overhead electrical trolley system, the gas mask, a device that lubricates moving train parts, and hair and beauty products for black people are only some of the inventions mentioned here. Many of these inventors died penniless and forgotten, but, hopefully, through books such as these, they will be remembered for their lasting contributions.

48pp   Paperback $3.99
0-590-48033-2   Cartwheel

By the same author in this series:
GREAT BLACK HEROES: FIVE BRAVE EXPLORERS
48pp   Paperback $3.99
0-590-48032-4   Cartwheel

Eva Moore
Illustrated by Don Bolognese
BUDDY: THE FIRST SEEING EYE DOG

In 1927, Dorothy Eustis, upon hearing that dogs in Germany were used to help lead blind soldiers around, was determined to start a school to train dogs for the blind in the United States. She started her project by training a dog for Morris Frank, a blind American. This is the story of how Morris learned to depend on Buddy, and how they opened the way for other blind people to find freedom in their lives through these wonderful dogs.

48pp   Paperback $3.99
0-590-26585-7   Cartwheel

Peggy Parish
Illustrated by Lynn Sweat
TEACH US, AMELIA BEDELIA

Amelia Bedelia, the literal-minded maid, is mistaken for the new teacher at the elementary school. The pupils are in hysterics as she calls the roll by yelling at a roll, plants bulbs by putting light bulbs into dirt, and gives highly creative math lessons involving the whole class and a whole lot of apples. The students never had a teacher like Amelia Bedelia before!

56pp   Paperback $3.99
0-590-53773-3   Cartwheel

Early Readers

I CAN READ BOOKS ®

In 1957, Harper published its first **I Can Read** title, *Little Bear*, written by Else Holmelund Minarik and illustrated by Maurice Sendak. Large type, simple vocabulary, chapter-like divisions, and decorative pictures made *Little Bear* perfect for emerging readers—they could read the story comfortably and not feel overwhelmed by the text. Following suit came such classics as Peggy Parish's *Amelia Bedelia* series, Lillian Hoban's books about Arthur the monkey, and Syd Hoff's popular *Danny and the Dinosaur*. Many books in this series are special in the depth of emotion evoked—*Little Bear*, the *Frog and Toad* books by Arnold Lobel, and *Daniel's Duck* by Clyde Bulla, to name a few—and all are enjoyed by children of all ages.

LEVEL 1: PRESCHOOL–GRADE 1

Esther Averill
THE FIRE CAT

Pickles, the cat with the big paws, can't help being bad—he keeps chasing little cats up trees. When his friend Mrs. Goodkind gives him to Joe, the fireman, Pickles decides a firehouse cat is what he wants to be. He tries hard to help the firemen at their jobs, but it isn't until Pickles proves he cares for the other cats that he earns his fire hat—and a seat on the fire truck.

64pp Paperback $3.75
0-06-444038-9 HarperTrophy

Syd Hoff
DANNY AND THE DINOSAUR

Danny goes to the museum where his wish comes true—a friendly dinosaur comes to life and spends the day playing with him. As the dinosaur says, after one hundred million years, it's good to play outside! The two have a monstrously good time eating ice cream, going to a ball game, and playing hide-and-seek with Danny's friends. When the day comes to an end, the dinosaur must return to the museum, even though Danny wants to keep him as a pet. After all, the museum needs him, and, Danny realizes, the dinosaur probably wouldn't fit in his house!

64pp Hardcover $14.95
0-06-022465-7 HarperCollins
Paperback $3.75
0-06-444002-8 HarperTrophy

By the same author in this series:
BARNEY'S HORSE
32pp Paperback $3.75
0-06-444142-3 HarperTrophy

MRS. BRICE'S MICE
32pp Paperback $3.75
0-06-444145-8 HarperTrophy

STANLEY
32pp Paperback $3.75
0-06-444010-9 HarperTrophy

Marco & Giulio Maestro
WHAT DO YOU HEAR WHEN COWS SING? AND OTHER SILLY RIDDLES

What child can resist a book of riddles? Each one-sentence riddle rests on a full-page color illustration, and the correct answer is revealed by turning the page. Bright and cheerful pictures of bugs and animals set off jokes that are appropriately silly for this age group. Oh, what *do* you hear when cows sing? *Moo*-sic!

48pp Hardcover $14.95
0-06-024948-X HarperCollins
Paperback $3.75
0-06-444227-6 HarperTrophy

Little Bear put his arms around Mother Bear.

He said, "Mother Bear, stop fooling.

You are my Mother Bear

and I am your Little Bear,

and we are on Earth, and you know it.

Now may I eat my lunch?"

"Yes," said Mother Bear,

"and then you will have your nap.

For you are my little bear,

and I know it."

FROM *Little Bear*

Else Holmelund Minarik
Illustrated by Maurice Sendak

LITTLE BEAR

Here are four stories about Little
Bear and his mother, who is
always there when Little Bear
needs her. Beginning readers will
feel a great sense of accomplish-
ment reading each story by
themselves, and will enjoy Little
Bear's adventures—flying to the
moon, making birthday soup, and
wishing for the impossible.
Minarik, formerly a first-grade
teacher, has captured the essence
of little children perfectly in this
funny, warm, and tender classic.

64pp Hardcover $14.95
0-06-024240-X HarperCollins
Paperback $3.75
0-06-444004-4 HarperTrophy

By the same author in this series:
FATHER BEAR COMES HOME
64pp Hardcover $14.95
0-06-024230-2 HarperCollins
Paperback $3.75
0-06-444014-1 HarperTrophy

A KISS FOR LITTLE BEAR
32pp Hardcover $14.95
0-06-024298-1 HarperCollins
Paperback $3.75
0-06-444050-8 HarperTrophy

LITTLE BEAR'S FRIEND
64pp Hardcover $14.95
0-06-024255-8 HarperCollins
Paperback $3.75
0-06-444051-6 HarperTrophy

LITTLE BEAR'S VISIT
64pp Hardcover $14.95
0-06-024265-5 HarperCollins
Paperback $3.75
0-06-444023-0 HarperTrophy

NO FIGHTING, NO BITING!
64pp Paperback $3.75
0-06-444015-X HarperTrophy

Peggy Parish
Illustrated by Arnold Lobel

DINOSAUR TIME

Eleven different dinosaurs are
introduced to young readers,
complete with basic facts and a
pronunciation guide. Just the
right amount of information is
presented, in a format that is
more advanced than most
preschool picture books about
dinosaurs. This is the perfect
"stepping stone" for children who
are both learning to read and
searching for knowledge about
these extinct behemoths.

32pp Paperback $3.75
0-06-444037-0 HarperTrophy

Alvin Schwartz
Illustrated by Paul Meisel

BUSY BUZZING BUMBLEBEES
AND OTHER TONGUE TWISTERS

Everyone loves a good tongue
twister, and *everyone* will have fun
with this collection! Here is an
excellent way for beginning
readers to sharpen their consonant
skills—and end up in a giggling
heap. Can you say this one three
times quickly: "Down the
slippery slide slid Sam"? The
cartoon-like art adds a lot of fun
to a very silly book.

64pp Paperback $3.75
0-06-444036-2 HarperTrophy

By the same author in this series:
Illustrated by Syd Hoff
I SAW YOU IN THE BATHTUB
AND OTHER FOLK RHYMES
64pp Paperback $3.75
0-06-444151-2 HarperTrophy

Illustrated by Karen Ann Weinhaus
THERE IS A CARROT IN MY EAR
AND OTHER NOODLE TALES
64pp Paperback $3.75
0-06-444103-2 HarperTrophy

If Stu chews shoes,
should Stu choose
the shoes he chews?

Alvin Schwartz, reteller
Illustrated by Dirk Zimmer
IN A DARK, DARK ROOM AND OTHER SCARY TALES

Seven tales with just the right amount of chill are gathered in this collection—perfect for a dark night read. Young readers will be introduced to such characters as the woman who always wears a green ribbon around her neck and the mysterious boy standing in the rain by the cemetery. *Brrrr!*

64pp   Hardcover $14.95
0-06-025271-5   HarperCollins
Paperback $3.75
0-06-444090-7   HarperTrophy

Bernard Wiseman
MORRIS THE MOOSE

When is a cow not a cow? When it's a moose! At least, Morris the moose *says* the cow is a moose. After all, she has four legs, a tail, and things on her head, just like he does. When the cow insists she is *not* a moose, Morris consults a deer. But the deer says Morris and the cow are both *deer*—after all, they both have four legs, a tail, and things on their heads, just like he does . . . Oh dear! Or should I say, Oh *deer!*

32pp   Paperback $3.75
0-06-444146-6   HarperTrophy

By the same author in this series:
MORRIS GOES TO SCHOOL
64pp   Paperback $3.75
0-06-444045-1   HarperTrophy

Harry was a white dog
with black spots.
He loved all his neighbors,
all except one.
He did not love the lady next door.

Gene Zion
Illustrated by Margaret Bloy Graham

HARRY AND THE LADY NEXT DOOR

Hooray! Fans of *Harry the Dirty Dog* can read a story about him by themselves! This time, the white dog with black spots is having trouble with the lady next door. She sings all day and all night, and she sings so loudly and so high that it hurts Harry's ears. Harry tries to drown her out with his howling, some mooing cows, and a marching band's tuba, but it takes a pair of croaking frogs to finally solve the problem. Zion's dry humor and Graham's expressive pictures create another winner.

64pp   Paperback $3.75
0-06-444008-7   HarperTrophy

Crosby Bonsall
THE CASE OF THE CAT'S MEOW

Snitch's cat Mildred has disappeared, but Snitch's friends in the Private Eyes Club will help find her! Well, they *do* find a lot of cats and dogs, but no Mildred! Even their trusty string-and-bucket-and-bell alarm doesn't catch anybody—except Snitch. Mildred, though, was close all along, and when they finally do find her, she has a surprise for them.

64pp   Paperback $3.75
0-06-444017-6   HarperTrophy

By the same author in this series:
THE CASE OF THE HUNGRY STRANGER
64pp   Paperback $3.75
0-06-444026-5   HarperTrophy

WHO'S AFRAID OF THE DARK?
32pp   Paperback $3.75
0-06-444071-0   HarperTrophy

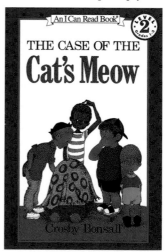

Early Readers

Doug Cushman
AUNT EATER LOVES A MYSTERY

Aunt Eater loves to read mysteries, and never goes anywhere without a couple of them in her bag. Sometimes this causes her to get carried away—like when she thinks her neighbor's cousin is a Mysterious Stranger, or the time she thinks a waiter's shadow is a monster. But sometimes her reading pays off, and she solves a mystery of her own!

64pp Paperback $3.75
0-06-444126-1 HarperTrophy

By the same author in this series:
AUNT EATER'S MYSTERY VACATION

64pp Paperback $3.75
0-06-444169-5 HarperTrophy

Lillian Hoban
ARTHUR'S LOOSE TOOTH

Arthur's tooth is loose, but he can't pull it out because he *hates* the sight of blood! He wiggles his tooth while his sister Violet and the baby-sitter get ready to prepare a surprise dessert. Later in the book, Violet, who is afraid of the dark, shows Arthur how to be brave—by facing her fears. Can Arthur be brave too and pull his tooth out so he can enjoy the surprise taffy apples?

64pp Paperback $3.95
0-06-444093-1 HarperTrophy

By the same author in this series:
ARTHUR'S BACK TO SCHOOL DAY

48pp Hardcover $14.95
0-06-024955-2 HarperCollins
Paperback $3.75
0-06-444245-4 HarperTrophy

ARTHUR'S FUNNY MONEY

64pp Paperback $3.75
0-06-444048-6 HarperTrophy

Russell Hoban
Illustrated by Lillian Hoban
A BARGAIN FOR FRANCES

Young readers familiar with the little badger can read this story without the help of an adult. Frances's friend Thelma tricks Frances into buying her plastic tea set, instead of the pretty china one that Frances has been saving for—and *no* backsies. Frances comes up with a clever scheme to hold her end of the bargain *and* still get the tea set she wants.

64pp Hardcover $14.95
0-06-022329-4 HarperCollins
Paperback $3.75
0-06-444001-X HarperTrophy

A BARGAIN FOR FRANCES
by Russell Hoban
Pictures by Lillian Hoban

Leonard Kessler
HERE COMES THE STRIKEOUT

Bobby loves to play baseball. He can run fast, slide into bases, and catch the ball, but he can't *hit* the ball. Whenever he's up to bat, all the other players laugh and jeer, "Here comes the strikeout!" Discouraged, Bobby asks his friend Willy for help. Under Willy's guidance, Bobby practices hitting for days on end. During the final game of the summer, who smashes the winning hit? Bobby! Hooray!

64pp Paperback $3.75
0-06-444011-7 HarperTrophy

By the same author in this series:
KICK, PASS, AND RUN

64pp Hardcover $14.95
0-06-027104-3 HarperCollins
Paperback $3.75
0-06-444210-1 HarperTrophy

Ethel & Leonard Kessler
STAN THE HOT DOG MAN

64pp Paperback $3.75
0-06-444192-X HarperTrophy

FROM *Frog and Toad Are Friends*

Arnold Lobel
FROG AND TOAD ARE FRIENDS

The inseparable Frog and Toad are introduced to readers through five wonderfully silly adventures. Like an innocent Laurel and Hardy, the two amphibians show the true meaning of friendship—Toad tells stories to Frog when Frog is sick, Frog helps search for Toad's lost button, and Frog writes a letter to Toad because he never receives any mail. These marvelous tales touch both the heart and the funny bone.

64pp   Hardcover $14.95
0-06-023957-3   HarperCollins
Paperback $3.95
0-06-444020-6   HarperTrophy

By the same author in this series:
DAYS WITH FROG AND TOAD
64pp   Hardcover $14.95
0-06-023963-8   HarperCollins
Paperback $3.95
0-06-444058-3   HarperTrophy

FROG AND TOAD ALL YEAR
64pp   Hardcover $14.95
0-06-023950-6   HarperCollins
Paperback $3.75
0-06-444059-1   HarperTrophy

FROG AND TOAD TOGETHER
64pp   Hardcover $14.95
0-06-023959-X   HarperCollins
Paperback $3.95
0-06-444021-4   HarperTrophy

MOUSE SOUP

A mouse is innocently sitting under a tree reading a book when a weasel grabs him by the tail and puts him in a pot to make mouse soup. The ingenious mouse tells the weasel that soup is not good without any stories in it, and then proceeds to tell him four very silly tales. The tales inspire the weasel to search for additional ingredients for the soup—and while he does, the mouse calmly climbs out of the pot, goes home, and finishes his book in peace.

64pp   Hardcover $14.95
0-06-023967-0   HarperCollins
Paperback $3.75
0-06-444041-9   HarperTrophy

MOUSE TALES
64pp   Hardcover $14.95
0-06-023941-7   HarperCollins
Paperback $3.75
0-06-444013-3   HarperTrophy

OWL AT HOME
64pp   Paperback $3.95
0-06-444034-6   HarperTrophy

Peggy Parish
Illustrated by Fritz Siebel
AMELIA BEDELIA

Meet Amelia Bedelia, the unflappable maid who does everything literally. With her purse on her arm and hat firmly on her head, Amelia Bedelia follows instructions to a tee: Change the towels? Nothing a pair of scissors can't do! Dust the furniture? That's when the perfumed dusting powder really comes in handy. Dress the chicken for dinner—well, do you want a boy chicken or a girl chicken? Amelia Bedelia's well-meaning gaffes cause readers to chuckle, but her employer to fume—it's a good thing she's such a good cook!

64pp   Hardcover $14.95
0-06-020186-X   HarperCollins
Paperback $3.75
0-06-444155-5   HarperTrophy

By the same author in this series:
Illustrated by Barbara Seibel Thomas
AMELIA BEDELIA AND THE SURPRISE SHOWER
64pp   Hardcover $14.95
0-06-024642-1   HarperCollins
Paperback $3.75
0-06-444019-2   HarperTrophy

Illustrated by Wallace Tripp
PLAY BALL, AMELIA BEDELIA
64pp   Hardcover $14.95
0-06-026700-3   HarperCollins
Paperback $3.75
0-06-444205-5   HarperTrophy

Illustrated by Barbara Siebel Thomas
THANK YOU, AMELIA BEDELIA
64pp   Hardcover $14.95
0-06-022979-9   HarperCollins
Paperback $3.75
0-06-444171-7   HarperTrophy

LEVEL 3: GRADES 2–4

Nathaniel Benchley
Illustrated by Don Bolognese

GEORGE THE DRUMMER BOY

There are many stories about what it was like for the colonists during the revolutionary war, but what was it like for the British soldiers? George, a British drummer boy, is involved in the first battle of the Revolution. He is cold, scared, confused, and oblivious that he is involved in a historical battle that would alter the birth of this nation.

64pp   Paperback $3.75
0-06-444106-7   HarperTrophy

By the same author in this series:
Illustrated by Arnold Lobel

SAM THE MINUTEMAN

It's the late 1700s in Lexington, Massachusetts, and tension is mounting between the colonists and the British. Sam's father is a minuteman—ready to fight at a minute's notice. When Paul Revere finally gives the call to arms, every man and boy is needed and Sam must fight too. Sam is frightened, but even after his best friend is wounded, he bravely fights on in the first battle of the revolutionary war.

64pp   Paperback $3.75
0-06-444107-5   HarperTrophy

Illustrated by Joan Sandin

SMALL WOLF

64pp   Paperback $3.75
0-06-444180-6   HarperTrophy

Barbara Brenner
Illustrated by Don Bolognese

WAGON WHEELS

64pp   Hardcover $14.95
0-06-020668-3   HarperCollins
Paperback $3.95
0-06-444052-4   HarperTrophy

Clyde Robert Bulla
Illustrated by Joan Sandin

DANIEL'S DUCK

The first thing Daniel ever carves out of wood is a duck, and he's so proud of it he enters it in the spring fair. Henry Pettigrew, the best wood-carver in the valley, might admire it. But when the duck is on display, Daniel sees the other settlers laughing at it. Hurt, Daniel tries to throw his duck into the river, but someone stops him—it's Henry Pettigrew. He shows Daniel that laughter can be a compliment, and that first efforts have value too.

64pp   Paperback $3.75
0-06-444031-1   HarperTrophy

Betsy Byars
Illustrated by Sue Truesdell

THE GOLLY SISTERS GO WEST

The squabbling, blundering Golly sisters, Rose and May-May, are off on tour in their covered wagon to dance and sing in different towns. But the sisters never seem to agree on anything: in their first show, they spend so much time arguing over who gets to wear the blue dress that their audience goes home. Then May-May mounts their horse and tries to get it to dance on stage—but the horse tears out of town with her on his back. These six hilarious tales are sure to have readers rolling in the aisles.

64pp   Paperback $3.95
0-06-444132-6   HarperTrophy

By the same author in this series:

THE GOLLY SISTERS RIDE AGAIN

64pp   Hardcover $14.95
0-06-021563-1   HarperCollins
Paperback $3.75
0-06-444207-1   HarperTrophy

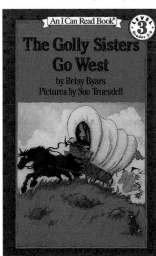

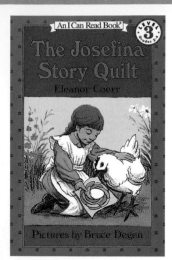

Eleanor Coerr
Illustrated by Bruce Degen

THE JOSEFINA STORY QUILT

Faith and her family are soon to travel west to California in a wagon train with other pioneers. Faith convinces her father to let her take Josefina, her beloved old hen. But her father warns her that if Josefina causes *any* trouble, then out she goes. There are many problems on the trail, many caused by the hen, but all is forgotten when Josefina scares away some robbers. Although Josefina dies soon thereafter, the tale is ultimately one of courage, love, and hope.

64pp Hardcover $14.95
0-06-021348-5 HarperCollins
Paperback $3.75
0-06-444129-6 HarperTrophy

By the same author in this series:
Illustrated by Carolyn Croll

THE BIG BALLOON RACE

64pp Paperback $3.75
0-06-444053-2 HarperTrophy

Illustrated by Don Bolognese

BUFFALO BILL AND THE PONY EXPRESS

64pp Hardcover $14.95
0-06-023372-9 HarperCollins
Paperback $3.75
0-06-444220-9 HarperTrophy

F. N. Monjo
Illustrated by Fred Brenner

THE DRINKING GOURD: A STORY OF THE UNDERGROUND RAILROAD

Upon being sent home for disrupting church services, Tommy Fuller is surprised to find a family of runaway slaves hiding in his barn. Unbeknownst to Tommy, his father's house is a stop on the Underground Railroad. Tommy and his father set off for the next safe haven with the former slave family hidden in a wagon of hay. But as Tommy's father leaves to find a hidden boat, a search party approaches the wagon. Can Tommy save the family from being caught?

64pp Hardcover $14.95
0-06-024329-5 HarperCollins
Paperback $3.95
0-06-444042-7 HarperTrophy

Joan Sandin

THE LONG WAY TO A NEW LAND

It is 1868, a time of drought and hunger in Sweden. Carl Erik and his family are on the brink of starvation when a letter from his uncle arrives, telling them of a better life in America. Erik and his family sell their possessions, bid farewell to their friends, and start their long and harrowing journey over both sea and land.

Young readers will witness the hardship emigrants were forced to endure before starting a promising new life.

64pp Paperback $3.95
0-06-444100-8 HarperTrophy

By the same author in this series:

THE LONG WAY WESTWARD

64pp Paperback $3.75
0-06-444198-9 HarperTrophy

Millicent E. Selsam
Illustrated by Arnold Lobel

GREG'S MICROSCOPE

When Greg gets a microscope, he—and the reader—learn what different things look like when magnified one hundred times. Greg examines things he finds at home: salt, sugar, hair, thread, cells from the inside of his cheek, and water from his aquarium. Fascinating illustrations show readers what Greg is seeing in this wonderful introduction to the hidden world.

64pp Paperback $3.75
0-06-444144-X HarperTrophy

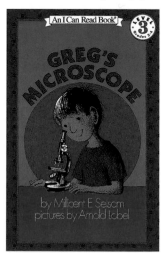

PUFFIN EASY-TO-READ

Using their cache of already published easy-to-read books, Puffin launched their **Easy-to-Read** program. Favorite stories by such beloved authors as James Marshall, Jean Van Leeuwen, and Harriet Ziefert are certain to attract readers to this series. Though the quality of stories in this series is uneven, some of them are superb. Like most other beginning-to-read series, Puffin **Easy-to-Read** is divided into reading levels. Level 1 uses sentences with clear and simple words and illustrations that help the reader understand the story line. Level 2 is the springboard for emerging readers: the stories use longer sentences, yet maintain a vocabulary easy enough for the child to feel comfortable on his or her own. Level 3 offers more challenging sentences and longer stories.

LEVEL 1 (JUST GETTING STARTED): PRESCHOOL-GRADE 2

Martin Silverman
Illustrated by Amy Aitken
MY TOOTH IS LOOSE!

Georgie is upset because his tooth is loose, and he doesn't know what to do. All his friends offer advice—bite an apple, eat some fudge, twist it out, pull it out with string—but all of these methods sound too scary to Georgie. His constant cry of "My tooth is loose, and I don't know what to do!" will find an anxious echo with many young readers about to loose their first tooth, and Georgie's mother's reassuring advice will help guide them through this important milestone.

32pp Paperback $3.99
0-14-037001-3 Puffin

Harriet Ziefert
Illustrated by Claire Schumacher
CAT GAMES

The cats Pat and Matt are two great friends who love to play hide-and-seek. Pat hides from Matt up a tree, and Matt can't see her. Can you? Then Matt climbs up too, and they are *both* hard to see! Soon a playful pup comes and wants to join their game. The simple story and hidden animals make this an appealing stepping stone from toddler book to first reader.

32pp Paperback $3.99
0-14-037857-X Puffin

By the same author in this series:
Illustrated by Mavis Smith
HARRY GETS READY FOR SCHOOL

Harry the hippo is very busy getting ready for school: he has his eyes to check and his hair to cut, school supplies and new clothes to buy, a checkup at both the doctor and the dentist, and lots of pencils to sharpen! Finally it's the first day of school. Is Harry ready? You bet he is!

32pp Paperback $3.99
0-14-036539-7 Puffin

HARRY GOES TO DAY CAMP
32pp Paperback $3.99
0-14-037000-5 Puffin

HARRY TAKES A BATH
32pp Paperback $3.99
0-14-036537-0 Puffin

LEVEL 2 (BEGINNING TO READ): KINDERGARTEN-GRADE 3

Edward Marshall
Illustrated by James Marshall
THREE BY THE SEA

Lolly, Spider, and Sam are having a picnic at the beach. Bored by the insipid story Lolly reads to them, Sam and Spider opt to take turns retelling the story, using the same rat and cat characters. Sam's version is good, but Spider's is even better—it gives them a good scare! Just the right thing before a swim!

48pp Paperback $3.99
0-14-037004-8 Puffin

FROM *Tales of Oliver Pig*

Jean Van Leeuwen
Illustrated by Ann Schweninger
TALES OF AMANDA PIG

After many published stories about her big brother Oliver, Amanda Pig finally gets five of her own! In them, she manages to eat a slippery, slimy egg; reconcile with Oliver after an argument; overcome her fear of a clock on the stairs; play with Oliver and Mother on a rainy day; and put a sleepy mother to bed. These gentle, loving tales are sure to strike a chord in young readers.

56pp   Paperback $3.99
0-14-036840-X   Puffin

By the same author in this series:
AMANDA PIG AND HER BIG BROTHER OLIVER
56pp   Paperback $3.99
0-14-037008-0   Puffin

AMANDA PIG ON HER OWN
56pp   Paperback $3.99
0-14-037144-3   Puffin

MORE TALES OF AMANDA PIG
56pp   Paperback $3.99
0-14-037603-8   Puffin

Illustrated by Arnold Lobel
TALES OF OLIVER PIG

Oliver Pig experiences a preschooler's life in a loving and understanding family. In this, the first of a series of books, he bakes cookies with Mother on a rainy day, convinces his little sister Amanda to eat dinner, gets ready to play in the snow, and hides from Father. Each wonderful story radiates comfort and warmth and feels just like a hug.

64pp   Paperback $3.99
0-14-036549-4   Puffin

MORE TALES OF OLIVER PIG
64pp   Paperback $3.99
0-14-036554-0   Puffin

Illustrated by Ann Schweninger
OLIVER, AMANDA AND GRANDMOTHER PIG
56pp   Paperback $3.50
0-14-037386-1   Puffin

OLIVER PIG AT SCHOOL
64pp   Paperback $3.99
0-14-037145-1   Puffin

LEVEL 3 (READING ALONE): GRADES 2-4

Mary Blount Christian
Illustrated by Marc Brown
SWAMP MONSTERS

Crag and Fenny, two swamp monsters, are tired of eating snail stew. They want to eat what those bad children eat, like pizza and ice cream. One day, while playing in their child masks, they find themselves surrounded by a class of children on a field trip. What a perfect chance to find out what children are *really* like! It's much more fun to be a child than just read about them . . . isn't it?

48pp   Paperback $3.99
0-14-036841-8   Puffin

Katy Hall and Lisa Eisenberg
Illustrated by Simms Tabac
BUGGY RIDDLES

Okay, there are books of riddles about school, camp, and other familiar situations, but here is a unique collection. Forty-two riddles about all sorts of creepy crawlies are sure to leave readers itching for more. How about "Why don't flies fly through screens? They don't want to strain themselves!" Though you may groan when your child stumps you, you just may find yourself trying a few out at the office!

48pp   Paperback $3.99
0-14-036543-5   Puffin

By the same authors in this series:
FISHY RIDDLES
48pp   Paperback $3.50
0-14-036546-X   Puffin

SNAKEY RIDDLES
48pp   Paperback $3.50
0-14-037141-9   Puffin

Illustrated by Nicole Rubel

GRIZZLY RIDDLES
48pp   Paperback $3.50
0-14-038028-0   Puffin

Edward Marshall
Illustrated by James Marshall

FOUR ON THE SHORE

Friends Lolly, Sam, and Spider have fled to the lake to do their homework and to escape Spider's pesky little brother, Willie. Even the lake isn't safe, because guess who shows up? In order to get rid of Willie, the three friends take turns telling scary stories, with Willie the victim each time. Is Willie scared? *Nah!* But when it's Willie's turn to tell a story, *watch out!*

48pp   Paperback $3.99
0-14-037006-4   Puffin

By the same author in this series:

FOX AND HIS FRIENDS

Fox wants to have a good time with his friends, but he keeps having to take care of his little sister, Louise. How can you have a good time with your little sister always tagging along? Somehow, Louise causes every situation to become much more exciting, *and* a little more than Fox bargained

for. Doesn't Louise remember that Fox hates to be in high places? Join Fox and his friends in these three silly stories.

56pp   Paperback $3.99
0-14-037007-2   Puffin

FOX ALL WEEK
32pp   Paperback $3.50
0-14-037708-5   Puffin

FOX AT SCHOOL
48pp   Paperback $3.50
0-14-036544-3   Puffin

FOX IN LOVE
48pp   Paperback $3.99
0-14-036843-4   Puffin

STEP INTO READING™

This series of affordable paperbacks offers an appealing variety of fiction and nonfiction by such popular authors as Jean Marzollo, Joyce Milton, Richard Scarry, and Joanna Cole—all carefully geared to the particular reading level of the reader. Using large, bright, full-page pictures and repetition to reinforce word comprehension, the Early Step Into Reading level is perfect for the just-beginning set. While Step 1 uses the same large type, this level offers greater story lines and more words per page. Step 2 moves into more complicated stories with an expanded vocabulary, and in Step 3, readers encounter paragraphs of text and a denser plot line. By Step 4, the books have chapters and feature many thrilling nonfiction topics.

EARLY STEP INTO READING: PRESCHOOL–KINDERGARTEN

Annie Cobb
Illustrated by Davy Jones

WHEELS!

Not just for vehicle lovers, this ode to man's greatest invention needs few words to get its point across. The catchy poem shows wheels being used in a variety of ways—such as on cars, trains, shopping carts, and dune buggies—then shows what it would be like if we didn't have any wheels at all.

32pp   Paperback $3.99
0-679-86445-8   Random House

Molly Coxe

CAT TRAPS

A hungry cat wants a snack, so he sets a mousetrap and traps a bug . . . *ugh!* He sets other traps, but keeps trapping the wrong animal, such as a pig, a dog, a giant fish, an angry duck, and finally, *himself.* Will he *ever* get his snack? The minimal rhyming text will bring smiles to novice readers.

32pp   Paperback $3.99
0-679-86441-5   Random House

STEP 1: PRESCHOOL–GRADE 1

Marsha Arnold
Illustrated by Lisa McCue

QUICK, QUACK, QUICK!

Mama Duck is continually calling "Quick, Quack, Quick!" to her tardy youngest duckling Quack. He's more interested in yummy berries, a hollow log, and a butterfly than in following his mother, brothers, and sisters. But this time, Quack's dawdling saves his family from a hungry cat!

32pp Paperback $3.99
0-679-87243-4 Random House

David L. Harrison
Illustrated by Hans Wilhelm

WAKE UP, SUN!

When the farm animals wake up in the middle of the night, they are distressed—the sun is gone! In vain the animals try to find the sun and wake it with their cries. All their noise wakes not the sun, but the farmer's baby, who starts crying—just as the sun finally rises. Now the foolish animals think only the baby can wake the sun!

32pp Paperback $3.99
0-394-88256-3 Random House

I love to drive!
I am a Toad.
Here I come—
Toad on the road!

Susan Schade and Jon Buller
Illustrated by Jon Buller

TOAD ON THE ROAD

Toad loves to drive, and in his spiffy red car, he can go anywhere. But it's more fun with friends along, so Toad picks up Cat, Pup, and Pig. Beginning readers will love the catchy rhymes and goofy illustrations of Toad and friends bopping along on the road!

32pp Paperback $3.99
0-679-82689-0 Random House

Cindy Wheeler

BOOKSTORE CAT

Mulligan the cat works in a bookstore. His various jobs are lying by the door, playing with his toys, and making children laugh. One day, during a puppet show, a pigeon strays into the shop and lands on stage next to a parrot puppet. Mulligan does his job—and ends up with a stuffed bird in his mouth. *Well done*, Mulligan!

32pp Paperback $3.99
0-394-84109-3 Random House

STEP 2: GRADES 1–3

Martha Brenner
Illustrated by Donald Cook

ABE LINCOLN'S HAT

Why did Abe Lincoln always wear a tall black hat? Why, to keep his important papers safe! This and other anecdotes about Lincoln as a young lawyer show just how fair and funny he was. Tall and lanky, always with a joke up his sleeve, Lincoln persevered to become one of the greatest presidents the United States ever had. Photographs of Lincoln, Stephen Douglas, Judge David Davis, and others are included.

48pp Paperback $3.99
0-679-84977-7 Random House

P. E. King
Illustrated by Alastair Graham

DOWN ON THE FUNNY FARM

A young man can't believe his good fortune when a silly old farmer sells him his farm for only one dollar. But something is funny about this farm—the rooster barks, the horse crows, the pig chases a mouse, and the chicken rolls in the mud and grunts! Patiently, the young man shows all the animals how to act. To complete his happiness, he finds a wife, and she asks if her father can live with them. But the father is the silly old farmer—and the farm is in confusion once more.

48pp Paperback $3.99
0-394-87460-9 Random House

Joan Heilbroner
Illustrated by Sal Murdocca
TOM THE TV CAT

Tom the cat helps his owner the fish man by cleaning the house and assisting in the store. One day, the fish man brings home a funny box that has *people* inside! Tom is fascinated and soon does nothing but watch TV. He wants to imitate all the people he sees on TV—a singer, a superhero, a wrestler—but when he tries, all the neighbors throw things out their windows at him. Finally, Tom decides that being a great fish cat is the best thing to be!

48pp   Paperback $3.99
0-394-86708-4   Random House

Joyce Milton
Illustrated by Richard Roe
DINOSAUR DAYS

Take a step back in time to when the dinosaurs roamed the earth. The lively text combines introductions with specific dinosaurs with facts about all. The book shows how some dinosaurs replaced others before they all died out, and how some other animals that live today lived back then, leaving readers a clear picture of the world millions of years ago.

48pp   Paperback $3.99
0-394-87023-9   Random House

By the same author in this series:
Illustrated by Alton Langford
WHALES: THE GENTLE GIANTS
48pp   Paperback $3.99
0-394-89809-5   Random House

FROM *Tom the TV Cat*

Annabelle Prager
Illustrated by Tomie de Paola
THE SURPRISE PARTY

Nicky is excited—it's almost his birthday! When he discovers he doesn't have enough money for the kind of party he wants, he convinces his best friend, Al, to throw him a *surprise* birthday party. Al has everything planned, but Nicky keeps telling him what he wants to have at the party. When the big day arrives, Nicky is ready to be surprised—but Al found a way to have a *real* surprise party, *his* way!

48pp   Paperback $3.99
0-394-89596-7   Random House

By the same author in this series:
THE SPOOKY HALLOWEEN PARTY
48pp   Paperback $3.99
0-394-84961-2   Random House

STEP 3: GRADES 2–3

Judy Donnelly
Illustrated by Keith Kohler
THE TITANIC LOST . . . AND FOUND

Readers will feel as if they are among the over two thousand passengers on board in this gripping account of the terrible disaster of the Titanic. Initially, no one believed the ship was really sinking. The band played on deck to keep people's spirits up, and then, as panic spread, there weren't enough lifeboats for everyone. Years later scientist Robert Ballard laboriously searched for and finally found the sunken ship, which he left at the bottom of the sea as a memorial.

48pp   Paperback $3.99
0-394-88669-0   Random House

FROM *The Mystery of the Pirate Ghost*

Geoffrey Hayes
THE MYSTERY OF THE PIRATE GHOST

Otto and his Uncle Tooth are on the lookout—there's a ghost in town, and it's causing trouble! It stole a clothesline, a box of taffy, and a silver trumpet. Worst of all, the ghost is wearing the hat of Blackeye Doodle, the notorious pirate! Could it be his ghost? And can Otto and his uncle stop him?

48pp Paperback $3.99
0-394-87220-7 Random House

Deborah Hautzig, adapter
Illustrated by Darcy May
THE LITTLE MERMAID

Of the Sea King's six daughters, the youngest is the most beautiful, and has a beautiful voice to match. She is happy as a mermaid until she catches sight of a handsome human prince, but the only way she can get to know him is to become human. To do this, she sacrifices her voice to the sea witch in exchange for a magic potion. She then meets her prince, but he marries another. Hans Christian Andersen's tale of love and sacrifice is faithfully adapted for beginning readers.

48pp Paperback $3.99
0-679-82241-0 Random House

Jean Marzollo
Illustrated by Blanche Sims
SOCCER SAM

Sam is excited when his cousin Marco from Mexico comes to spend a year with his family—they will get to play basketball and other fun sports together. But Marco keeps hitting the ball with his head and his feet without using his hands! Sam is embarrassed, but then Marco teaches him and his friends a wonderful new game—soccer! Can their team beat the big third graders in a game?

48pp Paperback $3.99
0-394-88406-X Random House

By the same author in this series:
CANNONBALL CHRIS
48pp Paperback $3.99
0-394-88512-0 Random House

STEP 4: GRADES 2–4

Judy Donnelly
Illustrated by Dennis Davidson
MOONWALK: THE FIRST TRIP TO THE MOON

The thrill of man's first steps on the moon is recreated for beginning readers. The suspense builds over five chapters, which cover the take-off, the history of the space race, the development of rockets, the astronauts' training, and finally the astronauts experience in space. Actual photographs taken from the space capsule are included in this exciting read.

48pp Paperback $3.99
0-394-82457-1 Random House

Andrew Gutelle
Illustrated by Cliff Spohn
BASEBALL'S BEST: FIVE TRUE STORIES

Baseball fans will gobble up the true stories of five Hall of Famers: Babe Ruth, Joe DiMaggio, Jackie Robinson, Roberto Clemente, and Hank Aaron. Each chapter focuses on an exciting moment that made these players legendary. Photographs and drawings help capture these fabulous sports stars for today's youth.

48pp Paperback $3.99
0-394-80983-1 Random House

Lynn Hall
Illustrated by Antonio Castro

BARRY: THE BRAVEST SAINT BERNARD

High in the mountains of Switzerland, where the snow is deep and avalanches are common, the monks of Saint Bernard are famous for their huge dogs. With their keen sense of smell, the Saint Bernards are trained to find a person buried in the snow, dig him out, and keep him from freezing by lying close to him. This is the true story of Barry, a Saint Bernard who rescued over forty people, and whose courage and kindness became legendary.

48pp   Paperback $3.99
0-679-83054-5   Random House

Emily Little
Illustrated by Michael Eagle

THE TROJAN HORSE: HOW THE GREEKS WON THE WAR

Trouble is brewing between Greece and Troy. The Trojans control a waterway important to the Greeks, and demand a toll every time the Greeks use it. When a Trojan king kidnaps the Greek queen Helen to be his son Paris's wife, this means war! After ten years of fighting, the Greeks play the greatest trick in military history—using the Trojan Horse. This fascinating tale, full of heroes, is based on truth and forever immortalized in Homer's *Iliad*.

48pp   Paperback $3.99
0-394-89674-2   Random House

Kate McMullan
Illustrated by John R. Jones

DINOSAUR HUNTERS

How did we find out about dinosaurs? How do scientists figure out what a dinosaur looked like? Who were the first scientists to discover these extinct giants? Dinosaur lovers will have all these questions and more answered in this fascinating look at paleontology.

48pp   Paperback $3.99
0-394-81150-X   Random House

Rolf Myller
HOW BIG IS A FOOT?

The king has the perfect idea for the queen's birthday present—a new bed! The carpenter's apprentice is chosen to build it, but how big must it be? The king takes off his shoe, measures around the queen (including her crown), and gives the measurements to the apprentice. But when the little apprentice builds the bed, he uses his *own* feet as a standard, and the bed is too small! How to solve the problem? How measurements became standardized is cleverly told in this amusing fable.

48pp   Paperback $3.99
0-440-40495-9   Yearling

Pat Ross
Illustrated by Marilyn Hafner
MEET M & M

Mandy and Mimi live in the same apartment building, they look alike, and both of their names start with M. How could they *not* be friends! They are such good friends that people mistake them for twins. That's fine with Mandy and Mimi—"Just call us M and M," they tell everyone. But even in the best of friendships, arguments happen. One awful day everything goes wrong and Mandy and Mimi storm off to their own separate floors. The girls don't speak to each other for *three whole days.* Will Mandy and Mimi ever be M and M again?

64pp Paperback $3.99
0-14-038731-5 Puffin

By the same author:
M & M AND THE BAD NEWS BABIES
48pp Paperback $4.50
0-14-031851-8 Puffin

M & M AND THE HALLOWEEN MONSTER
64pp Paperback $3.99
0-14-034247-8 Puffin

M & M AND THE HAUNTED HOUSE GAME
64pp Paperback $3.99
0-14-038730-7 Puffin

Cynthia Rylant
Illustrated by Arthur Howard
MR. PUTTER AND TABBY POUR THE TEA

Old Mr. Putter has much to do. In the morning he eats his muffin. Then he works in his garden until teatime, when he enjoys his cup of tea. In the evening he has lots of wonderful stories to tell. The problem is, Mr. Putter is lonely. There is no one to share his muffins, drink tea with him, enjoy the flowers in his garden, or listen to his stories. What Mr. Putter needs is a

friend—and he finds one at the animal shelter. Now Mr. Putter has Tabby, the old yellow cat, who loves muffins, tea and flowers, and purrs while Mr. Putter tells his stories. What a happy pair!

44pp Hardcover $11.00
0-15-256255-9 Harcourt Brace
Paperback $6.00
0-15-200901-9 Harcourt Brace

CYNTHIA RYLANT
Mr. Putter and Tabby
Pour the Tea

ILLUSTRATED BY
ARTHUR HOWARD

By the same author:
MR. PUTTER AND TABBY BAKE THE CAKE
44pp Hardcover $12.00
0-15-200205-7 Harcourt Brace
Paperback $6.00
0-15-200214-6 Harcourt Brace

MR. PUTTER AND TABBY PICK THE PEARS
44pp Hardcover $12.00
0-15-200245-6 Harcourt Brace
Paperback $6.00
0-15-200246-4 Harcourt Brace

MR. PUTTER AND TABBY WALK THE DOG
44pp Hardcover $13.00
0-15-256259-1 Harcourt Brace
Paperback $6.00
0-15-200891-8 Harcourt Brace

Marjorie Weinman Sharmat
Illustrated by Marc Simont
NATE THE GREAT

Nate the Great, boy detective and pancake lover, is on a case—who stole Annie's painting of her dog, Fang? Garbed in deerstalker hat, trench coat, and rubbers (his mother insists), Nate follows all leads. Could Fang have buried it in the backyard? Or did Rosamund, who has four cats all named Hex, take the picture? Then there's Annie's little brother, Harry, who is painting pictures himself. . . .With a deadpan style reminiscent of Sam Spade, Nate follows the clues and solves his case—and eats a lot of pancakes on the way.

64pp Hardcover $14.95
0-698-20627-4 Coward
Paperback $3.99
0-440-46126-X Yearling

By the same author in this series:
NATE THE GREAT AND THE BORING BEACH BAG
48pp Hardcover $14.95
0-698-20631-2 Coward
Paperback $3.99
0-440-40168-2 Yearling

NATE THE GREAT AND THE MISSING KEY
48pp Paperback $3.99
0-440-46191-X Yearling

NATE THE GREAT GOES UNDERCOVER
48pp Hardcover $16.95
0-399-23234-6 Putnam
Paperback $3.99
0-440-46302-5 Yearling

Fiction

WHEN WE ENTER THE WORLD OF FICTION, we leave behind colorful pictures and favorite characters, and subject matter becomes more complicated. Intermediate readers (covered in the first part of this section) are the stepping stones to these more advanced works.

The variety of subjects in the fiction section reflect children's expanding interests and personalities. Included are the genres of science fiction, fantasy, mystery, and tragedy, as well as books on relationships, humorous tales, horror stories, and sports titles.

Kids often become die-hard fans of certain authors and genres. Many of the better-known works, such as *The Chronicles of Narnia* and *The Little Prince*, are rediscovered by adults.

Kids will be exposed to many of the books in this section through school reading lists, community reading groups, and discussion at home.

What to look for . . .

• Books with a reading level that will challenge and stimulate

• Books with a subject that interests the young reader. Many children want to pick out their own books at this age.

• Books on your child's school reading lists

• Some of the more popular and enduring titles are available in different editions. The trim size of the books may vary, and the cover art may vary as well, but almost without exception the text remains the same.

• Some classic tales are available in abridged formats.

Fiction

David A. Adler
Illustrated by Susanna Natti

CAM JANSEN AND THE MYSTERY OF THE STOLEN DIAMONDS

Jennifer Jansen has a photographic memory, hence her nickname "the Camera," or "Cam" for short. Cam's talents come in handy when she and her friend Howie see a robber escape from a jewelry store. When the police catch the wrong man, it's up to Cam and Howie to find the real culprits! Fast action and cliffhanger chapter endings will keep readers on the edge of their seats in this first book of the popular series.

64pp   Hardcover $12.99
0-670-20039-5   Viking
64pp   Paperback $3.99
0-14-038580-0   Puffin
Ages 7-10

By the same author:
CAM JANSEN AND THE CHOCOLATE FUDGE MYSTERY

64pp   Hardcover $11.99
0-670-84968-5   Viking
64pp   Paperback $3.99
0-14-036421-8   Puffin
Ages 7-10

CAM JANSEN AND THE MYSTERY OF THE GOLD COINS

64pp   Paperback $3.99
0-14-038954-7   Puffin
Ages 7-10

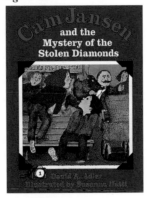

Judy Blume
Illustrated by Sonia O. Lisker

FRECKLE JUICE

Andrew *loves* Nicky Lane's freckles. He wishes he had freckles that covered his face and neck—then his mother would never know when he was dirty! So when Andrew's classmate Sharon offers to sell him a secret freckle juice recipe, Andrew can't resist. But when Andrew mixes up and drinks the awful concoction, he realizes he's been had. What can Andrew do? Why, think up the perfect comeback!

48pp   Paperback $3.99
0-440-42813-0   Yearling
Ages 6-9

By the same author:
Illustrated by Amy Aitken

THE ONE IN THE MIDDLE IS THE GREEN KANGAROO

Freddy Dissel is tired of being the middle child. His older brother Mike gets new clothes, while Freddy gets hand-me-downs; Ellen, his little sister, is small and cute and gets her own room, while Freddy has to share a room with Mike. Freddy wants to be noticed—not be just "the peanut butter part of the sandwich"—so he makes a stand for himself: he asks for a part in the fifth- and sixth-grade play! He lands the role of the green kangaroo—the *only* green kangaroo in the play, and he finds being the one in the middle isn't so bad after all.

48pp   Paperback $3.99
0-440-46731-4   Yearling
Ages 6-9

Jeff Brown
Illustrated by Steve Björkman

FLAT STANLEY

What is it like to be flat as a pancake? After a bulletin board falls on top of him, Stanley Lambchop knows! At only half an inch thick, Stanley is able to enjoy some unusual adventures—slipping under closed doors, traveling via airmail across the country, and flying in the air as a kite for his younger brother. This pun-filled, droll, and silly story is sure to entertain the most reluctant reader.

64pp   Paperback $3.95
0-06-442026-4   HarperTrophy
Ages 7-10

Clyde Robert Bulla
Illustrated by Thomas B. Allen

THE CHALK BOX KID

Nine-year-old Gregory isn't happy when he and his parents have to move. Now he has to adjust to a new house without a garden and a new school without his old friends. Worst of all, even though he has his own room for the first time, he must share it with his selfish Uncle Max. Luckily, Gregory has his artistic talents, and when he finds an abandoned chalk factory behind his house, he uses it to make a special room all his own.

64pp   Paperback $3.99
0-394-89102-3   Random House
Ages 7-9

By the same author:
Illustrated by Leigh Grant

SHOESHINE GIRL

Sarah Ida doesn't get along with her parents, but she didn't count on being palmed off to her aunt for the summer. She's even more upset when she finds out her aunt won't give her any money. Well, she'll show them! She'll just go find a job! But the only job she can find is helping Al shine shoes at his shoeshine stand. Little does Sarah know that this humble job will teach her valuable lessons about life and herself.

64pp   Paperback $4.50
0-06-440228-2   HarperTrophy
Ages 7-10

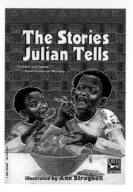

Ann Cameron
Illustrated by Ann Strugnell

THE STORIES JULIAN TELLS

Julian, the boy with the active imagination, loves to tell stories—especially to his younger brother Huey. Huey is good at believing everything Julian tells him, like the story about the catalog cats you can order through the mail. Or the way to grow tall like his fig tree is to eat all of its new leaves. Julian's parents wisely react to his stories with love and understanding—even when the stories result in some missing pudding!

80pp   Paperback $4.99
0-394-82892-5   Knopf
Ages 5-9

By the same author:
Illustrated by Diane Allison

JULIAN, SECRET AGENT
64pp   Paperback $3.99
0-394-81949-7   Random House
Ages 7-9

Patrick Skene Catling
Illustrated by Margot Apple

THE CHOCOLATE TOUCH

John Midas can never get enough chocolate. One day, he finds a

Fiction

funny coin with his initials on it, then finds a strange candy store, where he trades the coin for a box of chocolates. After John eats one of the chocolates, everything else he puts into his mouth turns to chocolate too! He has the chocolate touch! But then a kiss turns his mother into chocolate—how can he rid himself of this horrible curse?

96pp Paperback $4.50
0-440-41289-7 Yearling
Ages 8-12

Rebecca Caudill
Illustrated by Nancy Grossman
DID YOU CARRY THE FLAG TODAY, CHARLEY?

Charley Cornett's insatiable curiosity is preventing him from receiving the biggest honor at the Little School in the Appalachian Mountains. Each day, the most helpful five-year-old gets to carry the school flag to the school ahead of the other children. But Charley's enthusiasm for all the wonders of the school—the drinking fountain, the containers of clay, and all those books in the library—makes him forget to behave. Will Charley ever get to carry the flag?

96pp Hardcover $16.95
0-8050-1201-X Henry Holt
96pp Paperback $3.50
0-440-40092-9 Yearling
Ages 6-9

By the same author:
Illustrated by Elliot Gilbert
THE BEST-LOVED DOLL
64pp Paperback $6.95
0-8050-5467-7 Henry Holt
Ages 4-6

FROM *The Dog That Pitched a No-Hitter*

Matt Christopher
Illustrated by Daniel Vasconcellos
THE DOG THAT PITCHED A NO-HITTER

Mike, the pitcher for the Grand Avenue Giants, is worried. Can he pitch well enough to help his team beat the tough Peach Street Mudders? Just the thought of some of their players makes him sweat. Luckily, Mike has a secret weapon: his dog. Harry knows all about baseball and, via ESP, he passes on to Mike the weaknesses of the other teams' players. But this time Mike is so nervous Harry's advice doesn't help. Will Mike still be able to pitch a no-hitter?

48pp Paperback $3.95
0-316-14103-8 Little, Brown
Ages 5-8

By the same author:
THE DOG THAT CALLED THE PITCH
48pp Hardcover $14.95
0-316-14207-7 Little, Brown
Ages 5-8

Illustrated by Bill Ogden
THE DOG THAT STOLE FOOTBALL PLAYS
48pp Paperback $3.95
0-316-13423-6 Little, Brown
Ages 5-8

Barbara Cohen
Illustrated by Michael J. Deraney
MOLLY'S PILGRIM

Molly feels left out in her third-grade class—the American children aren't like her old friends in Russia, and tease Molly about her clothes and her accent. Molly wishes her family would move back, but her mother says they came to America to find freedom. At Thanksgiving, Molly's teacher asks each student to bring a Pilgrim doll to class—and the doll Molly's mother makes looks exactly like a Russian peasant! All at once, Molly and her classmates realize that Molly and her parents are Pilgrims too.

32pp Hardcover $16.00
0-688-02103-4 Lothrop
48pp Paperback $3.50
0-440-41057-6 Yearling
Ages 5-8

By the same author:
Illustrated by Jan Naimo Jones
MAKE A WISH, MOLLY
48pp Paperback $3.50
0-440-41058-4 Yearling
Ages 6-10

Roald Dahl
Illustrated by Quentin Blake
THE MAGIC FINGER

In his typically humorous style, Roald Dahl lambasts the practice of hunting. A girl who lives next door to the Greggs *hates* the fact that the whole family hunts, and not only do they shoot innocent animals, but they *enjoy* it too. When the Greggs don't listen to her when she tries to stop them, the girl sees red—and points her magic finger at them. The next morning the Gregg family wakes up to find they have wings instead of arms and are quickly shrinking to bird size. Meanwhile, a family of ducks is sprouting human arms—can the Greggs stop the ducks from hunting *them?*

64pp   Hardcover $14.99
0-670-85252-X   Viking
64pp   Paperback $3.99
0-14-038616-5   Puffin
Ages 8-12

By the same author:
THE TWITS

Mr. and Mrs. Twit are the nastiest couple around—not only do they play mean tricks on each other, they smear sticky glue on the branches of trees to capture poor birds and cook them in a pie. And that's not all! The Twits force their captive family of trained monkeys, the Muggle-Wumps, to stand on their heads all day. The Muggle-Wumps have had enough and are ready for revenge, and those terrible Twits are in for a topsy-turvy time!

96pp   Paperback $4.99
0-14-130107-4   Puffin
Ages 7-11

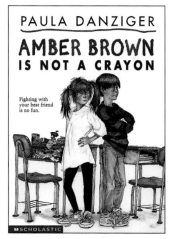

Paula Danziger
Illustrated by Tony Ross
AMBER BROWN IS NOT A CRAYON

Justin Daniels and sassy, messy Amber Brown have been best friends since preschool and sit together in their third-grade class. The two have been close for so long that they practically know what each other is thinking. But Amber and Justin don't want to share their thoughts right now—they are too sad. Justin is moving away to Alabama, and Amber will be losing her best friend.

Hilarious yet poignant, and with situations that every third-grader (and third-grader wannabe) can identify with, *Amber Brown* is right on target for its audience.

80pp   Hardcover $14.99
0-399-22509-9   Putnam
80pp   Paperback $3.50
0-590-45899-X   Little Apple
Ages 7-10

By the same author:
AMBER BROWN GOES FOURTH

112pp   Hardcover $13.95
0-399-22849-7   Putnam
112pp   Paperback $3.99
0-590-93425-2   Little Apple
Ages 7-10

YOU CAN'T EAT YOUR CHICKEN POX, AMBER BROWN

80pp   Hardcover $13.99
0-399-22702-4   Putnam
112pp   Paperback $3.50
0-590-50207-7   Little Apple
Ages 7-10

Eleanor Estes
Illustrated by Louis Slobodkin
THE HUNDRED DRESSES

One day, poor, motherless, and friendless Wanda Petronski, who always wears the same faded blue dress to school, announces that she has a hundred dresses at home. All the girls laugh at her, and Peggy, reluctantly followed by Maddie, start to tease her

daily. Then suddenly Wanda is gone—moved to the city where a Polish family will fit in better. But she leaves her class a gift: one hundred exquisite drawings of dresses, and two of the dresses are for Peggy and Maddie! This gentle tale about tolerance, written in the 1940s, teaches a lesson still relevant today.

88pp   Hardcover $16.00
0-15-237374-8   Harcourt Brace
88pp   Paperback $6.00
0-15-642350-2   Voyager
Ages 6-10

Ruth Stiles Gannett
Illustrated by Ruth Chrisman Gannett

MY FATHER'S DRAGON

Book 1 in *My Father's Dragon* Series

Elmer Elevator, the narrator's father, stows away on a ship bound for Wild Island to free a baby dragon from the tyranny of animals there. An old alley cat informed Elmer of the dragon's plight—how the wild animals have the dragon tied up, how they fly him as a ferry service over the river, and twist his wings when they get angry. Using both his wits and the unusual provisions from his knapsack—magnifying glasses, lollipops, hair ribbons, and a toothbrush and toothpaste—Elmer sidetracks the suspicious animals and makes a daring rescue of the captive dragon.

96pp   Paperback $4.99
0-394-89048-5   Random House
Ages 7-10

FROM *The Dragons of Blueland*

By the same author:

THREE TALES OF MY FATHER'S DRAGON

50th Anniversary Edition
260pp   Hardcover $15.99
0-679-88911-6   Random House
Ages 7-10

ELMER AND THE DRAGON

Book 2 in *My Father's Dragon* Series
96pp   Paperback $4.99
0-394-89049-3   Random House
Ages 7-10

THE DRAGONS OF BLUELAND

Book 3 in *My Father's Dragon* Series
96pp   Paperback $4.99
0-394-89050-7   Random House
Ages 7-10

Johanna Hurwitz
Illustrated by Sheila Hamanaka

CLASS CLOWN

Lucas Cott is forever getting in trouble in his third-grade class. He's always speaking without raising his hand, making jokes, and interrupting lessons. School just seems so boring to him if he doesn't. But when Cricket, the smartest girl in the class, bets him he can't be quiet for a whole day, Lucas discovers school isn't as boring as he thought. Then Lucas's father tells him Cricket isn't the smartest student in the class—*he* is! Can Lucas change from class clown to a perfect student?

112pp   Hardcover $16.00
0-688-06723-9   Morrow Junior
112pp   Paperback $3.99
0-590-41821-1   Little Apple
Ages 7-10

By the same author:

CLASS PRESIDENT

96pp   Hardcover $16.00
0-688-09114-8   Morrow Junior
96pp   Paperback $3.99
0-590-44064-0   Little Apple
Ages 7-10

SCHOOL'S OUT

128pp   Hardcover $12.95
0-688-09938-6   Morrow Junior
128pp   Paperback $3.99
0-590-45053-0   Little Apple
Ages 7-10

TEACHER'S PET

128pp   Hardcover $16.00
0-688-07506-1   Morrow Junior
Ages 7-10

Suzy Kline
Illustrated by Frank Remkiewicz

HORRIBLE HARRY IN ROOM 2B

Harry is *horrible!* He keeps the
whole second grade on its toes by
doing terrible things. Things like
showing Song Lee a pet snake that
makes her scream; shaking hands
with Sidney, then telling him that
the goop on his hand is a squashed
slug (it was really banana); and
demanding to play a dead fish to
be planted with the corn in the
Thanksgiving play. That Harry!

64pp   Paperback $3.99
0-14-038552-5   Puffin
Ages 7-10

By the same author:

HORRIBLE HARRY AND THE ANT INVASION

64pp   Paperback $3.99
0-14-032914-5   Puffin
Ages 7-10

HORRIBLE HARRY'S SECRET

64pp   Hardcover $11.99
0-670-82470-4   Viking
64pp   Paperback $3.99
0-14-032915-3   Puffin
Ages 7-10

John Peterson
Illustrated by Roberta Carter Clark

THE LITTLES

Meet the Little family: Mr.
Little, Mrs. Little, their two
children Tom and Lucy, Granny
Little, and Uncle Pete. They are
an ordinary family, except they
are all, well, little. *Very* little. In
fact, Mr. Little, all of six inches,
is the tallest of them all. The
Littles have tails and live inside
the walls of a house owned by
Mr. and Mrs. Bigg. Life is grand,
until the Biggs go on vacation
and rent their home to the
Newcombs—and their *cat!*

80pp   Paperback $3.99
0-590-46225-3   Scholastic
Ages 7-10

By the same author:

THE LITTLES AND THE TRASH TINIES

80pp   Paperback $3.50
0-590-46595-3   Scholastic
Ages 7-10

THE LITTLES GIVE A PARTY

96pp   Paperback $3.50
0-590-46597-X   Scholastic
Ages 7-10

THE LITTLES GO EXPLORING

96pp   Paperback $3.99
0-590-46596-1   Scholastic
Ages 7-10

THE LITTLES GO TO SCHOOL

80pp   Paperback $3.99
0-590-42129-8   Scholastic
Ages 7-10

THE LITTLES HAVE A WEDDING

96pp   Paperback $3.99
0-590-46224-5   Scholastic
Ages 7-10

THE LITTLES TAKE A TRIP

96pp   Paperback $3.99
0-590-46222-9   Scholastic
Ages 7-10

THE LITTLES TO THE RESCUE

96pp   Paperback $3.99
0-590-46223-7   Scholastic
Ages 7-10

Jon Scieszka
Illustrated by Lane Smith

KNIGHTS OF THE KITCHEN TABLE

The Time Warp Trio Series

It's Joe's birthday, and he, Fred,
and Sam open the present from
Joe's magician uncle who always
gives cool gifts. This time, the
present is just a book with the
stupid title of *The Book*. But on
the first page is an awesome
picture of a black knight with a
pointy lance. Before the three

know it, they are in the story, and the unfriendly knight is directing his lance right at them! How does this trio of very twentieth-century boys fit in to the Middle Ages, battling giants and matching wits with Merlin? This first in a series of fast-paced yet hilarious time-traveling adventures will keep readers howling.

64pp   Hardcover $11.99
0-670-83622-2   Viking
64pp   Paperback $3.99
0-14-034603-1   Puffin
Ages 7-11

By the same author:
2095
The Time Warp Trio Series
80pp   Hardcover $11.99
0-670-85795-5   Viking
80pp   Paperback $3.99
0-14-037191-5   Puffin
Ages 7-11

THE GOOD, THE BAD, AND THE GOOFY
The Time Warp Trio Series
80pp   Paperback $3.99
0-14-036170-7   Puffin
Ages 7-11

FROM *Harry Kitten and Tucker Mouse*

THE NOT-SO-JOLLY ROGER
The Time Warp Trio Series
64pp   Hardcover $14.99
0-670-83754-7   Viking
64pp   Paperback $3.99
0-14-034684-8   Puffin
Ages 7-11

YOUR MOTHER WAS A NEANDERTHAL
The Time Warp Trio Series
80pp   Paperback $3.99
0-14-036372-6   Puffin
Ages 7-11

George Selden
Illustrated by Garth Williams
HARRY KITTEN AND TUCKER MOUSE

The streets of New York City can be a jungle for a little mouse like Tucker. Where will his next meal come from? Where can he find a place to call home? Luckily, Tucker befriends Harry, a philosophical kitten with the same needs, and the two join forces. From the Empire State Building to the docks of the West Side, the two search for a safe haven, giving readers an unusual tour of the city. Finally, in the Times Square subway station, this unlikely duo finds a home.

80pp   Hardcover $16.00
0-374-32860-9   FSG
96pp   Paperback $3.99
0-440-40124-0   Yearling
Ages 7-11

By the same author:
CHESTER CRICKET'S PIGEON RIDE
80pp   Paperback $3.50
0-440-41389-3   Yearling
Ages 8-12

HARRY CAT'S PET PUPPY
176pp   Paperback $3.99
0-440-45647-9   Yearling
Ages 7-11

Fiction

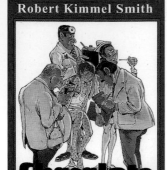

Robert Kimmel Smith
Illustrated by Gioia Fiammenghi
CHOCOLATE FEVER

Henry Green adores chocolate and consumes it in any shape or form—and at any time of day. For breakfast, he washes down his chocolate cereal and chocolate sprinkled pancakes with a glass of chocolate milk. On his way to school, he snacks on chocolate kisses—you get the idea. But one morning, Henry feels strange, and stranger still when he breaks out in a rash of mysterious brown spots. Oh my gosh! Henry has the world's first case of . . . *Chocolate Fever!*

96pp Paperback $3.99
0-440-41369-9 Yearling
Ages 7-11

Gloria Whelan
Illustrated by Stephen Marchesi
SILVER

Nine-year-old Rachel dreams of the day when she can race in the Iditarod—the dog-sled race in

Alaska—like her father. Now maybe she can, for Rachel's father gives her the runt of his lead dog's litter of puppies for her birthday! Rachel knows that with love and care, Silver will grow into a smart and strong dog like his mother. But one snowy night, Silver disappears into the wolf-infested woods. Rachel has to go after him—or she may never see her puppy again.

64pp Paperback $3.99
0-394-89611-4 Random House
Ages 7-9

By the same author:
Illustrated by Leslie Bowman
HANNAH

64pp Paperback $3.99
0-679-82698-X Random House
Ages 7-9

Illustrated by Pamela Johnson
NEXT SPRING AN ORIOLE

64pp Paperback $3.99
0-394-89125-2 Random House
Ages 7-9

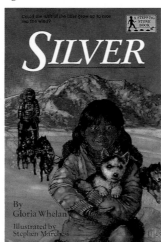

FICTION

Here, at last, are the coveted "chapter books," the books that all young readers strive for. These books hold the hidden surprise of allowing the imagination of their readers to blossom, for many of the books are without illustrations. Now the reader must supply all the pictures for himself or herself. In the private, cozy world of the written word, young minds can travel to the Alaskan tundra, visit a desert island, or fly to outer space—without moving from their chair!

Joan Aiken
Illustrated by Pat Marriott
THE WOLVES OF WILLOUGHBY CHASE

Wealthy, plucky Bonnie Green of Willoughby Chase is delighted her cousin Sylvia is coming to live with her. Unfortunately, there is a blight on Bonnie's happiness—her parents are departing on a cruise for three months, leaving them in the care of their new governess, Miss Slighcarp. *Alas!* No sooner has Sir Willoughby gone, than the evil governess takes over the mansion and banishes the two girls, sending them into the clutches of the horrible Mrs. Brisket! Hidden passages, howling wolves, faithful servants, and a trustworthy friend all play crucial roles in this gripping British melodrama.

176pp Paperback $4.99
0-440-49603-9 Yearling
Ages 10-14

Lloyd Alexander
THE CHRONICLES OF PRYDAIN

Inspired by Welsh legends, the five books that constitute *The Chronicles of Prydain* trace the evolution of a headstrong boy, eager for adventure and life beyond his narrow existence, into a young man fit to rebuild a land ravaged by war. By turns suspenseful and humorous, these thrilling stories take readers on a journey that is filled with the important issues we all must face in life.

THE BOOK OF THREE
Book 1 in *The Chronicles of Prydain*

The first book in this gripping series introduces Taran, the assistant pig-keeper who longs for adventure. When the oracular pig Hen Wen flees to the forest, Taran chases after her, only to lose his way in the gloomy woods. Suddenly Taran hears hoofbeats—the evil Horned King is preparing to take over Taran's beloved country, Prydain. Taran must stop him, but only Hen Wen knows the secret that will destroy the wicked king. As Taran's search for the pig progresses, he is joined by a bevy of unusual companions.

224pp   Hardcover $16.95
0-8050-0874-8   Henry Holt
224pp   Paperback $5.50
0-440-40702-8   Yearling
Ages 10 & up

By the same author:
THE BLACK CAULDRON
Book 2 in *The Chronicles of Prydain*
224pp   Hardcover $17.95
0-8050-0992-2   Henry Holt
240pp   Paperback $5.50
0-440-40649-8   Yearling
Ages 10 & up

THE CASTLE OF LLYR
Book 3 in *The Chronicles of Prydain*
208pp   Hardcover $16.95
0-8050-1115-3   Henry Holt
208pp   Paperback $5.50
0-440-41125-4   Yearling
Ages 10 & up

TARAN WANDERER
Book 4 in *The Chronicles of Prydain*
256pp   Hardcover $16.95
0-8050-1113-7   Henry Holt
272pp   Paperback $5.50
0-440-48483-9   Yearling
Ages 10 & up

THE HIGH KING
Book 5 in *The Chronicles of Prydain*
288pp   Hardcover $16.95   A
0-8050-1114-5   Henry Holt
304pp   Paperback $5.50
0-440-43574-9   Yearling
Ages 10 & up

TIME CAT
244pp   Paperback $4.99
0-14-037827-8   Puffin
Ages 10 & up

William H. Armstrong
Illustrated by James Barkley
SOUNDER

Told through the eyes of an African-American boy living in the South during the nineteenth century, this spare tale has a quiet power. The boy always feels secure when his tall, strong father is around—his father and his father's dog, Sounder. The boy loves that dog more than anything. But one winter there isn't any game for his father or the dog to catch. Love can't feed six hungry people, and after many nights of returning home empty-handed, the boy's father steals a ham out of desperation. White men come and take the father away, changing the lives of both the boy and his beloved Sounder forever.

128pp   Hardcover $14.95   A
0-06-020143-6   HarperCollins
128pp   Paperback $4.95
0-06-440020-4   HarperTrophy
Ages 10 & up

From Mr. Popper's Penguins

Charlotte finds herself torn, until she sees the captain shoot a man. Then Charlotte's choice is clear: she becomes one of the crew, works like a man, and sanctions the plot against the captain. But when Captain Jaggery accuses her of murder and sentences her to death, what can this thirteen-year-old do?

224pp Hardcover $16.95
0-531-05893-X Orchard
240pp Paperback $4.50
0-380-71475-2 Avon
Ages 8-12

By the same author:
BEYOND THE WESTERN SEA BOOK 1: THE ESCAPE FROM HOME
304pp Hardcover $18.95 (no illus.)
0-531-09513-4 Orchard
336pp Paperback $4.99 (no illus.)
0-380-72875-3 Camelot
Ages 10 & up

BEYOND THE WESTERN SEA BOOK 2: LORD KIRKLE'S MONEY
400pp Hardcover $18.95 (no illus.)
0-531-09520-7 Orchard
432pp Paperback $4.99 (no illus.)
0-380-72876-1 Camelot
Ages 10 & up

THE FIGHTING GROUND
160pp Paperback $4.95 (no illus.)
0-06-440185-5 HarperTrophy
Ages 8-12

Natalie Babbitt
TUCK EVERLASTING

When ten-year-old Winnie Foster kneels to drink from a spring, Jesse Tuck grabs her and carries her off. Little does Winnie know, the magical spring makes people live forever, and the Tuck family, having drunk the

By the same author:
SOUR LAND
128pp Paperback $4.95
0-06-440074-3 HarperTrophy
Ages 12 & up

Richard & Florence Atwater
Illustrated by Robert Lawson
MR. POPPER'S PENGUINS

Mr. Popper the housepainter has always dreamed of far-off places, especially the Arctic and Antarctica. Imagine his surprise when he receives a package from Admiral Drake, the famous explorer, containing a real live penguin! To keep Captain Cook from getting lonely, the Poppers get Greta, another lonely penguin from the aquarium. Before long, the Poppers are the proud owners of *twelve* curious, intelligent, and very comical penguins! Caring for all the birds is expensive, so

the family puts them to work—on the stage. Soon the whole country is clamoring to see Popper's Performing Penguins!

148pp Hardcover $16.95
0-316-05842-4 Little, Brown
148pp Paperback $4.95
0-316-05843-2 Little, Brown
Ages 9-12

Avi
Illustrated by Ruth E. Murray
THE TRUE CONFESSIONS OF CHARLOTTE DOYLE

Prim, ladylike Charlotte Doyle is leaving England to join her family in their new home in Providence, Rhode Island. But all is not smooth sailing—the vessel Charlotte boards is commanded by Captain Jaggery, who is hated and feared by the sailors for his cruelty. Thrust in the midst of a surly crew with mutinous plans,

water, knows what a curse that can be. Jesse introduces Winnie to his family and their strange, beautiful, yet sequestered life. Winnie vows the water will remain a secret, but she hadn't counted on the stranger who followed her and overheard everything. In this small jewel of a book, Babbitt raises intriguing questions about the loneliness of immortality, the thoughtless greed of man, and the important choices we must make in life.

144pp   Hardcover $15.00
0-374-37848-7   FSG
144pp   Paperback $4.95
0-374-48009-5   Sunburst
Ages 9 & up

By the same author:
THE DEVIL'S STORYBOOK
102pp   Hardcover $13.00
0-374-31770-4   FSG
112pp   Paperback $4.95
0-374-41708-3   Sunburst
Ages 9 & up

THE SEARCH FOR DELICIOUS
176pp   Hardcover $16.00
0-374-36534-2   FSG
176pp   Paperback $3.95
0-374-46536-3   Sunburst
Ages 9 & up

Lynne Reid Banks
Illustrated by Brock Cole
THE INDIAN IN THE CUPBOARD
Book 1 of the *Indian in the Cupboard* Series

Omri is delighted with the beat-up old medicine chest his brother gives him for his birthday, but he's not so pleased with the plastic Indian from his friend Patrick. After all, Omri's getting too big to play with those kinds of things. But when he puts the Indian in

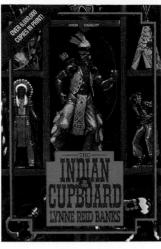

the cupboard and locks it with a special key, the *Indian comes alive!* How can Omri take care of an arrogant, proud, demanding three-inch Indian—not to mention his horse—*and* keep them secret? This masterful blend of fantasy, suspense, and compassion keeps readers enthralled up to the very last page.

192pp   Hardcover $15.95
0-385-17051-3   Doubleday
192pp   Paperback $4.99
0-380-60012-9   Camelot
Ages 8-12

By the same author:
Illustrated by William Geldart
THE RETURN OF THE INDIAN
Book 2 of the *Indian in the Cupboard* Series
192pp   Hardcover $15.95
0-385-23497-X   Doubleday
192pp   Paperback $4.99
0-380-70284-3   Camelot
192pp   Paperback $4.50 (no illus.)
0-380-72593-2   Avon
Ages 8-12

Illustrated by Ted Lewin
THE SECRET OF THE INDIAN
Book 3 of the *Indian in the Cupboard* Series
160pp   Hardcover $15.95
0-385-26292-2   Doubleday
160pp   Paperback $4.99
0-380-71040-4   Camelot
176pp   Paperback $3.99 (no illus.)
0-380-72594-0   Avon
Ages 8-12

Illustrated by Tom Newsom
THE MYSTERY OF THE CUPBOARD
Book 4 of the *Indian in the Cupboard* Series
256pp   Hardcover $16.00
0-688-12138-1   Morrow Junior
256pp   Paperback $4.99
0-380-72013-2   Camelot
208pp   Paperback $3.99
0-380-72595-9   Avon
Ages 8-12

Illustrated by James Watling
THE KEY TO THE INDIAN
Book 5 of the *Indian in the Cupboard* Series
240pp   Hardcover $16.00
0-380-97717-6   Avon
Ages 8-12

FROM *The House With a Clock in its Walls*

Marion Dane Bauer
ON MY HONOR

Joel and Tony have been uneasy friends their whole lives, always wanting to do opposite things. One day, Joel suggests they go swimming, but Tony, who wants to conceal that he can't swim well, would rather bike to the state park. When they get to the swirling, powerful Vermillion River, Tony suddenly suggests they go swimming after all. Though he knows it's forbidden, Joel agrees, and dares Tony in a race to a sandbar—but when he reaches the sandbar, he finds Tony is gone, pulled under by the strong current of the river. Feeling culpable and terrified, Joel conceals Tony's death from Tony's parents and his own. Bauer skillfully portrays Joel's struggle with grief and guilt in this gripping novel.

96pp   Hardcover $15.00
0-89919-439-7   Clarion
96pp   Paperback $4.50
0-440-46633-4   Yearling
Ages 9-12

By the same author:
FACE TO FACE
192pp   Paperback $3.99
0-440-40791-5   Yearling
Ages 9-12

John Bellairs
Illustrated by Edward Gorey
THE HOUSE WITH A CLOCK IN ITS WALLS
Book 1 of the *House With a Clock in its Walls* Trilogy

When newly orphaned Lewis Barnavelt goes to live at Uncle Jonathan's mansion on the hill, he is surprised to learn that Jonathan and his neighbor Mrs. Zimmerman are witches! Both assure Lewis that not all witches are bad. But some of them are, like Isaac Izard and his evil wife Selenna, who once lived in the house. Deep within its walls this wicked pair hid a horrible secret, whose ominous ticking measures the time left until the end of the world. Can Lewis and his friends find the source and save the world from destruction?

192pp   Paperback $4.50
0-14-036336-X   Puffin
Ages 8 & up

By the same author:
Illustrated by Mercer Mayer
THE FIGURE IN THE SHADOWS
Book 2 of the *House With a Clock in its Walls* Trilogy
160pp   Paperback $4.50
0-14-036337-8   Puffin
Ages 8 & up

Illustrated by Richard Egielski
THE LETTER, THE WITCH, AND THE RING
Book 3 of the *House With a Clock in its Walls* Trilogy
208pp   Paperback $4.50
0-14-036338-6   Puffin
Ages 8 & up

Illustrated by Edward Gorey

THE MUMMY, THE WILL, AND THE CRYPT

176pp   Paperback $3.99
0-14-038007-8   Puffin
Ages 9 & up

THE SPELL OF THE SORCERER'S SKULL

176pp   Paperback $3.99
0-14-038044-2   Puffin
Ages 9 & up

Joan W. Blos

A GATHERING OF DAYS: A NEW ENGLAND GIRL'S JOURNAL, 1830–32

The joys and hardships of life in early nineteenth-century New Hampshire are vividly captured in the journal entries of thirteen-year-old Catherine Hall. For two years after her mother dies, Catherine struggles to act as mistress of the house and to do well at school. Then, to her horror, her father marries a woman with a son Catherine's age! This remarriage causes her to struggle with feelings many girls of today would recognize. Gradually, Catherine lets go of her jealous grudge and allows herself to accept the new wife as the mother she badly needs.

160pp   Hardcover $15.00   **A**
0-684-16340-3   Atheneum
160pp   Paperback $3.95
0-689-71419-X   Aladdin
Ages 8–12

Judy Blume

ARE YOU THERE GOD? IT'S ME, MARGARET.

Published in 1970, this book broke many barriers in children's literature by dealing with the controversial subjects of religion and puberty. Eleven-year-old Margaret needs somebody to hear her worries and fears. For lack of a diary, and even though she has no religion, Margaret decides to confide in God. Her questions are those most girls her age have—such as, when are her breasts ever going to grow? What is it like to have a period, and when will she get hers? Blume writes with respect and compassion, and her frankness opened the way for a new kind of writing in children's books.

160pp   Paperback $4.50
0-440-40419-3   Yearling
Ages 9–13

By the same author:

BLUBBER

160pp   Paperback $4.99
0-440-40707-9   Yearling
Ages 9–12

IGGIE'S HOUSE

128pp   Paperback $4.50
0-440-44062-9   Yearling
Ages 9–12

Illustrated by Roy Doty

TALES OF A FOURTH GRADE NOTHING

Peter Hatcher would gladly trade in his two-year-old brother, Fudge. Fudge can be an absolute terror—throwing a tantrum in the shoe store, smearing mashed potatoes on the wall at a café, ruining the poster for Peter's project—yet his parents make a huge fuss over him all the time, just because he's little and cute. Well, what about Peter? Can't his parents ever notice *him*? Fudge makes Peter feel like a fourth-grade *nothing*, and when Fudge swallows Peter's turtle, it's the last straw!

128pp   Hardcover $13.99
0-525-40720-0   Dutton
128pp   Paperback $4.50
0-440-48474-X   Yearling
Ages 8–12

FUDGE-A-MANIA

160pp   Hardcover $13.99 (no illus.)
0-525-44672-9   Dutton
160pp   Paperback $4.50 (no illus.)
0-440-40490-8   Yearling
Ages 8–12

has disappeared. His parents have very little money, and they were counting on Mr. de Vere to come through. How are they going to pay the hotel bill when only one night costs $453, plus tax? Sam's father believes that the Big Bazoohley, the jackpot that always seems to come their way in time of need, will save them. Sam isn't so confident and decides to find the Big Bazoohley himself. Before he knows what's happening, Sam is kidnapped and forced to enter the Perfecto Kiddo competition!

144pp   Hardcover $14.95
0-8050-3855-8   Henry Holt
144pp   Paperback $3.95
0-698-11420-5   PaperStar
Ages 8-12

Sylvia Cassedy
BEHIND THE ATTIC WALL

Unwanted—that's how twelve-year-old Maggie feels. She's been thrown out of so many boarding schools that she despairs of ever finding a permanent home. Now

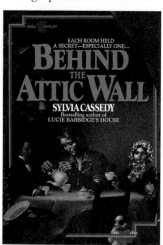

Maggie is stuck living in a gloomy mansion with her two great-aunts, who don't understand her, and her eccentric Uncle Morris, who speaks in riddles. But one day Maggie starts to hear whispers coming from behind her wall. There she finds the family she always wanted (one that accepts and loves her), even though they are only dolls. Does her eccentric Uncle Morris have anything to do with them?

320pp   Paperback $4.50
0-380-69843-9   Camelot
Ages 8-12

By the same author:
LUCIE BABBIDGE'S HOUSE
256pp   Paperback $4.50
0-380-71812-X   Camelot
Ages 8-12

John Christopher
THE TRIPODS TRILOGY

John Christopher was one of the first authors to write series science fiction for children. *The Tripods Trilogy* describes a futuristic world dominated by huge alien metal machines called

Tripods, who tame humans by "Capping" them—inserting a metal cap into people's heads to keep them brainwashed into docility. The trilogy traces the escape of three boys to a community of uncapped people, who then launch an attack on the Tripods to free mankind. These superbly written books are rich in the questions they raise about freedom and man's ultimate desire to think for himself.

THE WHITE MOUNTAINS
Book 1 in *The Tripods Trilogy*

Will lives in a peaceful world where everyone is happy and does the work that is expected of him or her without question. But he becomes anxious as the day of his Capping by the Tripods approaches. Why is everybody so obedient—by Capping people, do Tripods gain control of their minds? Then Will meets the Vagrant—one of those people on whom Capping doesn't work—and he confirms Will's fears. The Vagrant tells Will about a place in the far-off White Mountains where men roam uncapped. Determined to join them, Will and two other boys embark on the dangerous journey to freedom.

224pp   Paperback $3.95
0-02-042711-5   Aladdin
Ages 10-14

By the same author:
THE CITY OF GOLD AND LEAD
Book 2 in *The Tripods Trilogy*
224pp   Paperback $4.50
0-02-042701-8   Collier
Ages 10-14

THE POOL OF FIRE
Book 3 in *The Tripods Trilogy*
224pp   Paperback $4.50
0-02-042721-2   Aladdin
Ages 10-14

Matt Christopher
Illustrated by Harvey Kidder
THE KID WHO ONLY HIT HOMERS

Sylvester Coddmyer III is passionate about baseball, but the problem is, he's a terrible player! He's all butterfingers in the outfield, and as for hitting, he's lucky if his bat *ever* connects with the ball. Sylvester knows that if he signs up for Little League, he'd just be warming the bench. Suddenly, a Mr. George Baruth offers to help coach him—and before Sylvester knows it, he's socking homers over the fence every time at bat! Thanks to Mr. Baruth, Sylvester is the team's most valuable player. But how come nobody else ever sees his mysterious helper? Fast action and play-by-play narrative makes Sylvester's story a perfect read for sports fans.

160pp   Paperback $3.95
0-316-13987-4   Little, Brown
Ages 9-12

FROM *The Kid Who Only Hit Homers*

By the same author:
CATCH THAT PASS!
96pp   Paperback $3.95
0-316-13924-6   Little, Brown
Ages 9-12

FACE-OFF
96pp   Paperback $3.95
0-316-13994-7   Little, Brown
Ages 9-12

TOUGH TO TACKLE
152pp   Paperback $3.95
0-316-14058-9   Little, Brown
Ages 9-12

Illustrated by Barry Bomzer
DIRT BIKE RACER
96pp   Paperback $3.95
0-316-14053-8   Little, Brown
Ages 9-12

Illustrated by Foster Caddell
CATCHER WITH THE GLASS ARM
144pp   Paperback $3.95
0-316-13985-8   Little, Brown
Ages 9-12

Illustrated by Paul Casale
RETURN OF THE HOME RUN KID
96pp   Paperback $3.95
0-316-14273-5   Little, Brown
Ages 9-12

Illustrated by Byron Goto
ICE MAGIC
96pp   Paperback $3.95
0-316-13991-2   Little, Brown
Ages 9-12

Illustrated by Karen M. Swearingen
THE BASKET COUNTS
96pp   Paperback $3.95
0-316-14076-7   Little, Brown
Ages 9-12

DOUBLE PLAY AT SHORT
160pp   Paperback $3.95 (no illus.)
0-316-14201-8   Little, Brown
Ages 9-12

Roald Dahl

Roald Dahl (1916–1990) reigns as one of the most popular authors of children's books. With total disregard for the opinions of grown-ups, Dahl wrote whatever he thought would please his readers—children. Most of his books have a similar theme: innocent and defenseless children, oppressed by nasty adults, find a way to rid themselves of their oppressors and achieve happiness and freedom. Dahl peppers his wonderfully ingenious stories with hilarious made-up words and frank descriptions of the grosser things in life. By showing kids he is on *their* side, Dahl has given them books that not only make them laugh, but also make them feel empowered.

FROM *Charlie and the Chocolate Factory*

Illustrated by Joseph Schindelman

CHARLIE AND THE CHOCOLATE FACTORY

Honest but impoverished Charlie Bucket is the fifth and final winner of the golden ticket, allowing him a day's admittance to Willy Wonka's marvelous chocolate factory. The four other winners are decidedly disgusting: greedy Augustus Gloop, spoiled Veruca Salt, gum-chewing Violet Beauregard, and television-obsessed Mike Teavee. While led through the factory by the tiny Mr. Wonka, the children are overcome by greed—and disappear, one at a time. Finally only Charlie is left, and Mr. Wonka rewards the deserving boy and his family by giving Charlie the amazing and magical kingdom of candy, complete with Oompa-Loompas and chocolate rivers!

176pp   Hardcover $17.00
0-394-81011-2   Knopf
Illustrated by Quentin Blake
176pp   Paperback $4.99
0-14-130115-5   Puffin
Ages 8-12

By the same author:
CHARLIE AND THE GREAT GLASS ELEVATOR

176pp   Hardcover $17.00
0-394-82472-5   Knopf
Illustrated by Quentin Blake
176pp   Paperback $4.99
0-14-130112-0   Penguin
Ages 8-12

Illustrated by Quentin Blake
MATILDA

Matilda Wormwood started reading books at the age of four, but her crook father and bingo-playing mother regard book reading as a waste of time and much prefer watching television. In fact, they take no notice of their genius daughter at all! Only Miss Honey, Matilda's lovely and gentle teacher, recognizes her special gifts, and the two become friends. Yet Miss Honey has problems of her own—her aunt is the tyrannical Miss Trunchbull, the headmistress of Crunchem Hall, who bullies children and parents alike. The horrible Trunchbull has taken Miss Honey's house and money. Can Matilda, with her bounty of intelligence, help her friend get them back?

240pp   Hardcover $15.99
0-670-82439-9   Viking
240pp   Paperback $4.99
0-14-130106-6   Puffin
Ages 8-12

DANNY, THE CHAMPION OF THE WORLD

224pp   Paperback $4.99
0-14-130114-7   Puffin
Ages 8-12

THE WITCHES

208pp   Hardcover $16.00
0-374-38457-6   FSG
208pp   Paperback $4.99
0-14-130110-4   Puffin
Ages 8-12

Illustrated by Lane Smith
JAMES AND THE GIANT PEACH

144pp   Hardcover $16.00
0-679-88090-9   Knopf
144pp   Paperback $4.99
0-14-037424-8   Puffin
Ages 8-12

THE WONDERFUL STORY OF HENRY SUGAR AND SIX MORE

240pp   Paperback $4.99 (not illus.)
0-14-032874-2   Puffin
Ages 12 & up

Paula Danziger
THE CAT ATE MY GYMSUIT

Marcy Lewis—overweight, lonely, and suffering from the verbal abuses of an angry father—emerges from her protective shell when the radical and innovative Ms. Finney comes to teach English at Marcy's school. Not only does Marcy start to speak out in class, she also confronts her father and discovers she really *does* have something to say. This new Marcy even makes friends with a *boy!* Her newfound confidence strikes a chord in her mother, and the two forge an alliance against Marcy's tyrannical father. When Ms. Finney is suspended for not saying the Pledge of Allegiance and for angering some parents with her unusual teaching methods, Marcy defies both her father and the principal and stands up for what she feels is right. Danziger's upbeat humor lightens the tone in this story of a young girl's struggle to find strength and self-confidence.

154pp   Paperback $3.99
0-698-11684-4   PaperStar
Ages 10 & up

FROM *The Little Prince*

By the same author:
THERE'S A BAT IN BUNK FIVE
154pp   Paperback $3.99
0-698-11689-5   PaperStar
Ages 10 & up

Marguerite de Angeli
Illustrated by the author
THE DOOR IN THE WALL

Robin, son of Sir John de
Bureford, will never be as great a
knight as his father, for a sudden
illness has left his legs paralyzed.
Since his father must fight the
Scots, and his mother is chosen
as lady-in-waiting for the queen,
Robin is left in the care of the
good Brother Luke. Through the
kind monk's gentle lessons, Robin
learns the value of patience and
perseverance—and more

importantly, that all walls have
doors. When the Welsh lay siege
to the castle and the whole town
is threatened, Robin finds his
"door" and proves that, crippled
though he may be, he can still
save the town and serve his king.

128pp   Hardcover $16.95
0-385-07283-X   Doubleday
128pp   Paperback $4.99
0-440-40283-2   Yearling
Ages 9-12

Barthe DeClements
NOTHING'S FAIR IN FIFTH GRADE

Jenifer and her friends are
disgusted by how fat the new girl
is. Elsie will stop at nothing to
get food—she even steals people's
lunch money! No one in the class
likes Elsie—even her own mother

doesn't seem to like her. But
when Jenifer finds Elsie crying in
the bathroom and realizes that
Elsie has feelings too, she has a
brainstorm: Elsie is smart in math,
and she is having problems—why
not have Elsie tutor her? Then
Elsie could earn back the money
she stole, maybe make a friend,
and even prevent her mother
from sending her to boarding
school.

144pp   Paperback $4.50
0-14-034443-8   Puffin
Ages 8-12

By the same author:
THE FOURTH GRADE WIZARDS
128pp   Paperback $3.99
0-14-032760-6   Puffin
Ages 8-12

**SIXTH GRADE CAN REALLY
KILL YOU**
160pp   Paperback $3.99
0-14-037130-3   Puffin
Ages 8-12

Antoine de Saint-Exupéry
Illustrated by the author
THE LITTLE PRINCE

A pilot crash-lands in the Sahara,
where he meets the Little Prince.
The prince had recently fled from
his tiny planet where he owned
three volcanoes and a flower—a
flower whose love he had
misunderstood. A fable of love and
the mysteries we all share in life,
The Little Prince is a must-read not
only for children, but for everyone.

112pp   Hardcover $16.00
0-15-246503-0   Harcourt Brace
112pp   Paperback $10.00
0-15-646511-6   Harcourt Brace
128pp   Paperback $6.00
0-15-652820-7   Harcourt Brace
Ages 9 & up

Fiction

Edward Eager
Illustrated by N. M. Bodecker

HALF MAGIC

It seems like just a harmless coin, but when the four children discover its magic, they know their summer will be far from dull. The only drawback is the coin only grants *half* wishes, so the wisher must remember to wish for twice as much as he or she wants. And *oh!* How often do you say, "I wish . . ." without thinking? The children agree to take turns wishing, but mishaps always seem to occur. Like when Martha, bored at the movies, wishes she wasn't there, and is only *half* not there, transparent and ghostly. Or when one of the children wishes the family cat can talk, and she can only *half* speak, much to everyone's distress. What adventures the coin causes! It even finds them a new stepfather!

208pp   Paperback $6.00
0-15-233081-X   Odyssey
Ages 9-12

By the same author:

KNIGHT'S CASTLE

208pp   Paperback $6.00
0-15-202073-X   Odyssey
Ages 9-12

MAGIC BY THE LAKE

208pp   Paperback $6.00
0-15-250444-3   Odyssey
Ages 9-12

MAGIC OR NOT?

208pp   Paperback $6.00
0-15-251160-1   Odyssey
Ages 9-12

SEVEN-DAY MAGIC

208pp   Paperback $6.00
0-15-272916-X   Odyssey
Ages 9-12

THE TIME GARDEN

208pp   Paperback $6.00
0-15-288193-X   Odyssey
Ages 9-12

THE WELL-WISHERS

240pp   Paperback $6.00
0-15-294994-1   Odyssey
Ages 9-12

Nancy Farmer

THE EAR, THE EYE AND THE ARM

It's 2194 in Zimbabwe, and Tendai can't believe that in all his thirteen years, neither he nor his brother or sister has been allowed outside the house alone. Tendai's father, the powerful General Matsika, is in constant fear that his children will be kidnapped and keeps the house protected by robots. One day, the children's one human companion, Praise Singer, wangles a way to get them out of the house. Alas, General Matsika was right to worry—they are hardly gone an hour before they *are* kidnapped. The Ear, the Eye, and the Arm—

famed detectives with unusual powers—are hired to find them. But ultimately it is up to Tendai to draw on his ancestral powers to save himself and his siblings in this fast-paced futuristic adventure.

320pp   Hardcover $18.95
0-531-06829-3   Orchard
320pp   Paperback $4.99
0-14-037641-0   Puffin
Ages 10-14

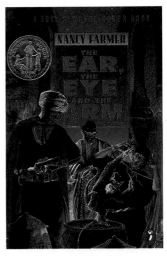

By the same author:

A GIRL NAMED DISASTER

320pp   Hardcover $19.95
0-531-09539-8   Orchard
320pp   Paperback $4.99
0-14-038635-1   Puffin
Ages 11 & up

THE WARM PLACE

160pp   Paperback $4.99
0-14-037956-8   Puffin
Ages 8-12

horde of wild hogs. But when Yeller gets in a fight with a rabid wolf, trouble strikes—and Travis is faced with the hardest decision in his life.

176pp Hardcover $23.00
0-06-011545-9 HarperCollins
192pp Paperback $5.50 (no illus.)
0-06-080971-X HarperPerennial
Ages 12 & up

By the same author:
SAVAGE SAM
160pp Paperback $6.00 (no illus.)
0-06-080377-0 HarperPerennial
Ages 12 & up

THE HOUSE OF DIES DREAR
VIRGINIA HAMILTON

—Illustrations by Eros Keith—

Virginia Hamilton
Illustrated by Eros Keith
THE HOUSE OF DIES DREAR

The huge house thirteen-year-old Thomas and his father move into was once a stop on the Underground Railroad. Full of hidden passageways, the house holds many secrets. Despite increasing danger, Thomas enthusiastically begins to uncover the secrets of the house—and secrets about the

past. This thoughtful, exciting, and provocative mystery will keep readers on edge through the dramatic final sequence.

256pp Hardcover $17.00
0-02-742500-2 Simon & Schuster
288pp Paperback $4.50
0-02-043520-7 Aladdin
Ages 11-14

By the same author:
THE MYSTERY OF DREAR HOUSE
224pp Hardcover $15.95
0-688-04026-8 Greenwillow
224pp Paperback $4.99
0-590-95627-2 Apple
Ages 9-12

M. C. HIGGINS, THE GREAT
288pp Hardcover $17.00
0-02-742480-4 Simon & Schuster
Illustrated by Symeon Shimin
288pp Paperback $4.50
0-689-71694-X Aladdin
Ages 8-12

Illustrated by Jerry Pinkney
THE PLANET OF JUNIOR BROWN
224pp Paperback $3.95
0-02-043540-1 Macmillan
Ages 9-12

Marguerite Henry
Illustrated by Wesley Dennis
MISTY OF CHINCOTEAGUE

On Assateague Island off the coast of Virginia live a herd of wild horses, descendants of a herd that was shipwrecked decades before. Paul and Maureen Beebe, who are staying with their grandparents on nearby Chincoteague Island, covet one of the horses—a wild mare people call the Phantom. Paul and Maureen have been saving their money in the hopes of buying her on Pony Penning Day. Much to everyone's

surprise, young Paul manages to round up the elusive Phantom *and* her beautiful newborn foal when the celebration finally comes! Will Paul and Maureen be able to keep both the Phantom and Misty?

176pp Paperback $3.95
0-689-71492-0 Aladdin
Ages 8-12

A NEWBERY HONOR BOOK
Marguerite Henry
MISTY of CHINCOTEAGUE

By the same author:
SEA STAR: ORPHAN OF CHINCOTEAGUE
176pp Paperback $3.95
0-689-71530-7 Aladdin
Ages 8-12

STORMY, MISTY'S FOAL
224pp Paperback $3.95
0-689-71487-4 Aladdin
Ages 8-12

Illustrated by Karen Haus Grandpré
MISTY'S TWILIGHT
160pp Paperback $3.99
0-689-80393-1 Aladdin
Ages 8-12

Fiction

S. E. Hinton
THE OUTSIDERS

Hinton wrote *The Outsiders* when
she was only sixteen years old,
and the book quickly became a
cult classic. Ponyboy, raised by his
older brother Darry, has a lot to
prove in the outside world. And
the outside world—where one is
either a Soc or a Greaser—is
where trouble lies. Tensions
escalate between the two gangs of
adolescent boys until one
particular rumble changes things
forever. With its rich setting and
enduring characters, Hinton's
classic has powerfully
communicated to several
generations of young teens. The
tone is rough and sometimes
violent, but the book abounds
with important messages.

192pp   Hardcover $15.99
0-670-53257-6   Viking
192pp   Paperback $4.99
0-14-038572-X   Puffin
Ages 10 & up

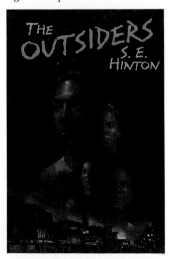

FROM *Bunnicula: A Rabbit-Tale of Mystery*

By the same author:
RUMBLE FISH
128pp   Paperback $4.50
0-440-97534-4   Laurel-Leaf
Ages 10 & up

TEX
208pp   Paperback $4.99
0-440-97850-5   Laurel-Leaf
Ages 10 & up

THAT WAS THEN, THIS IS NOW
160pp   Paperback $4.99
0-14-038966-0   Puffin
Ages 10 & up

Deborah & James Howe
Illustrated by Alan Daniel
BUNNICULA: A RABBIT-TALE OF MYSTERY

Harold the dog and Chester the
cat find their comfortable home
life disrupted when their owners
return from the movies with a
new pet. It's a bunny who was
left on one of the seats during the
showing of *Dracula*. In honor of
the movie, the family dubs their
new rabbit Bunnicula. Harold

accepts the cute bunny, but
Chester is suspicious: Bunnicula
has fangs, he sleeps all day (only
waking at sunset), and every
morning the vegetables in the
refrigerator are white and sucked
dry. Could Bunnicula be a—a—
vampire bunny?

112pp   Hardcover $15.00
0-689-30700-4   Atheneum
112pp   Paperback $3.99
0-689-80659-0   Aladdin
Ages 8-12

James Howe
Illustrated by Leslie Morrill
THE CELERY STALKS AT MIDNIGHT
128pp   Paperback $4.50
0-380-69054-3   Camelot
Ages 8-12

Illustrated by Lynn Munsinger
HOWLIDAY INN
208pp   Hardcover $16.00
0-689-30846-9   Atheneum
208pp   Paperback $4.99
0-380-64543-2   Camelot
Ages 8-12

Brian Jacques
Illustrated by Troy Howell
REDWALL

For over ten years children around the world have been discovering the exciting Redwall adventures. In the first and best known book of the series, it's mice versus rats! The peace-loving mice of Mossflower Abbey need to defend themselves against evil Cluny the Scourge, a one-eyed rat. In order to defeat the enemy, the unlikely hero Matthias will have to obtain the sword of Marin the warrior. It's not going to be an easy adventure! There are nine books in the Redwall series.

352pp   Anniversary Edition $22.95
0-399-23160-9   Philomel
Illustrated by Gary Chalk
352pp   Hardcover $21.99
0-399-21424-0   Philomel
352pp   Paperback $5.99 (no illus.)
0-441-00548-9   Ace
Ages 9 & up

By the same author:
Illustrated by Gary Chalk
MOSSFLOWER

432pp   Hardcover $21.99
0-399-21549-2   Philomel
384pp   Paperback $5.99
0-380-70828-0   Avon
Ages 9 & up

MATTIMEO

448pp   Hardcover $21.99
0-399-21741-X   Philomel
448pp   Paperback $5.99
0-380-71530-9   Avon
Ages 9 & up

Diana Wynne Jones
WITCH WEEK

Someone at Larwood House is a witch—at least, that's what the anonymous note left on the teacher's desk says. This is most alarming, because witchcraft is strictly forbidden and witches are burned. Could it just be a prank? Strange happenings, like flocks of birds flying in through the windows and all the shoes in the school disappearing, seem to confirm the note. Fat Nan Pilgrim, disliked by most of her classmates, is the immediate suspect, but *she* knows she's not a witch. Or is she? Or are there others in her class who also might be witches? Soon the school is in an uproar, and only the great enchanter Christomanci can save them.

224pp   Hardcover $14.00
0-688-12374-0   Greenwillow
224pp   Paperback $4.95
0-688-15545-6   Beech Tree
Ages 9-12

By the same author:
CART AND CWIDDER
Book 1 of *The Dalemark Quartet*
224pp   Hardcover $15.00
0-688-13360-6   Greenwillow
Ages 10 & up

DROWNED AMMET
Book 2 of *The Dalemark Quartet*
320pp   Hardcover $15.00
0-688-13361-4   Greenwillow
320pp   Paperback $4.95
0-688-13400-9   Beech Tree
Ages 12 & up

THE SPELLCOATS
Book 3 of *The Dalemark Quartet*
288pp   Hardcover $15.00
0-688-13362-2   Greenwillow
288pp   Paperback $4.95
0-688-13401-7   Beech Tree
Ages 12 & up

Norton Juster
Illustrated by Jules Feiffer
THE PHANTOM TOLLBOOTH

Puns and double entendres abound in this clever modern day classic. A bored boy named Milo spies a large box in his room containing "One Genuine Turnpike Tollbooth." For lack of anything else to do, Milo hops into his electric car, passes through the tollbooth, and immediately finds himself in the Kingdom of Wisdom. Therein lies the city Dictionopolis, where words reign; the city Digitopolis, where numbers rule; the island of Conclusions, which one can only jump to; and the scenic Point of View. Life is suddenly far from boring as Milo, Tock the Watchdog (complete with large watch in his side), and the Humbug embark on a dangerous mission to the Mountains of Ignorance to rescue the Princesses Rhyme and Reason.

256pp Hardcover $19.95
0-394-81500-9 Random House
264pp Paperback $4.99
0-394-82037-1 Bullseye
Ages 18-12

Dick King-Smith
Illustrated by Mary Rayner

BABE: THE GALLANT PIG

Mr. Hogget never owned a pig before he won Babe at the town fair. The taciturn sheep farmer takes the piglet back home, where Fly, the farm sheepdog, takes Babe under her paw and teaches him the rudiments of sheep herding. But Babe is appalled at how rude Fly is to the sheep, whom Fly considers stupid. Babe himself is polite and considerate, and soon the sheep do anything he asks them to. Mr. Hogget is amazed to see his pig herding the sheep better than Fly ever did, and he enters Babe in the Grand Challenge Sheepdog Trials. Will this unlikely sheep-pig have a chance of winning?

176pp Hardcover $15.00
0-517-55556-5 Crown
128pp Paperback $4.99
0-679-87393-7 Knopf
Ages 8-12

By the same author:
Illustrated by Lynette Hemmant

ACE: THE VERY IMPORTANT PIG

144pp Paperback $4.99
0-679-81931-2 Knopf
Ages 8-12

Illustrated by Cynthia Fisher

THE SCHOOL MOUSE

128pp Paperback $4.50
0-7868-1156-0 Hyperion
Ages 7-10

Illustrated by Mark Teague

THREE TERRIBLE TRINS

112pp Paperback $4.99
0-679-88552-8 Knopf
Ages 8-12

Eric Knight
Illustrated by Marguerite Kirmse

LASSIE COME-HOME

Lassie is well known in the small village in Yorkshire, England—not only because she is the most beautiful collie in the village, but also because she is extremely loyal to her young master, Joe Carraclough. But when Joe's father loses his job, he is forced to sell Lassie to the Duke of Rudling, who admires the dog. Joe is heartbroken, but he underestimates Lassie's fierce love for him—she escapes repeatedly from the Duke's estate to return to her boy. Finally the Duke takes Lassie to northern Scotland, but she escapes yet again. Her harrowing journey of nearly a thousand miles to return to Joe is one of the world's most beloved dog stories.

256pp Hardcover $16.95
0-8050-0721-0 Henry Holt
Ages 8-12

E. L. Konigsburg
Illustrated by the author

FROM THE MIXED-UP FILES OF MRS. BASIL E. FRANKWEILER

When Claudia and Jamie run away from home (just for a little while to make the parents take notice), they go to the perfect haven. With beds, food, and lots of places to hide, the Metropolitan Museum of Art is just right—until Claudia spies *the* statue. It's breathtaking, and nobody knows who the sculptor is! The mystery plagues Claudia until she has to solve it, and that is how she and her brother meet the formidable and rich Mrs. Basil E. Frankenweiler, the previous owner of the statue, who holds the key to its mystery.

176pp Hardcover $16.00
0-689-20586-4 Atheneum
176pp Paperback $4.50
0-689-71181-6 Aladdin
176pp Paperback $5.50
0-440-43180-8 Yearling
Ages 8-12

By the same author:
THE VIEW FROM SATURDAY

Mrs. Olinski, the sixth-grade teacher, can't explain why she chose these four very different students to be her Academic Bowl team. There's Noah, who likes to quote facts; Nadia, the red-haired lover of sea turtles; Ethan, the silent younger brother of Luke (the school's *Wunderkind*); and Julian, who is half East Indian, speaks with a British accent, and has a flair for magic tricks. The four have become the Souls, meeting weekly for tea at Julian's father's B and B. Not only do the Souls manage to beat the pants off their eighth-grade competitors, but the unlikely foursome give their paralyzed teacher something she has been missing for a long time—kindness and friendship.

176pp Hardcover $16.00 (no illus.)
0-689-80993-X Atheneum A
176pp Paperback $4.50 (no illus.)
0-689-81721-5 Aladdin
Ages 8-12

JENNIFER, HECATE, MACBETH, WILLIAM MCKINLEY, AND ME, ELIZABETH

128pp Paperback $4.50
0-440-44162-5 Yearling
Ages 9-12

A PROUD TASTE FOR SCARLET AND MINIVER

208pp Hardcover $17.00
0-689-30111-1 Atheneum
208pp Paperback $4.50
0-440-47201-6 Yearling
Ages 10-14

Robert Lawson
Illustrated by the author
BEN AND ME

Most people think that Benjamin Franklin invented the Franklin Stove, discovered the power of electricity, and was one of the authors of the Declaration of Independence. Well, he was—sort of. You see, he had a little help. In the brim of the ratty fur cap he always wore lived a very clever mouse, named Amos. Since Amos was always with Ben, he was privy to all his schemes—*and* their problems. As a matter of fact, it was *Amos* who solved most of the problems and thought up many of Ben's inventions—Ben only got the credit for them. But now it is revealed who really deserves the credit—Amos, Ben Franklin's Good Mouse.

128pp Hardcover $16.95
0-316-51732-1 Little, Brown
128pp Paperback $5.95
0-316-51730-5 Little, Brown
Ages 10 & up

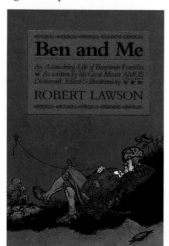

By the same author:
MR. REVERE AND I

160pp Paperback $5.95
0-316-51729-1 Little, Brown
Ages 10 & up

RABBIT HILL

128pp Hardcover $16.99 A
0-670-58675-7 Viking
128pp Paperback $4.50
0-14-031010-X Puffin
Ages 8-12

Madeleine L'Engle
THE TIME QUARTET

The four books that make up this fascinating series offer a heady combination of fantasy and science fiction. Meg Murry, her precocious little brother Charles Wallace, and Meg's friend Calvin must do battle against forces so evil they can only be conquered by the purest form of goodness: love. In each book the protagonist is aided by wise and benevolent creatures (who may or may not be angels). L'Engle's rousing stories all feature strong family ties, basic Christian tenets, and scientific exploration—and all are whopping good tales. The books in order are *A Wrinkle in Time*, *A Wind in the Door*, *A Swiftly Tilting Planet*, and *Many Waters*.

A WRINKLE IN TIME
Book 1 of *The Time Quartet*

Meg Murry's brilliant five-year-old brother Charles Wallace always seems to know just what she is feeling, especially when she is worrying about her father's absence. It's been two years since their physicist father left on a secret project, and a year since they've heard anything from him. Even

Fiction

Meg's mother is starting to worry, but it's Charles Wallace who takes action. His three mysterious friends Mrs. Whatsit, Mrs. Who, and Mrs. Which may be able to help, for they know the secret of the tesseract—a wrinkle in space and time. Before she knows it, Meg, her new friend Calvin, and Charles Wallace are all whisked away to join the strange trio on a dangerous quest for the children's father.

216pp   Hardcover $17.00
0-374-38613-7   FSG
240pp   Paperback $5.50
0-440-49805-8   Yearling
Ages 10 & up

By the same author:
A WIND IN THE DOOR
Book 2 of *The Time Quartet*
224pp   Hardcover $17.00
0-374-38443-6   FSG
240pp   Paperback $5.50
0-440-48761-7   Yearling
Ages 10 & up

A SWIFTLY TILTING PLANET
Book 3 of *The Time Quartet*
288pp   Hardcover $17.00
0-374-37362-0   FSG
304pp   Paperback $5.50
0-440-40158-5   Yearling
Ages 10 & up

MANY WATERS
Book 4 of *The Time Quartet*
310pp   Hardcover $17.00
0-374-34796-4   FSG
336pp   Paperback $5.50
0-440-40548-3   Yearling
Ages 10 & up

Gail Carson Levine
ELLA ENCHANTED
Ella, the spirited daughter of Lady Eleanor and Sir Peter of Kyrria, is given a gift at birth. *Some* gift! The well-meaning but bungling fairy Lucinda bestows on her the gift of obedience, and now Ella is cursed to obey *every* command, big and small. Even though Ella keeps the curse a

secret, it isn't long before her horrid stepsister guesses it, and Ella is trapped into satisfying her stepsister's selfish whims. Worst of all, the curse prevents Ella from marrying Prince Charmont—Char for short—for her forced obedience could cause his downfall. But Ella is spunky, and with the help of her fairy godmother *and* a repentant Lucinda, she makes it all come out right in the end. Elves, ogres, centaurs, and fairies abound in this delightful version of the Cinderella story.

240pp   Hardcover $14.95
0-06-027510-3   HarperCollins
Ages 8 & up

C. S. Lewis
THE CHRONICLES OF NARNIA
In 1950, Clive Staples Lewis wrote one of the finest fantasy stories in the history of children's literature—*The Lion, the Witch*

By the same author:
THE VOYAGES OF DOCTOR DOLITTLE
336pp   Paperback $4.99
0-440-40002-3   Yearling
Ages 9-12

Bette Bao Lord
Illustrated by Marc Simont
IN THE YEAR OF THE BOAR AND JACKIE ROBINSON

Ten-year-old Bandit is excited—she's leaving China with her mother to join her father in Brooklyn, NY. She even gets a new name in her new country—Shirley Temple (what could be more American?). But when the ten-year-old gets there, everything is so confusing. She can only speak two words of English, everything is foreign and new, and the other kids at school ignore her. Finally Mabel, the biggest girl in the class, takes Shirley under her wing and introduces her to the Brooklyn Dodgers and a new hero—Jackie Robinson. In December 1947 Jackie comes to visit the school. Who gets to present the key to

P.S. 8 to this great man? Why, a brave little immigrant named Shirley Temple Wong! This humorous look at a foreigner's adjustment to life in a new country is based on the author's own first years in America.

176pp   Paperback $4.95
0-06-440175-8   HarperTrophy
Ages 8-12

Maud Hart Lovelace
Illustrated by Lois Lenski
BETSY-TACY

Written in 1940, Betsy-Tacy evokes bygone days, when towns were small and children ran gaily about, holding hands and playing outside unsupervised until dark. Betsy, a little girl with a great imagination, lives at the end of a street that runs smack into a mountain. A new family moves in across the street, and, to Betsy's delight, they have a little girl her age. Soon Betsy and Tacy are inseparable—in fact, they are together so much that people regard them as one person: Betsy-Tacy. When a new girl Tib comes to town, the duo becomes a trio. This timeless book and its sequels have been—and will be—read and loved by generations of readers.

128pp   Hardcover $11.95
0-06-024415-1   HarperCollins
128pp   Paperback $4.95
0-06-440096-4   HarperTrophy
Ages 7-10

By the same author:
BETSY AND TACY GO DOWNTOWN
192pp   Paperback $4.95
0-06-440098-0   HarperTrophy
Ages 7-10

BETSY AND TACY GO OVER THE BIG HILL
176pp   Paperback $4.95
0-06-440099-9   HarperTrophy
Ages 7-10

BETSY-TACY AND TIB
144pp   Hardcover $11.95
0-06-024416-X   HarperCollins
144pp   Paperback $4.50
0-06-440097-2   HarperTrophy
Ages 7-10

Illustrated by Vera Neville
BETSY AND JOE
288pp   Paperback $4.95
0-06-440546-X   HarperTrophy
Ages 9-12

BETSY AND THE GREAT WORLD
336pp   Paperback $4.95
0-06-440545-1   HarperTrophy
Ages 9-12

BETSY IN SPITE OF HERSELF
288pp   Paperback $4.95
0-06-440111-1   HarperTrophy
Ages 9-12

BETSY WAS A JUNIOR
288pp   Paperback $4.95
0-06-440547-8   HarperTrophy
Ages 9-12

Fiction

BETSY'S WEDDING
272pp Paperback $4.95
0-06-440544-3 HarperTrophy
Ages 9-12

HEAVEN TO BETSY
288pp Paperback $4.95
0-06-440110-3 HarperTrophy
Ages 9-12

Lois Lowry
ANASTASIA KRUPNIK

Anastasia Krupnik is keeping a
running list of all her loves and
hates during her tenth year, but
the things she loves and the
things she hates keep changing
sides. How confusing! Her poet
father puts it best when he says
she's mercurial. Right now she's
mercurial all right, and her
mercury is rising, for her parents
just announced they are going to
have a baby! Guess who's on the
hate side of her list now? But
when Sam is born, Anastasia can't
help loving her new brother, and
forgives her parents as well. Soon
the only thing left on the hate
side is the one thing that will
never switch sides—liver!

128pp Hardcover $15.00
0-395-28629-8 Houghton Mifflin
128pp Paperback $4.50
0-440-40852-0 Yearling
Ages 9-12

By the same author:
ALL ABOUT SAM
144pp Paperback $3.99
0-440-40221-2 Yearling
Ages 8-12

ANASTASIA, ABSOLUTELY
128pp Paperback $3.99
0-440-41222-6 Yearling
Ages 9-12

ANASTASIA AGAIN!
160pp Paperback $3.99
0-440-40009-0 Yearling
Ages 9-12

ANASTASIA, ASK YOUR ANALYST
128pp Paperback $3.99
0-440-40289-1 Yearling
Ages 9-12

ANASTASIA AT THIS ADDRESS
144pp Paperback $3.99
0-440-40652-8 Yearling
Ages 9-12

ANASTASIA AT YOUR SERVICE
160pp Paperback $3.99
0-440-40290-5 Yearling
Ages 9-12

ANASTASIA HAS THE ANSWERS
128pp Paperback $3.99
0-440-40087-2 Yearling
Ages 9-12

ANASTASIA ON HER OWN
144pp Paperback $3.99
0-440-40291-3 Yearling
Ages 9-12

ANASTASIA'S CHOSEN CAREER
160pp Paperback $3.99
0-440-40100-3 Yearling
Ages 9-12

ATTABOY, SAM!
128pp Paperback $3.99
0-440-40816-4 Yearling
Ages 9-12

THE GIVER

Jonas lives with his assigned
mother, father, and little sister
Lily in an ordered world—one
devoid of conflict, feelings,
memories, colors, animals, or
even variation in weather. All is
safely organized into what is
known as Sameness. People are
content and cared for, and when
they turn old, they are "released."
When Jonas is twelve, he receives
his Life Assignment: he is to be
the next Giver, the one who
holds all the memories of the
past. The current Giver, an old
man, passes on to Jonas the
feelings from the past that the
current world cannot handle.
These include painful sights of
war, hunger, and death—but also
pictures of color, pleasure, joy,
and love. These revelations jar
Jonas out of his previous
complacency, and he plots, with
the Giver's aid, to escape to the
mysterious Elsewhere, and to
force his world to give up
Sameness. Lowry's tale of the
future is both unsettling and
thought-provoking.

208pp Hardcover $14.95 **A**
0-395-64566-2 Houghton Mifflin
192pp Paperback $5.50
0-440-21907-8 Laurel-Leaf
Ages 12 & up

NUMBER THE STARS
144pp Hardcover $14.95 **A**
0-395-51060-0 Houghton Mifflin
144pp Paperback $5.50
0-440-40327-8 Yearling
Ages 10-14

From Mrs. Piggle-Wiggle

Betty MacDonald
Illustrated by Hilary Knight
MRS. PIGGLE-WIGGLE

Whatever can parents do to handle their troublesome children? What can they do with sons who won't pick up their toys, or daughters who quarrel, hate baths, and who suddenly answer back? The answer? Just call Mrs. Piggle-Wiggle! She has a cure for everything! This roly-poly lady draws children like a magnet, and she knows just how to get them to shed their bad habits. For a girl who answers back, Mrs. Piggle-Wiggle sends over a parrot who answers back even more. As for the girl who refuses to take baths—well, Mrs. Piggle-Wiggle advises her parents to let her accumulate a good layer of dirt, then sprinkle

her with radish seeds! Readers will delight in the preposterous cures—and wish for some of them themselves!

132pp Hardcover $14.95
0-397-31713-1 HarperCollins
128pp Paperback $4.95
0-06-440148-0 HarperTrophy
Ages 6-10

By the same author:
HELLO, MRS. PIGGLE-WIGGLE

132pp Hardcover $14.95
0-397-31715-8 HarperCollins
128pp Paperback $4.95
0-06-440149-9 HarperTrophy
Ages 6-10

MRS. PIGGLE-WIGGLE'S MAGIC

132pp Hardcover $14.95
0-397-31714-X HarperCollins
144pp Paperback $4.95
0-06-440151-0 HarperTrophy
Ages 6-12

Illustrated by Maurice Sendak
MRS. PIGGLE-WIGGLE'S FARM

132pp Hardcover $14.95
0-397-31713-1 HarperCollins
128pp Paperback $4.95
0-06-440150-2 HarperTrophy
Ages 6-12

Patricia MacLachlan
SARAH, PLAIN AND TALL

This lyrical novel about a mail-order bride leaving her coastal home in Maine to go live on the prairie is poignant and moving. Anne and her brother Caleb, motherless since Caleb's birth, are lonely so Jacob, their father, places an ad in the newspaper for a bride. The answer is Sarah, plain and tall, who comes to the Wittings for a trial period to see if she can love them and live away from her beloved ocean. Each word of this novel is imbued with feeling; after a mere sixty-four pages, readers will come away teary-eyed yet immensely satisfied.

64pp Hardcover $14.95 **A**
0-06-024101-2 HarperCollins
64pp Paperback $4.95
0-06-440205-3 HarperTrophy
Ages 7 & up

By the same author:
Illustrated by Lloyd Bloom
ARTHUR, FOR THE VERY FIRST TIME

128pp Paperback $4.95
0-06-440288-6 HarperTrophy
Ages 8-11

Illustrated by Maria Pia Marrella
SEVEN KISSES IN A ROW

64pp Paperback $4.50
0-06-440231-2 HarperTrophy
Ages 7-10

Fiction

BABY
144pp   Paperback $4.99 (no illus.)
0-440-41145-9   Yearling
Ages 8 & up

THE FACTS AND FICTIONS OF MINNA PRATT
144pp   Paperback $4.50 (no illus.)
0-06-440265-7   HarperTrophy
Ages 8-12

SKYLARK
64pp   Paperback $4.95 (no illus.)
0-06-440622-9   HarperTrophy
Ages 8-10

Robert McCloskey
Illustrated by the author

HOMER PRICE

Six cheerfully humorous tales set in a small midwestern town during the 1940s tell of an inventive boy based on McCloskey himself. Homer lives just outside Centerburg, where his parents own a tourist camp and gas station. Though Centerburg is a fairly sleepy town where everybody knows everybody, a lot seems to happen here. When four robbers steal the prize money from an after-shave company's slogan contest, Homer and his pet skunk catch them. Homer's Uncle Ulysses invents a marvelous doughnut machine—but it won't stop making doughnuts! And don't forget Uncle Telly's incredible string collection! With tongue in cheek, McCloskey takes a fond look back, and readers of all ages will enjoy the antics.

160pp   Hardcover $15.99
0-670-37729-5   Viking
160pp   Paperback $4.99
0-14-030927-6   Puffin
Ages 8-12

FROM *Homer Price*

By the same author:
CENTERBURG TALES
192pp   Paperback $4.99
0-14-031072-X   Puffin
Ages 8-12

Eloise Jarvis McGraw
THE GOLDEN GOBLET

Ranofer longs to be a goldsmith, just as his father was. Indeed Zau, the greatest goldsmith in Egypt, had told his father that the boy shows promise. But with his father's death, Ranofer is forced to live with his cruel half-brother Gebu and to work in Gebu's stone-cutting shop, cutting stones for coffins and tombs. Ranofer has long suspected that Gebu is a thief, and when he finds a golden goblet in Gebu's room, Ranofer realizes with horror that it is stolen from a Pharaoh's tomb in the City of the Dead! Yet the only way for Ranofer to prove Gebu's guilt is to follow him, and catch him in the act. Filled with details of daily life, this thrilling adventure brings ancient Egypt to today's readers.

248pp   Paperback $5.99
0-14-030335-9   Puffin
Ages 9-12

By the same author:
MARA, DAUGHTER OF THE NILE
280pp   Paperback $4.99
0-14-031929-8   Puffin
Ages 10-14

MOCCASIN TRAIL
256pp   Paperback $4.99
0-14-032170-5   Puffin
Ages 10-14

THE MOORCHILD
256pp   Paperback $4.50
0-689-82033-X   Aladdin
Ages 9-12

A. A. Milne

Alan Alexander Milne (1882–1956), British author and playwright, has given children's literature some of its most endearing characters. Inspired by the stuffed animals owned by his son, Christopher Robin, Milne created the Hundred Acre Wood. Therein resides Winnie-the-Pooh, a bear of "very little brain"; his timid friend Piglet; the gloomy donkey Eeyore; the indefatigable Tigger; the matronly Kanga; her little Roo; and their friend, Christopher Robin. Milne's writing style evokes wonder. With gentle humor, he captures stereotypes in his characters—Rabbit is a bossy know-it-all, and Owl a blustery intellectual—and he treats these foibles not with censure, but with affection. Captured in these tales is the essence of childhood, its innocence and imaginative play.

Sing Ho! for the life of a Bear!
Sing Ho! for the life of a Bear!
I don't much mind if it rains or snows,
'Cos I've got a lot of honey on my nice
    new nose,
I don't much care if it snows or thaws,
'Cos I've got a lot of honey on my nice
    clean paws!
Sing Ho! for a Bear!
Sing Ho! for a Pooh!
And I'll have a little something in an hour
    or two!

TEXT AND IMAGES FROM *Winnie-the-Pooh*

Fiction

Illustrated by Ernest H. Shepard

WINNIE-THE-POOH

Meet Winnie-the-Pooh, the bear who always gets peckish around eleven o'clock, loves to eat "hunny," and makes up little songs called "hums." He has a kind heart, and a tendency to pretend to know things that he really doesn't know. As a result, Christopher Robin must perpetually rescue him from fixes! One day Pooh uses a balloon to disguise himself as a cloud and get honey from a bee's hive (he doesn't succeed). Another day Pooh eats so much at Rabbit's house that he gets stuck in Rabbit's hole. And in yet another adventure, Pooh and Piglet hunt for Heffalumps, but Pooh falls into their trap and scares Piglet half to death! These and other tales about Pooh have charmed generations of readers, and Shepard's exquisite line drawings are such an integral part of *Winnie-the-Pooh* that one can't imagine the book without them.

176pp Full-Color Gift Edition
$22.50 0-525-44776-8 Dutton
176pp Hardcover $10.99
0-525-44443-2 Dutton
176pp Paperback $4.99
0-14-036121-9 Puffin
Ages 4 & up

By the same author:

THE HOUSE AT POOH CORNER

192pp Full-Color Gift Edition
$22.50 0-525-44774-1 Dutton
192pp Hardcover $10.99
0-525-44444-0 Dutton
192pp Paperback $4.99
0-14-036122-7 Puffin
Ages 4 & up

FROM *The House At Pooh Corner*

NOW WE ARE SIX

112pp Hardcover $20.00
0-525-44960-4 Dutton
112pp Paperback $4.99
0-14-036124-3 Dutton

WHEN WE WERE VERY YOUNG

112pp Hardcover $20.00
0-525-44961-2 Dutton
112pp Paperback $4.99
0-14-036123-5 Dutton

POOH'S LIBRARY 4 BOOK BOXED SET: WINNIE-THE-POOH, THE HOUSE AT POOH CORNER, NOW WE ARE SIX, AND WHEN WE WERE VERY YOUNG

Hardcover $44.00
0-525-44451-3 Dutton
Paperback $20.00
0-14-095560-7 Puffin
Ages 4 & up

FROM *Anne of Green Gables*

They ask the orphanage to send a boy, but when Matthew goes to pick him up at the train station, he finds a skinny red-haired girl instead. And how this girl can talk! By the time Matthew returns to Green Gables, he has been completely charmed. Marilla is sterner and wants to send Anne back: she knows a girl won't be much help with heavy work. But the irrepressible eleven-year-old has a knack for worming her way into people's hearts. Anne's naiveté and earnest desire to do right make up for her impulsive plunges into trouble, and soon even Marilla can't imagine life at Green Gables without her. This turn-of-the-century novel's spunky heroine is enormously popular and has enchanted generations of readers.

384pp   Hardcover $15.95
0-448-06030-2   Grosset
(Illustrated Junior Library®)
320pp Paperback $3.99 (no illus.)
0-553-21313-X   Bantam
Ages 10 & up

L. M. Montgomery
THE ANNE OF GREEN GABLES NOVELS

Canadian author Lucy Maud Montgomery's *Anne of Green Gables* was an instant bestseller when first published in 1908, and has been charming readers ever since. In the imaginative and garrulous Anne Shirley, one can see bits of the author; like Montgomery, a young Anne longs to have her work published and suffers many rejections before her first story is sold to a magazine. Over the eight books in the series, Anne's antics die down—she grows up, teaches, marries the local boy, and has her own children who are as imaginative as she. While sentimental, the books are a strong voice for female independence, and are humorous and immensely satisfying.

Illustrated by Jody Lee
ANNE OF GREEN GABLES
Book 1 in *The Anne of Green Gables Novels*

Marilla Cutbert and her brother Matthew are getting old and need someone to help them manage their farm at Green Gables on Prince Edward Island.

By the same author:
Illustrated by Clare Sieffert
ANNE OF AVONLEA
Book 2 in *The Anne of Green Gables Novels*
320pp   Hardcover $14.95
0-448-40063-4   Grosset
(Illustrated Junior Library®)
288pp   Paperback $3.99
0-553-21314-8   Bantam
Ages 10 & up

ANNE OF THE ISLAND
Book 3 in *The Anne of Green Gables Novels*
256pp   Paperback $3.99
0-553-21317-2   Bantam
Ages 10 & up

ANNE OF WINDY POPLARS
Book 4 in *The Anne of Green Gables Novels*
272pp   Paperback $3.99
0-553-21316-4   Bantam
Ages 10 & up

ANNE'S HOUSE OF DREAMS
Book 5 in *The Anne of Green Gables Novels*
240pp   Paperback $3.99
0-553-21318-0   Bantam
Ages 10 & up

ANNE OF INGLESIDE
Book 6 in *The Anne of Green Gables Novels*
288pp   Paperback $3.99
0-553-21315-6   Bantam
Ages 10 & up

RAINBOW VALLEY
Book 7 in *The Anne of Green Gables Novels*
240pp   Paperback $3.99
0-553-26921-6   Bantam
Ages 10 & up

RILLA OF INGLESIDE
Book 8 in *The Anne of Green Gables Novels*
288pp   Paperback $4.50
0-553-26922-4   Bantam
Ages 10 & up

EMILY OF NEW MOON
Book 1 in *The Emily Novels*
352pp   Paperback $4.99
0-553-23370-X   Bantam
Ages 10 & up

EMILY CLIMBS
Book 2 in *The Emily Novels*
336pp   Paperback $4.99
0-553-26214-9   Bantam
Ages 10 & up

EMILY'S QUEST
Book 3 in *The Emily Novels*
240pp   Paperback $4.50
0-553-26493-1   Bantam
Ages 10 & up

Phyllis Reynolds Naylor
THE AGONY OF ALICE
It's bad enough that Alice McKinley is in a new house in a new town, ready to start sixth grade, but not having a mother to help her cope is even worse. All she has is her father and nineteen-year-old brother Lester, and what can *they* do? Alice is *determined* to find a mother. Miss Cole, one of the sixth-grade teachers, would be perfect—she's slim, beautiful, and laughs all the time. Of course, Alice doesn't get her for a teacher; she gets the dowdy Mrs. Plotkin instead. But as time goes on, Alice finds that Mrs. Plotkin has hidden attributes. Alice's agonies over growing up (or, as she feels, "growing *backwards*") are divulged with compassion and humor.

144pp   Hardcover $16.00
0-689-31143-5   Atheneum
144pp   Paperback $3.99
0-689-81672-3   Aladdin
Ages 9-13

By the same author:
ALICE IN APRIL
176pp   Paperback $3.99
0-440-40944-6   Yearling
Ages 9-12

ALICE IN-BETWEEN
160pp   Paperback $3.99
0-440-41064-9   Yearling
Ages 9-12

ALICE IN RAPTURE, SORT OF
176pp   Paperback $3.50
0-440-40462-2   Yearling
Ages 8-12

ALICE THE BRAVE
144pp   Paperback $3.99
0-689-80598-5   Aladdin
Ages 9-13

ALL BUT ALICE
160pp   Paperback $3.99
0-440-40918-7   Yearling
Ages 9-12

SHILOH
From the moment softhearted Marty sees the scared and scrawny beagle, he wants him. But his parents won't let him keep the dog Marty dubs Shiloh, for Shiloh belongs to Judd Travers, a man known for his rudeness and bad temper. In desperation, Marty hides the dog and pretends not to know where he is—he *won't* let Judd have Shiloh back! Judd Travers abuses his dogs—just look at how frightened Shiloh was at first. What's more, Marty found a dog with a bullet in its head last year, and he's sure the dog belonged to Judd! Not merely a boy-and-dog story, this compelling novel depicts the wrenching struggles of a boy forced to compromise his values to defend what he really loves.

144pp   Hardcover $15.00   Ⓐ
0-689-31614-3   Atheneum
144pp   Paperback $4.99
0-440-40752-4   Yearling
Ages 8-12

SAVING SHILOH
144pp   Hardcover $15.00
0-689-81460-7   Atheneum
Ages 8-12

SHILOH SEASON
128pp Hardcover $15.00
0-689-80647-7 Atheneum
128pp Paperback $4.50
0-689-80646-9 Aladdin
Ages 8-12

THE BOYS START THE WAR AND THE GIRLS GET EVEN
134pp Paperback $5.99
0-440-40971-3 Yearling
Ages 8-12

THE FEAR PLACE
128pp Hardcover $16.00
0-689-31866-9 Atheneum
128pp Paperback $3.95
0-689-80442-3 Aladdin
Ages 9-14

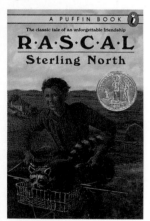

Sterling North
Illustrated by John Schoenherr

RASCAL

In May 1918, eleven-year-old Sterling finds a baby raccoon he names Rascal and takes him home to join the other animals in his menagerie. It isn't long before the boy and animal are inseparable friends—they go camping and fishing together, eat from the same spoon, and even share a bed.

Rascal is clever—he watches whatever Sterling does, and then imitates him. But Rascal's unusual antics cause trouble—such as when he discovers corn and samples the crops of the whole neighborhood! Despite this, Sterling loves his pet—so much so, that when Rascal reaches maturity, the boy allows the raccoon to choose between staying with him or returning to the wild.

192pp Hardcover $14.99
0-525-18839-8 Dutton
192pp Paperback $4.99
0-14-034445-4 Puffin
Ages 10-14

Mary Norton
Illustrated by Beth & Joe Krush

THE BORROWERS

Fourteen-year-old Arietty lives with her mother Homily and her father Pod Clock under the floorboards in a comfortable house. It's not their house—it belongs to the creature called Aunt Sophy, the only "human bean" (as they call her) the Clock family lets see them. For the Clocks are Borrowers—little people only inches high—who "borrow" from the humans all they need to live. Because it is so dangerous, only Pod is allowed to go on borrowing expeditions. But Arietty is bored and lonely; she wants a friend, even if it is a forbidden human bean. She's so desperate that she risks being seen, and before she knows it, her family is in serious danger!

192pp Hardcover $17.00
0-15-209987-5 Harcourt Brace
192pp Paperback $6.00
0-15-209990-5 Odyssey
Ages 8 & up

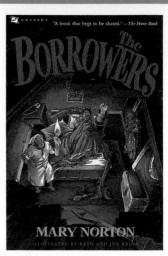

"A book that begs to be shared."—*The Horn Book*

MARY NORTON
ILLUSTRATED BY BETH AND JOE KRUSH

By the same author:

THE BORROWERS AFIELD
224pp Hardcover $17.00
0-15-210166-7 Harcourt Brace
224pp Paperback $6.00
0-15-210535-2 Odyssey
Ages 8 & up

THE BORROWERS AFLOAT
192pp Hardcover $17.00
0-15-210345-7 Harcourt Brace
192pp Paperback $6.00
0-15-210534-4 Odyssey
Ages 8 & up

THE BORROWERS ALOFT
208pp Hardcover $17.00
0-15-210524-7 Harcourt Brace
208pp Paperback $6.00
0-15-210533-6 Odyssey
Ages 8 & up

THE BORROWERS AVENGED
384pp Hardcover $17.00
0-15-210530-1 Harcourt Brace
384pp Paperback $6.00
0-15-210532-8 Odyssey
Ages 8 & up

Scott O'Dell
Illustrated by Ted Lewin

ISLAND OF THE BLUE DOLPHINS

When their tribe flees the Aleuts, the twelve-year-old Ghalas-at Indian Karana and her six-year-old brother Ramo find themselves stranded on their island home without weapons or food. Karana tries her best to care for her brother, but Ramo is killed three days later by the leader of a pack of wild dogs. Now Karana is truly alone, and must teach herself the rudiments of survival. To ward off loneliness, she captures and tames the dog that killed her brother. Set in the early 1800s, this fascinating and true adventure covers the eighteen years Karana spent with her dog and other animals on the Island of the Blue Dolphins, seventy-five miles southwest of Los Angeles. Her struggles, courage, and compassion are an inspiration to readers of all ages.

192pp   Hardcover $20.00 [A]
0-395-53680-4   Houghton Mifflin
192pp   Hardcover $16.00 (no illus.)
0-395-06962-9   Houghton Mifflin
192pp   Paperback $5.50 (no illus.)
0-440-94000-1   Laurel-Leaf
Ages 10 & up

By the same author:
BLACK PEARL
96pp   Paperback $4.50 (no illus.)
0-440-41146-7   Yearling
Ages 10 & up

MY NAME IS NOT ANGELICA
144pp   Paperback $4.50 (no illus.)
0-440-40379-0   Yearling
Ages 10-14

SING DOWN THE MOON
144pp   Paperback $4.99 (no illus.)
0-440-40673-0   Yearling
Ages 10 & up

ZIA
192pp   Paperback $4.50 (no illus.)
0-440-41001-0   Yearling
Ages 9-12

Katherine Paterson
Illustrated by Donna Diamond
BRIDGE TO TERABITHIA

Jess Aarons has been practicing all summer to be the fastest runner in the fifth grade. But Leslie Burke, the new kid at school, is faster than he is—and Leslie's a *girl*. Before Jess knows it, he and Leslie are friends, and the two find a place in the woods they dub Terabithia. A creek surrounds their secret kingdom, and in order to get there they must swing across the water on a rope. But as the spring rains come, Jess is tormented—he's afraid to swing over the rushing water. Then one fateful morning, while Jess is out of town, it is Leslie who falls into the torrent and is drowned. Stunned and angered, Jess can't face the fact that Leslie, the brave, imaginative leader, is suddenly wrenched from his life. Only when he finally comes to terms with her death can Jess fully appreciate the

legacy Leslie gave him. Eloquent, quietly powerful, and beautifully written, *The Bridge to Terabithia* deals with a difficult subject with dignity and respect.

144pp   Hardcover $15.95 [A]
0-690-01359-0   HarperCollins
144pp   Paperback $4.95
0-06-440184-7   HarperTrophy
Ages 10 & up

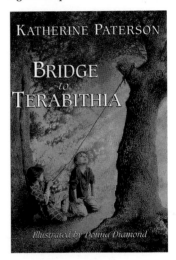

By the same author:
THE GREAT GILLY HOPKINS

Paterson tackles the volatile issues of abandonment and prejudice in this outstanding novel. Tough, smart, and arrogant Gilly Hopkins is tired of moving from foster family to foster family—she just wants to be with her mother. At her third foster home in less than three years, Gilly is placed with the fat Maime Trotter. Gilly is disgusted to find that Maime also cares for a wimpy boy named William Ernest and the elderly Mr. Randolph, who's not only blind, he's black. To her surprise, Gilly finds the love Trotter, William Ernest, and Mr. Randolph offer her is far stronger than the empty memories she has of her mother. But Gilly stubbornly hangs on to her dream of being united with her mother, and it is only when she succeeds that she realizes whom she really loves.

192pp Hardcover $14.95 (no illus.)
0-690-03837-2 HarperCollins
160pp Paperback $4.95 (no illus.)
0-06-440201-0 HarperTrophy
Ages 10 & up

Illustrated by Peter Landa
SIGN OF THE CHRYSANTHEMUM
144pp Paperback $4.95
0-06-440232-0 HarperTrophy
Ages 10 & up

JACOB HAVE I LOVED
256pp Paperback $4.95 (no illus.)
0-06-440368-8 HarperTrophy A
Ages 10 & up

LYDDIE
192pp Paperback $4.99 (no illus.)
0-14-037389-6 Puffin
Ages 12 & up

PARK'S QUEST
160pp Paperback $3.99 (no illus.)
0-14-034262-1 Puffin
Ages 10 & up

Gary Paulsen
HATCHET
In this gripping survival novel, a city-bred boy, still suffering from the sting of his parents' divorce, finds himself suddenly stranded in the wilderness when the two-seater plane he was on crashes. The hatchet his mother gave him, which he thought was so nerdy, becomes the only thing keeping him alive. Written in a terse you-

are-there style, *Hatchet* shows thirteen-year-old Brian's forced transformation from ignorant youth to competent manhood.

208pp Hardcover $16.00
0-02-770130-1 Simon & Schuster
208pp Paperback $4.50
0-689-80882-8 Aladdin
Ages 11-13

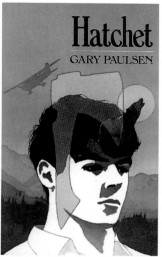

By the same author:
DOGSONG
192pp Paperback $4.50
0-689-80409-1 Aladdin
Ages 12 & up

RIVER
144pp Paperback $4.99
0-440-40753-2 Yearling
Ages 10-14

THE VOYAGE OF THE FROG
160pp Paperback $4.50
0-440-40364-2 Dell
Ages 10-14

WOODSONG
144pp Paperback $4.99
0-14-034905-7 Puffin
Ages 12 & up

William Pène du Bois
Illustrated by the author
THE TWENTY-ONE BALLOONS
Professor William Waterman Sherman leaves San Francisco on August 15, 1883, determined to be the first man to fly across the Pacific Ocean in a hot air balloon. But after seven days, disaster strikes—a sea gull pecks a hole in his balloon! Professor Sherman crashes on the volcanic island of Krakatoa; where, to his amazement, he finds a secret community of twenty American families all living in great comfort—for the island is filled with diamond mines! The families have perfected many wonderful inventions to help them enjoy the isolation, and the Professor happily joins their life of leisure. But on August 26th, the volcano Krakatoa erupts and all must make a thrilling escape—on a huge wooden platform lifted by twenty-one hot air balloons!

192pp Paperback $4.99 A
0-14-032097-0 Puffin
Ages 10-14

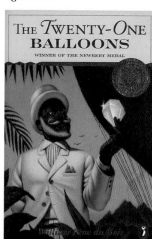

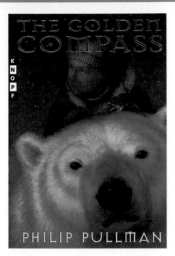

Philip Pullman
THE GOLDEN COMPASS
Book 1 in *His Dark Materials*

Pullman's complex fantasy revolves around a girl who lives in an alternate world—a world where a person's soul lives as a separate being outside of his or her body. Called daemons, the souls take on the shape of an animal and are integrally attached to their people. Lyra, a young girl, and her daemon Pantalaimon find their life takes a sudden change when the beautiful Arctic explorer Mrs. Coulter takes Lyra on to be her helper. Mrs. Coulter is involved in a mysterious thing called Dust—but with Dust is linked a terrible danger. Children have been disappearing, to be used in some horrible experiments involving their daemons and Dust. Though Lyra doesn't trust her beautiful patroness, she must pretend she knows nothing, and *must* keep her invaluable golden compass a secret. Before she knows it, Lyra is involved in a life-threatening race with Mrs. Coulter to save children from a horrible fate. With action at a breakneck pace, this novel pulls out all the emotional stops!

416pp   Hardcover $20.00
0-679-87924-2   Knopf
368pp   Paperback $6.99
0-345-41335-0   Del Rey
Ages 10 & up

By the same author:
THE SUBTLE KNIFE
Book 2 in *His Dark Materials*
304pp   Paperback $5.99
0-345-41336-9   Del Ray
Ages 10 & up

THE RUBY IN THE SMOKE
240pp   Paperback $4.99
0-394-89589-4   Knopf
Ages 12 & up

Ellen Raskin
THE WESTING GAME

It's no coincidence that these six families were chosen to live in the glamorous Sunset Towers— all sixteen tenants had some connection with the eccentric millionaire, Samuel Westing. Not until Westing is discovered dead in his house do the tenants learn that they are his heirs, and they gather to hear the most unusual will ever read—not only does it claim that Westing was murdered by one of them, but the will is a game! The heirs are paired into eight teams, each provided with written clues to help identify the murderer. The pair that solves the clues will get Westing's vast fortune. But watch out—in this clever and very humorous mystery, full of red herrings and wordplay, it's what you *don't* know that counts, and no one is who he or she claims to be.

192pp   Hardcover $15.99
0-525-42320-6   Dutton
224pp   Paperback $4.99
0-14-038664-5   Puffin
Ages 10 & up

By the same author:
FIGGS AND PHANTOMS
160pp   Paperback $5.99
0-14-032944-7   Puffin
Ages 10-14

THE MYSTERIOUS DISAPPEAR-ANCE OF LEON (I MEAN NOEL)
160pp   Paperback $4.99
0-14-032945-5   Puffin
Ages 10-14

Wilson Rawls
WHERE THE RED FERN GROWS: THE STORY OF TWO DOGS AND A BOY

Billy and his coon dogs Old Dan and Little Anne are the best hunting team in the Ozarks. Old Dan is brave and strong while Little Anne is smart, but it is the devotion between the three that makes them special. The dogs' hunting abilities are so great, they win a countywide raccoon hunt. But their victory is short-lived, for in the hills of Cherokee County lurks a great danger—the mountain lion. The day Old Dan trees one of these devil cats, Billy knows it's a fight to the death.

208pp   Hardcover $16.95
0-385-32330-1   Delacorte
256pp   Paperback $5.50
0-553-27429-5   Bantam
Ages 10 & up

By the same author:
SUMMER OF THE MONKEYS
240pp   Hardcover $15.95
0-385-11450-8   Doubleday
304pp   Paperback $5.50
0-553-29818-6   Bantam
Ages 10 & up

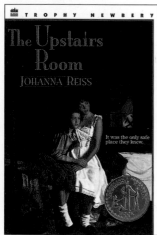

Johanna Reiss
THE UPSTAIRS ROOM

Annie de Leeuw has a false sense of security—though she and her family are Jewish, they live far from Hitler's War. But when the Germans invade Holland in 1941, things get ugly. Annie's father

can't work anymore, nor can Sini or Rachel, Annie's older sisters. Forced to flee, Annie and Sini find space with the Oostervelds—a humble farmer, his wife, and mother. For two years, the sisters stay hidden in a small room upstairs, with little to do and in constant fear of being caught. Will the war ever end, and will they ever see their father and Rachel again? Based on the author's childhood, this chronicle of constant fear is, like Anne Frank's famous diary, a testament to the sufferings of wartime Europe.

208pp   Paperback $4.95
0-06-440370-X   HarperTrophy
Ages 12 & up

By the same author:
THE JOURNEY BACK
224pp   Paperback $4.95
0-06-447042-3   HarperTrophy
Ages 12 & up

Barbara Robinson
THE BEST SCHOOL YEAR EVER

There's hardly a dull moment at Woodrow Wilson School with the six horrible Herdman kids. Everyone knows they're bad: they tell incredible lies, steal the craziest stuff, and scare the other kids—and yet they always seem to get away with it. Take for example the time they steal Louella McClusky's baby brother Howard while he is still as bald as a cue ball. They paint his head with *waterproof* felt-tip pens and charge kids a quarter to see the famous tattooed baby. And what happens? Louella is grounded, but the Herdmans get six dollars and fifty cents. They put their perpetually angry and spitting cat

in the dryer at the new Laundromat, Gladys Herdman bites everyone, and Leroy put a dead snake in the pencil sharpener. For goodness sake! The whole town can only throw up their hands and say, What can you do?

128pp   Hardcover $14.95
0-06-023039-8   HarperCollins
128pp   Paperback $4.95
0-06-440492-7   HarperTrophy
Ages 8 & up

By the same author:
Illustrated by Judith Gwyn Brown
THE BEST CHRISTMAS PAGEANT EVER
96pp   Hardcover $14.95
0-06-025043-7   HarperCollins
96pp   Paperback $4.95
0-06-440275-4   HarperTrophy
Ages 8 & up

Cynthia Rylant
MISSING MAY

Summer is six years old when she finally finds a loving home with her elderly Aunt May and Uncle Ob. But six years later, May suddenly dies while working in her garden—May, whose heart was as big as a house and whose love allowed Summer and Ob the freedom to be who they are. With May's death, Ob feels he doesn't have a reason to live, until he senses May's spirit visit him. Now he wants to contact her, and with the help of Cletus, an odd boy from school, Summer and Ob set out to try and reach May one last time. Poetic and moving, *Missing May* tells of the journey an old man and a young girl take together to find peace and acceptance after losing the person they love.

96pp   Hardcover $14.95
0-531-05996-0   Orchard
96pp   Paperback $4.50
0-440-40865-2   Yearling
Ages 10 & up

By the same author:
A FINE WHITE DUST
112pp   Paperback $3.95
0-689-80462-8   Aladdin
Ages 11-13

I HAD SEEN CASTLES
112pp   Paperback $5.00
0-15-200374-6   Harcourt Brace
Ages 12 & up

THE VAN GOGH CAFE
64pp   Paperback $3.99
0-590-90717-4   Apple
Ages 8-12

Louis Sachar
Illustrated by Julie Brinckloe
SIDEWAYS STORIES FROM WAYSIDE SCHOOL

Wayside School was built wrong—instead of being a one-story building with thirty classrooms, Wayside School is thirty stories tall with one room on each floor! Like the school, the book itself has thirty stories—each one about a different pupil in the class taught by Mrs. Jewls (Mrs. Gorf, the previous teacher, hated kids so much she turned her whole class into apples—then turned into an apple herself and was eaten!). There's the story about Mauricea who doesn't like *anyone* in the class. She only likes ice cream—that is, until Mrs. Jewls creates ice cream that tastes like each of the other pupils! And then there's Nancy, who hates his name so much that he trades names with a girl named Mac. These wacky tales about this unconventional school will have readers laughing out loud.

128pp   Paperback $4.50
0-380-69871-4   Camelot
Ages 8-12

By the same author:
SIDEWAYS ARITHMETIC FROM WAYSIDE SCHOOL
96pp   Paperback $3.99 (no illus.)
0-590-45726-8   Apple
Ages 10-14

MORE SIDEWAYS ARITHMETIC FROM WAYSIDE SCHOOL
112pp   Paperback $3.99 (no illus.)
0-590-47762-5   Apple
Ages 10-14

Illustrated by Joel Schick
WAYSIDE SCHOOL GETS A LITTLE STRANGER
176pp   Paperback $4.50
0-380-72381-6   Camelot
Ages 8-12

WAYSIDE SCHOOL IS FALLING DOWN
192pp   Paperback $4.50
0-380-75484-3   Camelot
Ages 8-12

FROM *Sideways Stories from Wayside School*

Fiction

THERE'S A BOY IN THE GIRLS' BATHROOM

Bradley Chalkers sits in the last seat of the last row, away from everyone. No one likes him, not even his teacher Mrs. Ebbels—but that's okay, because he doesn't like anyone either. His only friends are the toy animals he has in his bedroom at home. When the new boy Jeff Fishkin offers to be friends, Bradley doesn't know how to act. It's all too confusing and scary. Anyway, he knows it won't last. Sure enough, soon Jeff joins the other boys in taunting Bradley. Then Bradley meets Carla, the new school counselor, who seems to like him no matter what he says or does. Carla believes his lies, likes his stories, and hangs a picture he drew on her wall. She even thinks he's nice! Gradually, Bradley starts to believe in himself and finds some real and lasting friends.

204pp   Paperback $4.99 (no illus.)
0-394-80572-0   Knopf
Ages 8-12

DOGS DON'T TELL JOKES

216pp   Paperback $4.99 (no illus.)
0-679-83372-2   Knopf
Ages 8-12

JOHNNY'S IN THE BASEMENT

128pp   Paperback $4.50 (no illus.)
0-380-83451-0   Camelot
Ages 8-12

SIXTH GRADE SECRETS

208pp   Paperback $4.50 (no illus.)
0-590-46075-7   Apple
Ages 8-12

Illustrated by Barbara Samuels

SOMEDAY ANGELINE

160pp   Paperback $4.50
0-380-83444-8   Camelot
Ages 8-12

George Selden
Illustrated by Garth Williams

THE CRICKET IN TIMES SQUARE

Business has not been good at the Bellini's newspaper stand in the Times Square subway station. Tucker the mouse, who lives in a drainpipe near the newsstand, wishes he could help. One night, Mario Bellini hears a beautiful sound—it is Chester, a cricket from Connecticut, who is accidentally brought to New York City and plays music with his wings. After Mario convinces his parents to let him keep Chester; Tucker, his friend Harry the cat, and the cricket come up with a plan to help the Bellinis keep their newsstand—Chester can give concerts!

144pp   Hardcover $16.00
0-374-31650-3   FSG
160pp   Paperback $4.99
0-440-41563-2   Yearling
Ages 8-12

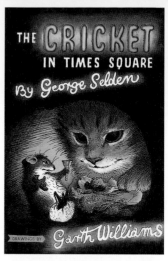

By the same author:

CHESTER CRICKET'S NEW HOME

160pp   Paperback $3.99
0-440-41246-3   Yearling
Ages 8-12

TUCKER'S COUNTRYSIDE

176pp   Paperback $4.50
0-440-40248-4   Yearling
Ages 10-14

Doris Buchanan Smith
Illustrated by Mike Wimmer

A TASTE OF BLACKBERRIES

Jamie's such a ham—always exaggerating and showing off. He's a daredevil too, doing things his best friend would never dream of. Still, the two have a lot of special times together, like when they pick blackberries, and they sure laugh a lot! One day, while working in a neighbor's yard, Jamie falls writhing to the ground after a bee stings him. But this time Jamie isn't fooling around . . . and suddenly, Jamie is gone forever. In just a few pages, *A Taste of*

Blackberries brilliantly captures the emotions a nameless young boy goes through after the death of his best friend—bewilderment, grief, and finally, a gradual acceptance that life must continue.

96pp Paperback $4.95
0-06-440238-X HarperTrophy
Ages 7-10

Zilpha Keatley Snyder
Illustrated by Alton Raible
THE EGYPT GAME

April is lonely when her glamorous mother goes off to Hollywood, leaving her to live in an apartment with her grandmother. But Melanie Ross, a girl with an imagination as active as April's, lives in the building too, and the two quickly find out they have a lot in common. Both girls love Egypt, so when they discover a bust of Nefertiti in an abandoned storage yard, they invent the Egypt Game—complete with costumes, altars, statues, ceremonies, prayers, and rites. April and Melanie play the game whenever they can, and soon let other kids in on the secret. But then something strange happens—when the children write a question for the oracle, the oracle writes back! Is the Egypt Game just a game?

224pp Paperback $5.50
0-440-42225-6 Yearling
Ages 10-14

By the same author:
THE GYPSY GAME
240pp Paperback $4.99 (no illus.)
0-440-41258-7 Yearling
Ages 8-12

THE HEADLESS CUPID
208pp Paperback $4.50
0-440-43507-2 Yearling
Ages 9-12

THE WITCHES OF WORM
192pp Paperback $4.50
0-440-49727-2 Yearling
Ages 9-12

Elizabeth George Speare
THE SIGN OF THE BEAVER

Matt is left all alone in his family's cabin during the summer of 1769 as his father retrieves his mother and sister from Massachusetts. After a vagrant steals Matt's rifle and a bear takes all his flour and molasses, Matt begins to worry about food. Foolishly, he tries to steal honey from a bee's nest, and ends up being rescued by an elderly Penobscot Indian and his sullen grandson. Matt is grateful for Saknis's aid, and gets a chance to return the favor when the old man insists he teach his grandson Attean to read the white man's words. Attean's scorn for the white man's ways is in sharp contrast to the pride he feels as he teaches Matt the rudiments of survival Native American style. Gradually, as Matt gains insight into the Penobscots's views of life, the boys' uneasy alliance turns into friendship.

144pp Hardcover $16.00
0-395-33890-5 Houghton Mifflin
144pp Paperback $5.50
0-440-47900-2 Yearling
Ages 9-12

By the same author:
THE BRONZE BOW
256pp Paperback $6.95
0-395-13719-5 Houghton Mifflin
Ages 12 & up

THE WITCH OF BLACKBIRD POND

At sixteen, Kit Tyler is forced to leave her pampered life in Barbados and live with her Aunt Rachel and Uncle Matthew in a strict Puritan settlement in Connecticut. But Kit just can't fit in to the community's rigid ways, and, unhappy and homesick, she roams the swamps around Blackbird Pond. There she befriends the Widow Hannah Tupper, a lonely old woman with a knowledge of herbs and healing. But most of the Puritans believe that Hannah is a witch, and when a dreadful illness hits the colony, the ignorant townsfolk blame the Witch of Blackbird Pond. Knowing that Hannah is innocent, Kit helps her friend escape—only to be tried as a witch herself! This romantic adventure gives a lively portrayal of an early America on the eve of the Revolution.

256pp Hardcover $16.00
0-395-07114-3 Houghton Mifflin
256pp Paperback $5.50
0-440-49596-2 Yearling
Ages 12 & up

Fiction

FROM *Abel's Island*

Jerry Spinelli
MANIAC MAGEE

Jeffrey Lionel Magee is three when his parents die in a tragic trolley crash just outside of Two Mills, Pennsylvania. After living eight years with his horrible aunt and uncle, Jeffrey takes off running—and doesn't stop until he finishes the two hundred miles back to Two Mills. It's here that this shabby homeless boy makes the transformation from ordinary Jeffrey into mythical Maniac Magee. And Maniac Magee can do more than just run! He alone can hit John McNab's blistering fastball, intercept the football from eleventh-grader James "Hands" Down, and stand up to Mars Bar Thompson, head of the East End kids. Most amazing of all is how Maniac Magee breaks down the lines of prejudice separating the East and West Ends of Two Mills. Yes, he's a legend indeed.

192pp   Hardcover $15.95
0-316-80722-2   Little, Brown
192pp   Paperback $4.95
0-06-440424-2   HarperTrophy
Ages 9-12

By the same author:
SPACE STATION SEVENTH GRADE
240pp   Paperback $5.95
0-316-80804-0   Little, Brown
Ages 12 & up

WHO PUT THAT HAIR IN MY TOOTHBRUSH?
232pp   Paperback $5.95
0-316-80841-5   Little, Brown
Ages 12 & up

WRINGER
240pp   Hardcover $14.95
0-06-024913-7   HarperCollins
Ages 9-12

William Steig
Illustrated by the author
ABEL'S ISLAND

While picnicking, Abel the mouse and his wife Amanda are caught in a rainstorm and are forced to take shelter in a cave. When the wind rips Amanda's scarf from her neck, Abel reaches out to grab it, but falls into a torrential stream and is helplessly swept away to an island far from home. During his year stranded on the island, this proper and gentlemanly mouse builds a home, finds food, and develops his newfound talent as a sculptor—all the while dreaming of Amanda and trying to find a way to get back. Steig tells Abel's story with his usual elegance, and the hero's reunion with his beloved wife is especially poignant.

128pp   Hardcover $15.00
0-374-30010-0   FSG
128pp   Paperback $4.95
0-374-40016-4   Sunburst
Ages 7 & up

By the same author:
DOMINIC
160pp   Paperback $4.95
0-374-41826-8   FSG
Ages 9-12

THE REAL THIEF
64pp   Paperback $3.95
0-374-46208-9   Sunburst
Ages 6 & up

Mildred D. Taylor
ROLL OF THUNDER, HEAR MY CRY

The Logan family has owned four hundred acres of Mississippi land for almost fifty years and nothing is going to make them sell it. Papa tells Cassie that living on one's own land is what

Fiction

matters most—it gives a sense of pride and belonging, and holds a family together. Cassie doesn't understand the importance of sticking together until her ninth year, when she encounters prejudice for the first time. Why do the white people look down on her and her family? Taylor's powerful and searing novel about the South during the Depression tells of one family's strength, courage, and sacrifice in the face of racial hatred.

288pp   Hardcover $15.99   A
0-8037-7473-7   Dial
288pp   Paperback $4.99
0-14-034893-X   Puffin
288pp   Paperback $4.99
0-14-038451-0   Puffin
Ages 10 & up

By the same author:
LET THE CIRCLE BE UNBROKEN
400pp   Paperback $4.99   A
0-14-034892-1   Puffin
Ages 10 & up

THE ROAD TO MEMPHIS
302pp   Paperback $4.99   A
0-14-036077-8   Puffin
Ages 12 & up

Illustrated by Max Ginsberg
MISSISSIPPI BRIDGE
64pp   Paperback $3.99
0-553-15992-5   Skylark
Ages 7-11

Illustrated by Jerry Pinkney
SONG OF THE TREES
56pp   Hardcover $15.99
0-8037-5452-3   Dial
Ages 7-10

Sydney Taylor
Illustrated by Helen John
ALL-OF-A-KIND FAMILY

All-of-a-Kind Family gives readers a glimpse of a time when family and community were central to life. Growing up in the Lower East Side in 1912 is difficult, and Papa's junk shop doesn't make much money. Yet Mama's loving guidance and Papa's gentle understanding give their five girls more than money could ever buy. There's the friendship the girls have among themselves, Papa's way of making the Jewish holidays special for each child, and the wonderful example both parents give by their kindness to others. Still popular today, these adventures of turn-of-the-century New York are based on the author's own childhood.

192pp   Paperback $4.50
0-440-40059-7   Yearling
Ages 8-12

Theodore Taylor
THE CAY
Eleven-year-old Phillip Enright and his mother are fleeing Curaçao from a German invasion when the ship they are on is torpedoed. Phillip is knocked unconscious by a falling timber,

and wakens to find himself floating on a raft with a huge elderly black man and a cat. Phillip has always been taught that black people are inferior, but when Phillip loses his sight from the injury, it is the old man who saves them all. When the raft finally comes to rest on a small island, Timothy patiently teaches Phillip how to take care of himself, and gradually Phillip realizes how wrong his feelings of superiority are. This story quietly yet powerfully unfolds a young boy's revelation and an old man's sacrifice in the face of racism.

144pp   Hardcover $15.95
0-385-07906-0   Doubleday
144pp   Paperback $4.50
0-380-00142-X   Camelot
144pp   Paperback $4.50
0-380-01003-8   Flare
Ages 8-12

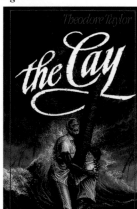

By the same author:
Illustrated by Richard Cuffari
STRANGER FROM THE SEA: TEETONCEY
160pp   Paperback $3.99
0-380-71024-2   Camelot
Ages 8-12

TIMOTHY OF THE CAY: A PREQUEL-SEQUEL

176pp   Hardcover $13.95 (no illus.)
0-15-288358-4   Harcourt Brace
160pp   Paperback $4.50 (no illus.)
0-380-72119-8   Harcourt Brace
Ages 10-14

THE TROUBLE WITH TUCK

128pp   Paperback $4.50 (no illus.)
0-380-62711-6   Camelot
Ages 9-12

TUCK TRIUMPHANT

160pp   Paperback $4.50 (no illus.)
0-380-71323-3   Camelot
Ages 8-12

P. L. Travers
Illustrated by Mary Shepard

MARY POPPINS

Prim, proper, and haughty Mary Poppins has only to direct her special look, and her charges shake in their shoes. But the day the Banks children see her slide *up* the banister, they know this formidable personage is no ordinary nanny! On outings with her, *anything* can happen! When visiting Mary Poppins's uncle Mr. Wigg, Jane and Michael are magically filled with laughing gas, and float bobbing and laughing near the ceiling. They take a nocturnal visit to the zoo, where the animals host Mary Poppins's birthday party. The children even witness Mary Poppins and her old friend Mrs. Corry paste foil stars to the night sky. Mary Poppins staunchly denies these wonderful adventures after they happen, causing readers to feel as though they have just been included in the most wonderful secrets.

224pp   Hardcover $18.00
0-15-252595-5   Harcourt Brace
224pp   Paperback $6.00
0-15-201717-8   Odyssey
Ages 8 & up

By the same author:
MARY POPPINS COMES BACK

320pp   Paperback $6.00
0-15-201719-4   Odyssey
Ages 8 & up

MARY POPPINS IN THE PARK

288pp   Paperback $6.00
0-15-201721-6   Odyssey
Ages 8 & up

MARY POPPINS OPENS THE DOOR

272pp   Paperback $6.00
0-15-201722-4   Odyssey
Ages 8 & up

Cynthia Voigt
HOMECOMING

When the Tillerman children's momma abandons them during a car trip, thirteen-year-old Dicey finds herself suddenly responsible for her three younger siblings. Jamie, at ten, is smart and practical; but nine-year-old Maybeth is painfully shy, rarely speaks, and is often thought to be retarded; and six-year-old Sammy is stubborn and likes his own way. But the Tillermans are a family, and the resourceful Dicey is determined they will not be separated. With little more than eleven dollars between them, the four start walking to find a place they can call home. Readers will root for Dicey with her fierce pride, sense of honesty, and love for her siblings in this absorbing novel.

384pp   Paperback $4.99
0-449-70254-5   Fawcett Juniper
Ages 10 & up

By the same author:
THE CALLENDER PAPERS

192pp   Paperback $4.50
0-449-70184-0   Fawcett Juniper
Ages 10 & up

COME A STRANGER

256pp   Paperback $4.99
0-689-80444-X   Aladdin
Ages 11 & up

DICEY'S SONG

224pp   Paperback $4.50
0-449-70276-6   Fawcett Juniper
Ages 12 & up

IZZY, WILLY-NILLY
288pp Paperback $4.99
0-689-80446-6 Aladdin
Ages 12 & up

ON FORTUNE'S WHEEL
304pp Paperback $4.50
0-449-70391-6 Fawcett Juniper
Ages 12 & up

THE RUNNER
288pp Paperback $4.99
0-590-48380-3 Scholastic
Ages 12 & up

A SOLITARY BLUE
320pp Paperback $4.99
0-590-47157-0 Scholastic
Ages 12 & up

THE VANDEMARK MUMMY
224pp Paperback $4.50
0-449-70417-3 Fawcett Juniper
Ages 10 & up

Barbara Brooks Wallace
PEPPERMINTS IN THE PARLOR

When recently orphaned Emily Luddock arrives at Sugar Hill Hall to live with her aunt and uncle, she's in for a surprise—her uncle is missing, her aunt is a frightened shadow of her former self, and Emily is immediately forced to become a servant! The sinister Mrs. Meeching and her accomplice Mrs. Plumly have taken over the mansion and turned it into a home for the unfortunate aged whom no one wants. The only bright spot in the house is a bowl of red and white peppermints, but cruel punishment awaits anyone who so much as *touches* one. Emily is terrified, but must find out why the two women have control over her aunt, and where they have hidden her uncle. Complete with

secret passages, smuggling sea captains, a courageous heroine, and her stalwart friend, this is a satisfying Dickensian read for the younger set.

208pp Paperback $3.95
0-689-71680-X Aladdin
Ages 8-12

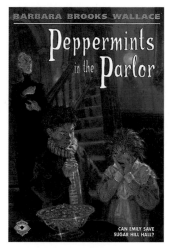

By the same author:
COUSINS IN THE CASTLE
160pp Paperback $3.99
0-689-80778-3 Aladdin
Ages 8-12

THE TWIN IN THE TAVERN
192pp Paperback $3.95
0-689-80167-X Aladdin
Ages 8-12

Sylvia Waugh
THE MENNYMS

The Mennyms have lived their calm and predictable lives undisturbed at Number 5, Brocklehurst Grove for forty years. They never need to eat or sleep, hardly ever go outside, and never age—for the Mennyms are a family of life-sized rag dolls. They

were created by the previous tenant of the house, and came to life after her death. There is Sir Magnus and his wife Tulip, their son Joshua and his wife Vinetta, and the grandchildren—the surly adolescent Appleby; her pensive brother, Soobie; the twins Wimpey and Poopie; and Googles, the baby. Residing in the hall closet as a permanent guest is Miss Quigley, who makes weekly appearances for a pretend tea. Each day is boringly like the next until they receive the letter—the new owner of the house would like to come for a visit. What are the Mennyms to do? This quirky and amusing fantasy has plenty of tongue-in-cheek wit.

240pp Paperback $4.50
0-380-72528-2 Camelot
Ages 8-12

By the same author:
MENNYMS ALIVE
224pp Hardcover $16.00
0-688-15201-5 Greenwillow
Ages 8-12

MENNYMS ALONE
192pp Hardcover $16.00
0-688-14702-X Greenwillow
Ages 8-12

MENNYMS IN THE WILDERNESS
256pp Hardcover $15.00
0-688-13820-9 Greenwillow
240pp Paperback $4.50
0-380-72529-0 Camelot
Ages 8-12

MENNYMS UNDER SIEGE
224pp Paperback $4.50
0-380-72584-3 Camelot
Ages 8-12

E. B. White

Elwyn Brooks White (1899–1985) is best known for his
brilliant and witty articles which appeared in the *New Yorker*
magazine over a span of almost fifty years. But in the world of
children's books White is most remembered for his three
moving novels: *Stuart Little*, *Charlotte's Web*, and *The Trumpet of
the Swan*. In *Stuart Little*, a mouse born to a family of humans
has many humorous adventures. But the story also has an
underlying sadness as Stuart searches for his missing friend, the
beautiful—and in his mind, perfect—bird, Margalo. *Charlotte's
Web* is about friendship, sacrifice, and death—all under the
guise of a tale about a little pig and his arachnid pal, Charlotte.
The Trumpet of the Swan explores a friendship between a boy
and a trumpeter swan who cannot trumpet, but makes up for
this deficiency by learning to play a real one. White's books,
though written for children, touch readers of all ages, and are
truly classics in the world of literature.

FROM *Charlotte's Web*

Illustrated by Garth Williams

CHARLOTTE'S WEB

The day Fern Arable stops her
father from killing the runt of his
sow's litter marks the beginning
of the wonderful story of Wilbur
the pig. After being saved Wilbur
is sent to Fern's uncle's farm. The
naive pig is lonely, so it is with
delight that he makes the
acquaintance of Charlotte the
spider, a lover a words. Being
literate and wise, she teaches her
porcine friend much about life,
especially when the other animals
in the barnyard tease him. When
the sensitive Wilbur discovers he
is to be fattened and eventually
slaughtered, it is Charlotte who
vows to save him, and she does it
in the most surprising way. Garth
Williams's exceptional black-and-
white illustrations add to the genius
of one of the most famous and
beloved books in children's
literature.

*192pp   Hardcover $14.95
0-06-026385-7   HarperCollins
192pp   Paperback $4.95
0-06-440055-7   HarperTrophy
Ages 7 & up*

Fiction

By the same author:

E. B. WHITE 3 BOOK BOXED SET:
CHARLOTTE'S WEB, STUART
LITTLE,* AND *THE TRUMPET OF
THE SWAN
Hardcover $44.85
0-06-026399-7   HarperCollins
Paperback $14.85
0-06-440061-1   HarperTrophy
Ages 7 & up

STUART LITTLE
144pp   Hardcover $14.95
0-06-026395-4   HarperCollins
144pp   Paperback $5.95
0-06-440056-5   HarperTrophy
Ages 8-12

Illustrated by Edward Frascino

THE TRUMPET OF THE SWAN
224pp   Hardcover $14.95
0-06-026397-0   HarperCollins
224pp   Paperback $4.95
0-06-440048-4   HarperTrophy
Ages 8-12

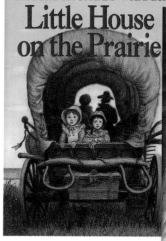

Laura Ingalls Wilder

Laura Ingalls Wilder (1867–1957) did not start writing her immensely popular *Little House* books until she was in her sixties. Under the guidance of her journalist daughter Rose Lane, Wilder chronicled not only her own life, but the childhood of her husband Almanzo (in *Farmer Boy*) as well. Wilder's first book, *Little House on the Prairie*, describes her life with her family in their snug home in Pepin, Wisconsin, in the 1860s. Here we are introduced to jovial violin-playing Pa, wise and gentle Ma, obedient and diligent Mary, the baby Carie, and Laura, the daring one in the family. The later books go on to chronicle the family's move west: first to Kansas, then to Minnesota, and finally, to South Dakota. A boon to history teachers, the *Little House* books painlessly teach children about pioneer life in America—its daily routines, chores, and hardships as well as customs, food, and music. The books, in chronological order, are: *Little House in the Big Woods, Little House on the Prairie, Farmer Boy, On the Banks of Plum Creek, By the Shores of Silver Lake, The Long Winter, Little Town on the Prairie, These Happy Golden Years,* and *The First Four Years.* Garth Williams' warm black-and-white drawings enhance all of the books.

Special Needs

What to look for . . .

- A book you feel comfortable with

- A book that is sensitive to the subject you are trying to deal with

- A book that answers questions in an easy, straightforward manner

- Art or photos that capture the idea and feelings you would like conveyed to a child

- A book that will not frighten off a child who is struggling with a particular subject

Special Needs

ADOPTION

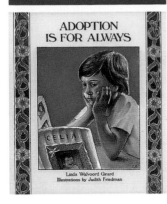

Linda Walvoord Girard
Illustrated by Judith Friedman
ADOPTION IS FOR ALWAYS

Celia's parents have always told her that she is adopted, but the meaning of the word only hits her when she's older. Suddenly Celia feels different, lonely, and full of unanswered questions. With support and understanding, Celia's adoptive parents patiently answer all her questions, letting her know that she is their daughter for always.

32pp   Hardcover $13.95
0-8075-0185-9   Albert Whitman
Paperback $5.95
0-8075-0187-5   Albert Whitman

By the same author:
Illustrated by Linda Shute
WE ADOPTED YOU, BENJAMIN KOO

This helpful resource on interracial adoption reassures readers that it is the family that counts, not how you are different. Nine-year-old Benjamin Koo Andrews was born Koo Hyun Soo in Korea. He describes the

difficulties in being both adopted and from another country: he looks different from his adoptive parents, he must deal with people's unfeeling remarks, and he has a hard time understanding why he was given up to begin with. Benjamin's parents adopt another child when Benjamin is eight, and readers see the process of adoption through an older Benjamin's eyes.

32pp   Hardcover $14.95
0-8075-8694-3   Albert Whitman
Paperback $5.95
0-8075-8695-1   Albert Whitman

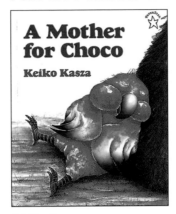

Keiko Kasza
A MOTHER FOR CHOCO

The little bird Choco is looking for a mother. But since Choco doesn't look like any of the other animals, none of the mothers are willing to take him—that is, except Mrs. Bear. Mrs. Bear knows a mother hugs, kisses, plays with, and loves her baby—no matter what he looks like. This suits Choco just fine, and Mrs. Bear adds Choco to her adopted brood. Endearing pictures and a reassuring text are

a comfort to adopted children, especially those in a blended family.

32pp   Hardcover $15.99
0-399-21841-6   Putnam
Paperback $5.95
0-698-11364-0   PaperStar

Karen Katz
OVER THE MOON: AN ADOPTION TALE

Loving text and ebullient art express the joy a couple feels when going overseas to meet their adopted infant for the very first time. This is a timeless momento of a special day for an adopted child.

28pp   Hardcover $15.95
0-8050-5013-2   Henry Holt

Phoebe Koehler
THE DAY WE MET YOU

Soft, muted illustrations create a tender mood as a couple prepares to meet their adopted baby for the first time. All the anticipation, joy, and excitement of this special day is captured in the simple line "The minute we saw you we knew that we loved you."

48pp   Hardcover $15.00
0-02-750901-X   Simon & Schuster
Paperback $5.99
0-689-80964-6   Aladdin

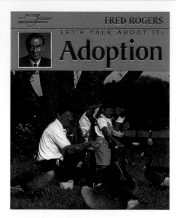

Fred Rogers
Illustrated by Jim Judkis

LET'S TALK ABOUT IT: ADOPTION

In his gentle and reassuring manner, Mr. Rogers looks at adoption by emphasizing the importance of family, no matter how you come to be in one. Emotions that come up in adoptive families—anger, sadness, happiness, and a feeling of belonging—happen in *all* families. No matter what the feelings, the love never goes away. This is a good book for adoptive families to use as a starting point for discussions.

32pp   Hardcover $15.95
0-399-22432-7   Putnam
Paperback $5.99
0-698-11625-9   PaperStar

Maxine B. Rosenberg
Illustrated by George Ancona

BEING ADOPTED

The stories of these three adopted children bring up many interracial and transcultural adoptive issues. The fact that children look different from their friends, peers, *and* family can

make them feel uncomfortable. The author stresses that adoption is just another way a baby can join a family, and that love is the glue that holds the family together. A helpful afterward is included.

48pp   Hardcover $16.00
0-688-02672-9   Lothrop

Ann Turner
Illustrated by James Graham Hale

THROUGH MOON AND STARS AND NIGHT SKIES

A young Asian boy recounts the oft-told story of his adoption: how he received the photographs of his house-to-be, his adoptive parents, and their red dog—and how these photos comforted him as he flew through "night and moon and stars" to reach his new home. The boy's fears at being in a strange place with unknown people are banished by the kindness of his new parents. The gentle, soothing poem evokes a feeling of love and belonging.

32pp   Hardcover $13.95
0-06-026189-7   HarperCollins
Paperback $5.95
0-06-443308-0   HarperTrophy

DEALING WITH DEATH

Aliki

THE TWO OF THEM

From the moment she is born, a girl and her grandfather have a special relationship. When she is little, he makes her a silver ring, sings her lullabies, and tells her stories of his youth. Years later, when he gets sick, the girl takes care of him with the same love that he always showed her. But the day comes when he isn't there anymore, and the pain of his death is sharp. Sitting in their garden, the girl sees that life must go on, and her grandfather would want her to go on doing the things they always did together. Aliki's gentle illustrations give warmth to this poignant remembrance of a loved one.

32pp   Paperback $4.95
0-688-07337-9   Mulberry

Special Needs

Laurene Krasny Brown
Illustrated by Marc Brown

WHEN DINOSAURS DIE: A GUIDE TO UNDERSTANDING DEATH

Using dinosaurs, the Browns help make difficult subjects accessible to young children. Here they explain what death means, and answer common questions, fears, and concerns children have when a loved one dies. Readers will be reassured that feelings about death other than grief—like anger and fear—are okay to have. A helpful section on "Ways to Remember Someone" offers solace to those feeling lost.

32pp Hardcover $14.95
0-316-10917-7 Little, Brown
Paperback $5.95
0-316-11955-5 Little, Brown

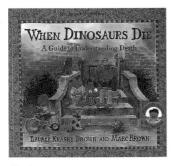

Jo Carson
Illustrated by Annie Cannon

YOU HOLD ME AND I'LL HOLD YOU

A young girl, whose only previous experience with death was when her sister's pet hamster died, is frightened and saddened by the mourning at her great-aunt's funeral. Like the others around her, the girl starts to cry. Her understanding father gathers her in his arms and says, "You

hold me and I'll hold you." The girl finds her pain is lessened when it is shared, and young readers will feel comforted by this introduction to a painful subject presented through a child's eyes.

32pp Paperback $6.95
0-531-07088-3 Orchard

Janice Cohn, D.S.W.
Illustrated by Gail Owens

I HAD A FRIEND NAMED PETER: TALKING TO CHILDREN ABOUT THE DEATH OF A FRIEND

The difficult subject of the death of a playmate is handled with great sensitivity in this story. Disbelief, anger, grief, guilt, and fear are among the feelings children are apt to have in this situation, and the author—a psychotherapist—approaches these feelings in a reassuring and comforting manner. In the end, Betsy sees that Peter will always live in her memories. A helpful introduction advises how to communicate with young children on this painful topic.

32pp Hardcover $16.00
0-688-12312-0 Morrow

Bryan Mellonie
Illustrated by Robert Ingpen

LIFETIMES: THE BEAUTIFUL WAY TO EXPLAIN DEATH TO CHILDREN

This sensitive book explains death in a comforting yet realistic manner. It presents death as part of the process of life, the end of each living thing's own special lifetime. Ingpen's beautiful illustrations form an integral part of this gentle explanation.

48pp Paperback $10.95
0-553-34402-1 Bantam

Fred Rogers
Illustrated by Jim Judkis

WHEN A PET DIES

In his usual straightforward and caring style, Mr. Rogers helps children overcome the death of a beloved pet. Using a boy and his dog and a girl and her cat in this photo essay, he assures readers that all the emotions a child may feel when a pet dies are acceptable. Above all, the book helps children and parents talk with one another about death.

32pp Paperback $5.99
0-698-11666-6 PaperStar

Judith Viorst
Illustrated by Erik Blegvad

THE TENTH GOOD THING ABOUT BARNEY

A young boy is inconsolable when his cat Barney dies. To help the boy assuage his grief, his mother suggests he think of ten good things to say about Barney at Barney's funeral. After much thinking, the boy can only come up with nine, but after Barney is buried in the ground, he thinks of one more, and the tenth good thing helps ease the boy's sorrow.

32pp Hardcover $14.00
0-689-20688-7 Atheneum
Paperback $4.99
0-689-71203-0 Aladdin

Hans Wilhelm
I'LL ALWAYS LOVE YOU

This sweet and moving story prepares children for the sad realization that pets don't live forever. A boy loves his dog Elfie, but as Elfie gets older, he grows less active and eventually dies. Looking back, the boy takes solace that every night he told Elfie he would always love her.

32pp Hardcover $17.00
0-517-55648-0 Crown
Paperback $5.99
0-517-57265-6 Crown

DEALING WITH DIVORCE

Laurene Krasny Brown
Illustrated by Marc Brown
DINOSAURS DIVORCE: A GUIDE FOR CHANGING FAMILIES

A superb children's book on divorce, *Dinosaurs Divorce* deals in positive ways with the confusion and anxiety that comes from this difficult situation. "Divorce Words and What They Mean," "Having Two Homes," and "Telling Your Friends" are among the subjects covered.

32pp Hardcover $15.95
0-316-11248-8 Little, Brown
Paperback $6.95
0-316-10996-7 Little, Brown

Linda Walvoord Girard
Illustrated by Judith Friedman
AT DADDY'S ON SATURDAYS

This realistic, yet comforting story covers the worries, fears, and guilt a young girl named Katie feels when her parents get divorced and her father moves out. Told from Katie's perspective, the reader sees firsthand how Katie feels and how her fears are allayed. Her understanding parents show her they both still love her, and though they are apart, will both always be there for her.

32pp Hardcover $14.95
0-8075-0475-0 Albert Whitman
Paperback $6.95
0-8075-0473-4 Albert Whitman

Fred Rogers
Illustrated by Jim Judkis
LET'S TALK ABOUT IT: DIVORCE

In a simple, straightforward text, Mr. Rogers offers young readers reassurance that divorce is the result of differences between parents, and is not the result of anything a child might have done. He lets kids know that it is important to be able to talk about feelings, and that all feelings arising from divorce are acceptable. As the title suggests, the book is meant to encourage discussion between children and parents.

32pp Hardcover $15.95
0-399-22449-1 Putnam

Kathy Stinson
Illustrated by Nancy Lou Reynolds
MOM AND DAD DON'T LIVE TOGETHER ANY MORE

A little girl is sad that her parents are divorced. Now she lives with her mother and brother during the week, and with her father on the weekends. The brief text captures the essence of a child's feelings about divorce—the guilt, and the wishes and fears. It also manages to convey the positive message that parents still love their children after a divorce, even if they can't do it living together.

32pp Hardcover $15.95
0-920236-92-8 Firefly
Paperback $5.95
0-920236-87-1 Annick

Special Needs

SPECIAL ISSUES

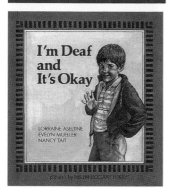

Lorraine Aseltine, Evelyn Mueller, and Nancy Tait
Illustrated by Helen Cogancherry

I'M DEAF AND IT'S OKAY

Small vignettes illustrate the feelings and experiences of a deaf boy in a hearing world. Often the lively boy feels left out, and is frustrated that he can't use the telephone and always must use hearing aids. But when Brian (a deaf teenager) comes to visit, the boy learns that even though he's deaf, there are still lots of things he can do. This book serves as a reminder that deaf children are just as capable as hearing children. A short picture dictionary of sign words is included.

40pp   Hardcover $13.95
0-8075-3472-2   Albert Whitman

Kathleen M. Dwyer
Illustrated by Gregg A. Flory

WHAT DO YOU MEAN I HAVE ATTENTION DEFICIT DISORDER?

Patrick is always in trouble at home and at school. His teachers and parents are constantly yelling at him to sit still and finish his work. A visit to the doctor identifies the problem—Patrick has Attention Deficit Disorder. With support from parents and teachers, special classes, and such helpful tools as a timer and some pasted reminders, Patrick shows that he can get his work done— and done well!

48pp   Hardcover $14.95
0-8027-8392-9   Walker

Virginia Fleming
Illustrated by Floyd Cooper

BE GOOD TO EDDIE LEE

Christy and JimBud don't want Eddie Lee tagging after them when they go to the pond to look for tadpoles. Christy feels bad— after all, her mother always told her to be kind to their neighbor with Down's syndrome. Eddie Lee follows them anyway, and it is he who shows Christy the hidden pond covered with water lilies and hiding tadpole eggs. Christy finally realizes that even though he looks different, Eddie Lee really is special.

32pp   Hardcover $16.99
0-399-21993-5   Philomel
Paperback $5.95
0-698-11582-1   PaperStar

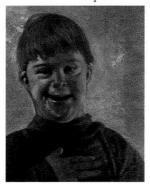

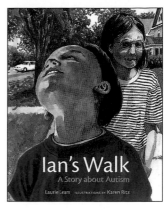

Laurie Lears
Illustrated by Karen Ritz

IAN'S WALK: A STORY ABOUT AUTISM

Julie is embarrassed by her younger brother Ian's odd behavior when they go for a walk together. Sometimes he makes her so angry! Yet when Ian suddenly disappears in the park, Julie's anger is replaced by worry—and when she finally finds him, by relief and love. On the way home, Julie allows him to do whatever odd thing he wants, and Ian rewards her with a rare smile.

32pp   Hardcover $14.95
0-8075-3480-3   Albert Whitman

Bill Martin Jr. and John Archambault
Illustrated by Ted Rand

KNOTS ON A COUNTING ROPE

A blind Native American boy is again treated to the story of his birth by his loving and supportive grandfather. In telling the story, the grandfather speaks proudly of the boy's courage and accomplishments. Each time the grandfather

FROM *Moses Goes to a Concert*

MY   FRIEND

Jeanne Whitehouse Peterson
Illustrated by Deborah Kogan Ray
I HAVE A SISTER, MY SISTER IS DEAF

In this loving tribute, the author describes what it is like for her younger sister to be deaf. Even though her sister cannot hear, she loves to do everything all children do—she enjoys playing the piano, climbing on the monkey bars, and holding a cat in her lap. As the author says, "My little sister can say more with her face and her shoulders than anyone else I know."

32pp   Paperback $5.95
0-06-443059-6   HarperTrophy

Berniece Rabe
Illustrated by Diane Schmidt
WHERE'S CHIMPY?

After her father reads her a story, Misty is ready for bed. But Chimpy, her stuffed monkey, is missing. Misty and her father search all over the place, but Misty finds everything *but* Chimpy. Finally the missing monkey is found—but now Daddy can't find his glasses! Misty has Down's syndrome, yet acts like any other child in the same situation. This cheerful story shows how all children are alike.

32pp   Hardcover $15.95
0-8075-8928-4   Albert Whitman
Paperback $5.95
0-8075-8927-6   Albert Whitman

tells the story, he ties another knot in a rope, so that when he is no longer alive, the child will be able to remember the story and his grandfather's everlasting love. This poetic and moving tale is ideal for children and their grandparents to share.

32pp   Hardcover $15.95
0-8050-0571-4   Henry Holt
Paperback $5.95
0-8050-5479-0   Henry Holt

Isaac Millman
MOSES GOES TO A CONCERT

When Moses and his classmates (who are all deaf) go to a concert, they are surprised to see that the percussionist has no shoes on! She's deaf too, and she plays by feeling the vibrations under her feet. By holding balloons in their laps, Moses and his classmates can also feel the vibrations. After the concert, the percussionist allows the class to play some of her instruments. The experience makes Moses

realize that he can do *anything* he wants when he grows up. The story is told in both written English and American Sign Language.

40pp   Hardcover $16.00
0-374-35067-1   FSG

Nicola Moon
Illustrated by Alex Ayliffe
LUCY'S PICTURE

Lucy is making a picture for her grandpa. All the other preschoolers are painting their pictures, but Lucy has something else in mind. Carefully and thoughtfully, she creates a collage using different textures. Each texture represents an item in the picture. When she proudly presents the picture to her grandpa, the blind man can "see" it perfectly!

28pp   Hardcover $15.99
0-8037-1833-0   Dial
Paperback $5.99
0-14-055769-5   Puffin

Barnes & Noble Books

FOR TWENTY YEARS, the Barnes & Noble Books publishing division has offered a diverse and exciting selection of books. We scour archives, search through stacks of out-of-print books, and review new titles from hundreds of international publishers to find what you, the reader, would like to see in our stores. Our goal is to bring important books to children at a price every family can afford. Keep reading!

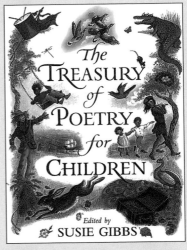

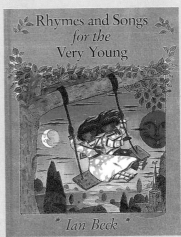

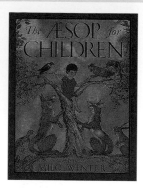

Aesop
Illustrated by Milo Winter

THE AESOP FOR CHILDREN

Who can forget such famous fables as *The Ants and the Grasshopper*, *The Town Mouse and the Country Mouse*, and *The Hare and the Tortoise?* All of Aesop's fables are gathered here and adorned with Milo Winter's beautiful illustrations.

112pp   Hardcover $7.98
1-56619-292-7   Barnes & Noble

Ian Beck, illustrator

RHYMES AND SONGS FOR THE VERY YOUNG

Ian Beck, one of Europe's best children's book artists, provides gorgeous illustrations for this volume of poems and song verses.

96pp   Hardcover $7.98
0-7607-0360-4   Barnes & Noble

Kay Chorao

KAY CHORAO'S BIG BOOK FOR BABIES

The Baby's Good Morning Book, The Baby's Lap Book, and *The Baby's Bedtime Book* are three of the most beautiful books for little ones around. Poems old and new—by

Emily Dickinson, Robert Louis Stevenson, William Wordsworth, and others—are included.

192pp   Hardcover $14.95
0-7607-1172-0   Barnes & Noble

Lucy Coats
Illustrated by Selina Young

FIRST RHYMES: A DAY OF RHYMES WITH A DIFFERENT TWIST

"It's raining, it's pouring, / Staying indoors is boring. / I want to kersplosh / In my new galoshes / And run off to Russia exploring." Familiar rhymes are even funnier and more charming when they are given unexpected twists!

64pp   Hardcover $6.98
0-7607-0359-0   Barnes & Noble

Alexandra E. Fischer
Illustrated by Bettina Paterson

A TO Z ANIMALS AROUND THE WORLD

Endangered animals from all around the globe are the subject of this fanciful alphabet book. A handy world map with a "who's who" glossary helps locate where each animal is from.

32pp   Hardcover $5.98
0-7607-0640-9   Barnes & Noble

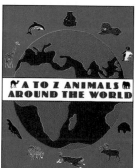

Don Freeman

ALL ABOUT CORDUROY

The two original adventures of one of the best-loved bears in children's literature are gathered in this one special volume. Both *Corduroy* and *A Pocket for Corduroy* are surefire hits with kids.

64pp   Hardcover $7.98
0-7607-1124-0   Barnes & Noble

Susie Gibbs, editor
Illustrated by Diz Wallis

THE TREASURY OF POETRY FOR CHILDREN

As gift editions go, this book is hard book to beat. Great works by poets from around the globe are complemented by soft, enchanting illustrations. Each member of the family can enjoy this treasury for years to come.

384pp   Hardcover $14.98
0-7607-0754-5   Barnes & Noble

Mother Goose
Illustrated by Blanche Fisher Wright

THE REAL MOTHER GOOSE

Blanche Fisher Wright's delicate illustrations are the perfect complement to this volume of the age-old Mother Goose rhymes. "Little Boy Blue, come, blow your horn! / The sheep's in the meadow, the cow's in the corn. / Where's the little boy that looks after the sheep? / Under the haystack, fast asleep!"

128pp Hardcover $7.98
0-88029-771-9 Barnes & Noble

Homer
THE ILIAD AND THE ODYSSEY

All the adventure and grandeur of Homer's immortal stories come alive in this exciting volume, written especially for the young reader.

152pp Hardcover $12.98
0-88029-621-6 Barnes & Noble

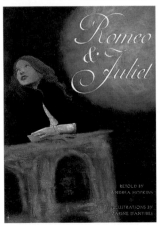

Andrea Hopkins, reteller
Illustrated by Marine D'Antibes
ROMEO & JULIET

The classic play by William Shakespeare is carefully retold for children. The text (which includes major excerpts from the play) is accompanied by magnificent illustrations that convey all the love and angst of teenage romance.

56pp Hardcover $9.95
0-7607-0807-X Barnes & Noble

Philip S. Jennings
Illustrated by Severo Baraldi
THE BIBLE FOR CHILDREN

Prepared especially for children, this magnificent volume contains the best-loved stories from both the Old and New Testaments.

312pp Hardcover $12.98
1-56619-985-9 Barnes & Noble

Erich Kästner
EMIL AND THE DETECTIVES

In Erich Kästner's classic children's mystery, Emil must deliver an envelope full of his mother's hard-earned money to his grandmother in Berlin. But there is trouble . . . and Emil and his merry band of detectives must track down the skulking thief! This terrific story keeps kids on the edge of their seats.

208pp Hardcover $5.98
0-7607-0638-7 Barnes & Noble

Mercer Mayer
THERE'S SOMETHING THERE!
THREE BEDTIME CLASSICS BY
MERCER MAYER

What's that in my attic? . . . And in my closet? . . . Or under my

bed? Mercer Mayer removes all bedtime fears in this charming three-book bind-up!

112pp Hardcover $12.95
0-7607-1173-9 Barnes & Noble

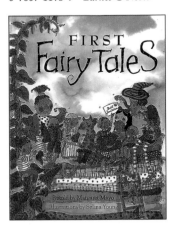

Margaret Mayo
Illustrated by Selina Young
FIRST FAIRY TALES

So you think you've heard these fairy tales? Well, think again, because these versions are chock-full of surprises and laugh-out-loud humor!

96pp Hardcover $7.98
0-7607-0358-2 Barnes & Noble

Robert McCloskey
THE COMPLETE ADVENTURES
OF HOMER PRICE

The delightful *Homer Price* and *Centerburg Tales*, bound in this one volume, are a treat for any fan of McCloskey.

344pp Hardcover $9.98
0-7607-1122-4 Barnes & Noble

Barnes & Noble Books

FROM *The Velveteen Rabbit*

Margaret Evans Price, illustrator
A CHILDREN'S TREASURY OF MYTHOLOGY

Twenty ageless Greek and Roman myths, beautifully illustrated, introduce the child to such immortals as Narcissus, Hercules, Atalanta, and of course Cupid.

158pp   Hardcover $7.98
1-56619-646-9   Barnes & Noble

E. B. White
Illustrated by Garth Williams
CHARLOTTE'S WEB

At some point this timeless classic becomes part of every child's reading experience. Our oversized, unabridged edition has large type and all the delightful illustrations of Charlotte, Wilbur, and friends. It is perfect for story time and read-alongs.

192pp   Hardcover $9.98
0-7607-0725-1   Barnes & Noble

Margery Williams
Illustrated by Robyn Officer
THE VELVETEEN RABBIT

How does a toy become real? The answer can be found in this beautifully illustrated version of an enduring classic. A stuffed rabbit is loved, very much, by a little boy. When the little boy gets sick with scarlet fever all his toys and books, including the old and worn rabbit, must be destroyed. Left in a sack, the Velveteen Rabbit cries a single tear and is transformed by a fairy into a live, hopping bunny.

40pp   Hardcover $6.98
0-7607-0301-9   Barnes & Noble

Gene Zion
Illustrated by Margaret Bloy Graham
A HARRY THE DIRTY DOG TREASURY

Harry is quite a dog—always finding himself in a bit of mischief! Three Harry books, graced with the original old-school illustrations, make this a very fun read.

96pp   Hardcover $12.98
0-7607-0742-1   Barnes & Noble

BARNES & NOBLE CLASSICS

Louisa May Alcott
LITTLE WOMEN

With their father off to the war, the four March sisters must take on greater responsibility to become "little women." Each sister is unique, yet together they fight and fret, fall in love, heed the wise words of their mother, and win over the hearts of readers.

544pp   Hardcover $5.98
1-5661-9475-X   Barnes & Noble

James M. Barrie
PETER PAN

Peter takes the Darling children on a fantastic adventure filled with pirates, mermaids and the Lost Boys. Readers both young and old will find this book consistently entertaining and just as readable as it was in Victorian times.

240pp   Hardcover $4.98
1-5661-9713-9   Barnes & Noble

L. Frank Baum
Illustrated by W.W. Denslow
THE WIZARD OF OZ

Dorothy and her little dog, Toto, are whisked away from their home in Kansas for a magical journey to Oz. She meets a host of unforgettable characters, and finally learns that "There is no place like home."

218pp   Hardcover $4.98
1-5661-9712-0   Barnes & Noble

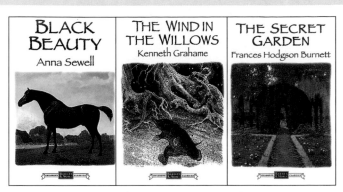

BLACK BEAUTY — Anna Sewell

THE WIND IN THE WILLOWS — Kenneth Grahame

THE SECRET GARDEN — Frances Hodgson Burnett

Frances Hodgson Burnett
A LITTLE PRINCESS

Seven-year-old Sara Crewe is the most adored and envied student at her school until a great tragedy strikes and she is forced to persevere under extremely difficult living conditions. This classic pays tribute to the power of compassion, and makes a great addition to every child's library.

256pp   Hardcover $4.98
1-5661-9715-5   Barnes & Noble

By the same author:
THE SECRET GARDEN

When a robin unearths the key to a secret garden, a whole world of mystery and delight unfolds. This magical story is one of the most beloved in children's literature.

240pp   Hardcover $4.98
1-5661-9481-4   Barnes & Noble

Lewis Carroll
Illustrated by John Tenniel
ALICE'S ADVENTURES IN WONDERLAND

"Down, down, down. Would the fall *never* come to an end?" Alice shoots down the rabbit hole and enters a brand-new world. Off-beat plot twists and a cast of utterly bizarre and captivating characters make Lewis Carroll's *Alice's Adventures in Wonderland* a feast for a child's imagination.

192pp   Hardcover $4.98
1-5661-9477-6   Barnes & Noble

Sir Arthur Conan Doyle
CLASSIC ADVENTURES OF SHERLOCK HOLMES

The Red-Headed League and six other thrilling Sherlock Holmes cases are presented in this one volume. Will the brilliant British sleuth meet his match?

224pp   Hardcover $4.98
0-7607-1104-6   Barnes & Noble

Kenneth Grahame
THE WIND IN THE WILLOWS

Whether scampering through the Wild Wood or floating down to the backwater, Grahame's lively, personable, sensitive animals tap the yearnings and fears of readers of all ages. A true classic!

368pp   Hardcover $4.98
1-5661-9714-7   Barnes & Noble

Lucy Maud Montgomery
ANNE OF GREEN GABLES

Delightfully unpredictable Anne Shirley has been charming readers for nearly a century. This beloved book continues to be read all around the world.

288pp   Hardcover $4.98
1-5661-9483-0   Barnes & Noble

Anna Sewell
BLACK BEAUTY

Told from a horse's point of view, *Black Beauty* is a testament to simple values and a plea for kindness to all creatures.

256pp   Hardcover $4.98
1-5661-9591-8   Barnes & Noble

Robert Louis Stevenson
TREASURE ISLAND

Who will get the treasure, and who will survive? The ultimate pirate story takes the reader on the high seas with the infamous Long John Silver.

320pp   Hardcover $4.98
1-5661-9473-3   Barnes & Noble

Mark Twain
THE ADVENTURES OF TOM SAWYER

Tom asks, "Does a boy get a chance to whitewash a fence every day?" To which Ben answers, "Say, Tom, let me whitewash a little." Tom Sawyer, Huckleberry Finn, and their gang of rapscallions make *The Adventures of Tom Sawyer* a joyous tale of boyhood.

224pp   Hardcover $4.98
1-5661-9479-2   Barnes & Noble

Award Winners

The Newbery Medal (named for eighteenth-century bookseller John Newbery) is awarded annually by the American Library Association for the most distinguished American children's book published the previous year.

NEWBERY MEDAL WINNERS, 1922–1999

YEAR	TITLE	AUTHOR
1999	*Holes*	Louis Sachar
1998	*Out of the Dust*	Karen Hesse
1997	*The View from Saturday*	E. L. Konigsburg
1996	*The Midwife's Apprentice*	Karen Cushman
1995	*Walk Two Moons*	Sharon Creech
1994	*The Giver*	Lois Lowry
1993	*Missing May*	Cynthia Rylant
1992	*Shiloh*	Phyllis Reynolds Naylor
1991	*Maniac Magee*	Jerry Spinelli
1990	*Number the Stars*	Lois Lowry
1989	*Joyful Noise: Poems for Two Voices*	Paul Fleischman
1988	*Lincoln: A Photobiography*	Russell Freedman
1987	*The Whipping Boy*	Sid Fleischman
1986	*Sarah, Plain and Tall*	Patricia MacLachlan
1985	*The Hero and the Crown*	Robin McKinley
1984	*Dear Mr. Henshaw*	Beverly Cleary
1983	*Dicey's Song*	Cynthia Voigt
1982	*A Visit to William Blake's Inn: Poems for Innocent and Experienced Travelers*	Nancy Willard
1981	*Jacob Have I Loved*	Katherine Paterson
1980	*A Gathering of Days: A New England Girl's Journal, 1830–1832*	Joan W. Blos
1979	*The Westing Game*	Ellen Raskin
1978	*Bridge to Terabithia*	Katherine Paterson
1977	*Roll of Thunder, Hear My Cry*	Mildred D. Taylor
1976	*The Grey King*	Susan Cooper
1975	*M. C. Higgins, the Great*	Virginia Hamilton
1974	*The Slave Dancer*	Paula Fox
1973	*Julie of the Wolves*	Jean Craighead George
1972	*Mrs. Frisby and the Rats of NIMH*	Robert C. O'Brien
1971	*The Summer of the Swans*	Betsy Byars
1970	*Sounder*	William H. Armstrong
1969	*The High King*	Lloyd Alexander
1968	*From the Mixed-up Files of Mrs. Basil E. Frankweiler*	E. L. Konigsburg
1967	*Up a Road Slowly*	Irene Hunt

Award Winners

1966	*I, Juan de Pareja*	Elizabeth Borton de Trevino
1965	*Shadow of a Bull*	Maia Wojciechowska
1964	*It's Like This, Cat*	Emily Cheney Neville
1963	*A Wrinkle in Time*	Madeleine L'Engle
1962	*The Bronze Bow*	Elizabeth George Speare
1961	*Island of the Blue Dolphins*	Scott O'Dell
1960	*Onion John*	Joseph Krumgold
1959	*The Witch of Blackbird Pond*	Elizabeth George Speare
1958	*Rifles for Watie*	Harold Keith
1957	*Miracles on Maple Hill*	Virginia Sorensen
1956	*Carry On, Mr. Bowditch*	Jean Lee Latham
1955	*The Wheel on the School*	Meindert DeJong
1954	*. . . And Now Miguel*	Joseph Krumgold
1953	*Secret of the Andes*	Ann Nolan Clark
1952	*Ginger Pye*	Eleanor Estes
1951	*Amos Fortune, Free Man*	Elizabeth Yates
1950	*The Door in the Wall*	Marguerite de Angeli
1949	*King of the Wind*	Marguerite Henry
1948	*The Twenty-One Balloons*	William Pène du Bois
1947	*Miss Hickory*	Carolyn Sherwin Bailey
1946	*Strawberry Girl*	Lois Lenski
1945	*Rabbit Hill*	Robert Lawson
1944	*Johnny Tremain*	Esther Forbes
1943	*Adam of the Road*	Elizabeth Janet Gray
1942	*The Matchlock Gun*	William D. Edmonds
1941	*Call it Courage*	Armstrong Sperry
1940	*Daniel Boone*	James Daugherty
1939	*Thimble Summer*	Elizabeth Enright
1938	*The White Stag*	Kate Seredy
1937	*Roller Skates*	Ruth Sawyer
1936	*Caddie Woodlawn*	Carol Ryrie Brink
1935	*Dobry*	Monica Shannon
1934	*Invincible Louisa: The Story of the Author of Little Women*	Cornelia L. Meigs
1933	*Young Fu of the Upper Yangtze*	Elizabeth Foreman Lewis
1932	*Waterless Mountain*	Laura Adams Armer
1931	*The Cat Who Went to Heaven*	Elizabeth Coatsworth
1930	*Hitty, Her First Hundred Years*	Rachel Field
1929	*The Trumpeter of Krakow*	Eric P. Kelly
1928	*Gay-Neck: The Story of a Pigeon*	Dhan Gopal Mukerji
1927	*Smoky, the Cowhorse*	Will James
1926	*Shen of the Sea*	Arthur Bowie Chrisman
1925	*Tales from Silver Lands*	Charles Joseph Finger
1924	*The Dark Frigate*	Charles Boardman Hawes
1923	*The Voyages of Dr. Dolittle*	Hugh Lofting
1922	*The Story of Mankind*	Hendrik Willem van Loon

Award Winners

THE CALDECOTT MEDAL

The Caldecott Medal (named after the nineteenth-century English illustrator Randolph J. Caldecott) is awarded annually by the American Library Association to the artist who has created the most distinguished picture book published the previous year.

CALDECOTT MEDAL WINNERS, 1938–1999:

YEAR	TITLE	ILLUSTRATOR
1999	*Snowflake Bentley*	Mary Azarian
1998	*Rapunzel*	Paul O. Zelinsky
1997	*Golem*	David Wisniewski
1996	*Officer Buckle and Gloria*	Peggy Rathmann
1995	*Smoky Night*	David Diaz
1994	*Grandfather's Journey*	Allen Say
1993	*Mirette on the High Wire*	Emily Arnold McCully
1992	*Tuesday*	David Wiesner
1991	*Black and White*	David Macaulay
1990	*Lon Po Po: A Red-Riding Hood Story from China*	Ed Young
1989	*Song and Dance Man*	Stephen Gammell
1988	*Owl Moon*	John Schoenherr
1987	*Hey, Al!*	Richard Egielski
1986	*The Polar Express*	Chris Van Allsburg
1985	*Saint George and the Dragon*	Trina Schart Hyman
1984	*The Glorious Flight: Across the Channel with Louis Blériot*	Alice & Martin Provensen
1983	*Shadow*	Marcia Brown
1982	*Jumanji*	Chris Van Allsburg
1981	*Fables*	Arnold Lobel
1980	*Ox-Cart Man*	Barbara Cooney
1979	*The Girl Who Loved Wild Horses*	Paul Goble
1978	*Noah's Ark*	Peter Spier
1977	*Ashanti to Zulu: African Traditions*	Leo & Diane Dillon
1976	*Why Mosquitoes Buzz in People's Ears: A West African Tale*	Leo & Diane Dillon
1975	*Arrow to the Sun*	Gerald McDermott
1974	*Duffy and the Devil*	Margot Zemach
1973	*The Funny Little Woman*	Blair Lent
1972	*One Fine Day*	Nonny Hogrogian
1971	*A Story, a Story*	Gail E. Haley
1970	*Sylvester and the Magic Pebble*	William Steig
1969	*The Fool of the World and the Flying Ship*	Uri Shulevitz
1968	*Drummer Hoff*	Ed Emberley
1967	*Sam, Bangs & Moonshine*	Evaline Ness
1966	*Always Room for One More*	Nonny Hogrogian

1965	*May I Bring a Friend?*	Beni Montresor
1964	*Where the Wild Things Are*	Maurice Sendak
1963	*The Snowy Day*	Ezra Jack Keats
1962	*Once a Mouse*	Marcia Brown
1961	*Baboushka and the Three Kings*	Nicolas Sidjakov
1960	*Nine Days to Christmas*	Marie Hall Ets and Aurora Labastida
1959	*Chanticleer and the Fox*	Barbara Cooney
1958	*Time of Wonder*	Robert McCloskey
1957	*A Tree Is Nice*	Marc Simont
1956	*Frog Went A-Courtin'*	Feodor Rojankovsky
1955	*Cinderella*	Marcia Brown
1954	*Madeline's Rescue*	Ludwig Bemelmans
1953	*The Biggest Bear*	Lynd Ward
1952	*Finders Keepers*	Nicolas Mordvinoff
1951	*The Egg Tree*	Katherine Milhous
1950	*Song of the Swallows*	Leo Politi
1949	*The Big Snow*	Berta & Elmer Hader
1948	*White Snow, Bright Snow*	Roger Duvoisin
1947	*The Little Island*	Leonard Weisgard
1946	*The Rooster Crows*	Maude & Miska Petersham
1945	*Prayer for a Child*	Elizabeth Orton Jones
1944	*Many Moons*	Louis Slobodkin
1943	*The Little House*	Virginia Lee Burton
1942	*Make Way for Ducklings*	Robert McCloskey
1941	*They Were Strong and Good*	Robert Lawson
1940	*Abraham Lincoln*	Ingri & Edgar Parin d'Aulaire
1939	*Mei Li*	Thomas Handforth
1938	*Animals of the Bible*	Dorothy P. Lathrop

Award Winners

CORETTA SCOTT KING AWARD BOOKS, 1970–1999: AUTHOR

YEAR	TITLE	AUTHOR
1999	*Heaven*	Angela Johnson
1998	*Forged by Fire*	Sharon Draper
1997	*Slam!*	Walter Dean Myers
1996	*Her Stories! African American Folktales, Fairy Tales and True Stories*	Virginia Hamilton
1995	*Christmas in the Big House, Christmas in the Quarters*	Patricia & Fredrick McKissack
1994	*Toning the Sweep*	Angela Johnson
1993	*The Dark-Thirty: Southern Tales of the Supernatural*	Patricia McKissack
1992	*Now is Your Time! The African-American Struggle For Freedom*	Walter Dean Myers
1991	*The Road to Memphis*	Mildred D. Taylor
1990	*A Long Hard Journey: The Story of the Pullman Porter*	Patricia & Fredrick McKissack
1989	*Fallen Angels*	Walter Dean Myers
1988	*The Friendship*	Mildred D. Taylor
1987	*Justin and the Best Biscuits in the World*	Mildred Pitts Walter
1986	*The People Could Fly: American Black Folktales*	Virginia Hamilton
1985	*Motown and Didi: A Love Story*	Walter Dean Myers
1984	*Everett Anderson's Goodbye*	Lucille Clifton
1983	*Sweet Whispers, Brother Rush*	Virginia Hamilton
1982	*Let the Circle Be Unbroken*	Mildred D. Taylor
1981	*This Life*	Sidney Poitier
1980	*The Young Landlords*	Walter Dean Myers
1979	*Escape to Freedom; A Play about Young Frederick Douglass*	Ossie Davis
1978	*Africa Dream*	Eloise Greenfield
1977	*The Story of Stevie Wonder*	James Haskins
1976	*Duey's Tale*	Pearl Bailey
1975	*The Legend of Africania*	Dorothy Robinson
1974	*Ray Charles*	Sharon Bell Mathis

Award Winners

1973	*I Never Had It Made: The Autobiography of Jackie Robinson*	Alfred Duckett
1972	*17 Black Artists*	Elton Fax
1971	*Black Troubadour: Langston Hughes*	Charlemae Rollins
1970	*Dr. Martin Luther King, Jr.: Man of Peace*	Lillie Patterson

CORETTA SCOTT KING AWARD BOOKS, 1979–1999:
ILLUSTRATOR

YEAR	TITLE	ILLUSTRATOR
1999	*I See the Rhythm*	Michele Wood
1998	*In Daddy's Arms I Am Tall: African Americans Celebrating Fathers*	Javaka Steptoe
1997	*Minty: A Story of Young Harriet Tubman*	Jerry Pinkney
1996	*The Middle Passage: White Ships / Black Cargo*	Tom Feelings
1995	*The Creation*	James E. Ransome
1994	*Soul Looks Back in Wonder*	Tom Feelings
1993	*The Origin of Life on Earth: An African Creation Myth*	Kathleen Atkins Wilson
1992	*Tar Beach*	Faith Ringgold
1991	*Aida*	Leo & Diane Dillon
1990	*Nathaniel Talking*	Jan Spivey Gilchrist
1989	*Mirandy and Brother Wind*	Jerry Pinkney
1988	*Mufaro's Beautiful Daughters*	John Steptoe
1987	*Half a Moon and One Whole Star*	Jerry Pinkney
1986	*The Patchwork Quilt*	Jerry Pinkney
1985	No Award Given	
1984	*My Mama Needs Me*	Pat Cummings
1983	*Black Child*	Peter Magubane
1982	*Mama Crocodile*	John Steptoe
1981	*Beat the Story Drum, Pum-Pum*	Ashley Bryan
1980	*Cornrows*	Carole Byard
1979	*Something on My Mind*	Tom Feelings

Author/Title Index

Author/Title Index

Author/Title Index

Author/Title Index

Author/Title Index

Author/Title Index

Author/Title Index

Author/Title Index

Author/Title Index

Author/Title Index

Author/Title Index

Author/Title Index

Author/Title Index

Author/Title Index

Author/Title Index

Subject Index

Subject Index

Subject Index

Subject Index

Subject Index

Subject Index

Subject Index

Subject Index

Subject Index

Subject Index